OVERCOME
UNHEALTHY RELATIONSHIPS, GASLIGHTING, ANXIOUS ATTACHMENT AND CODEPENDENCY

4 BOOKS IN 1

MASTER SELF-COMPASSION AND SELF-CARE TO EASE NARCISSISTIC ABUSE RECOVERY AND ENJOY LIFE

ROBERT J. CHARLES, PHD, DMIN

Overcome Unhealthy Relationships, Gaslighting, Anxious Attachment and Codependency

(4 Books in 1)

Master Self-Compassion and Self-Care to Ease Narcissistic Abuse Recovery and Enjoy Life

By Robert J. Charles, PhD, DMin

Contents

Your Free Gifts

Breathtaking BONUS! #1

Master the Art of Building Stronger Bonds with Loves Ones

In this Bonus, you'll find:

- How to Develop Effective Communication Strategies
- Ways to Build a Healthy Relationship Plan
- Exercises to Establish Healthy Boundaries for Personal Growth

Discover Powerful Strategies to Elevate Your Relationships to New Heights!
Click here to get this BONUS.

Amazing BONUS! #2

Companion Worksheets

<u>7 Transformative Worksheets</u> for Cultivating a New Mindset for a Better Life

Inside this BONUS, you'll discover:

- How to Cultivate Self-Compassion for True Happiness?
- How to Unleash Your Happy Hormones?
- How to Create Your ideal Self-Care Routine?

    If you want to start a better life with self-compassion and self-care
    <u>Download this BONUS.</u>

Join Our Facebook Support Group

Join our affectionate community of *Anxiety, Depression, and Emotional Regulation Support Group* on Facebook. You will be able to connect and share tips and strategies with other like-minded people. If you want to achieve your goals, don't take this journey alone.

It would be great to connect with you there,

Robert

>> Click Here to Join our Anxiety, Depression, and Emotional Regulation Support Group <<

BOOK #1

Fixing Avoidant and Anxious Attachment in Your Relationship

Attachment Styles Workbook to Stop Overthinking and Relationship Anxiety and Build a Secure Attachment

Introduction

Sophia was a curious and playful child who loved to explore the world around her. However, she tended to get scared quickly, especially when away from her mother. She would cling to her mother's hand whenever she felt afraid, seeking comfort and security.

Sophia's mother loved her deeply and always responded to her daughter's need for comfort by holding her tightly and soothing her fears. This interaction between Sophia and her mother was the foundation of their attachment, and it was the first time Sophia learned what it was like to feel secure and loved in a relationship.

As Sophia grew older, she developed relationships with other people, including friends, teachers, and eventually romantic partners. However, no matter how much she loved these people, she always felt a sense of unease and insecurity when she was away from them. She often sought their comfort and reassurance, just as she had done with her mother.

Years later, Sophia met Dave. Dave was kind, funny, and understanding, and Sophia soon fell in love with him. However, her old attachment patterns returned, and she constantly sought Dave's approval and comfort. Unfamiliar with attachment theory, Dave soon became frustrated with Sophia's behavior and started withdrawing from the relationship.

Sophia, feeling hurt and rejected, started doing some research and learned about attachment theory. She discovered that her early attachment experiences with her mother impacted her need for comfort and fear of abandonment. She also found that her behavior with Dave was a manifestation of her attachment style and that she could modify it.

Sophia started to work on her attachment issues, and over time, she became more secure in her relationship. She learned to trust that he loved her, even when they were apart, and she became more comfortable seeking comfort and support from others when she needed it. In the end, Sophia and Dave built a solid and loving relationship founded on understanding the principles of attachment theory.

Like Sophia, do you feel you have difficulty forming connections with others? Do you find yourself feeling lonely, even when surrounded by people? Are you struggling to find a sense of security in your relationships? If so, you are not alone.

Attachment theory is a powerful and transformative tool that can help unlock the secrets of your relationships, heal past wounds, and create more fulfilling connections with others. However, for many of us, delving into the complexities of human attachment can be overwhelming, primarily when our relationships have caused us pain and frustration.

That is why I have created this guide to attachment theory, to help you navigate this often-confusing world and find the answers you have been seeking. I can assure you that on these pages, you will learn about attachment theory, how it works, and how to use it to transform your relationships and create more happiness and fulfillment. Whether you are struggling with attachment issues in your romantic relationships, struggling to connect with others, or just seeking a deeper understanding of the human condition, this book is right for you.

As you read, you will get a comprehensive overview of attachment theory, allowing you to understand the subject more deeply. Also, you will learn to identify your attachment style, develop strategies to better interact with different attachment styles, and learn how to reprogram them for healthier relationships.

In addition, you will gain insight into how to overcome codependency and cultivate healthier relationships. You will also learn how to deal with jealousy and insecurity in your relationships and manage anxiety and avoidance. All of these benefits can help you gain a better understanding of attachment theory and improve your relationships.

You will have the opportunity to comprehensively understand this fascinating subject, including the impact of early childhood relationships on adult attachment, the different attachment styles, and the role of emotions in attachment.

However, that is not all! You will gain knowledge and receive practical tools and strategies to help you better manage your emotions and behaviors in relationships, ultimately leading to healthier and more secure attachments.

In the pages ahead, I will provide expert advice and guidance on identifying and addressing any attachment-related issues you may be facing, making this book a valuable and comprehensive resource for anyone looking to improve their relationships.

This book was written with you in mind and is filled with valuable information and practical insights that will help you gain a deeper understanding of attachment theory. As a seasoned attachment theory expert, I can assure you that I will lead you on your journey to understanding this fascinating subject.

You can trust that I have put my years of experience and learning into every page of this book, ensuring you receive the most up-to-date and accurate information. In the chapters ahead, I cover everything from the impact of early childhood relationships on adult attachment to the different attachment styles to the role of emotions in attachment.

Finally, throughout the book, I have applied a biblical approach to addressing these issues, and at the end of each chapter, you'll find a quick workbook to help you integrate what you've learned.

So, if you're looking for a trusted guide to help you navigate the world of attachment theory, look no further. This book is the right choice for you.

Ready?

Then let's get started.

PART ONE

THE WORKINGS OF ATTACHMENT THEORY

Are you someone who struggles with attachment anxiety in your relationships? Do you find yourself constantly worrying about whether your partner loves you or feeling fearful about being abandoned? If so, *Fixing Avoidant and Anxious Attachment in Your Relationship* might be the book you need. As someone who has dealt with several individuals who have experienced attachment anxiety, I understand the pain and frustration that come with it.

Part 1 of this book, "The Workings of Attachment Theory," provides readers with a comprehensive understanding of attachment theory and its impact on our relationships. Through Chapter 1, "An Overview of Attachment Theory," you'll learn about the different attachment styles and how they develop. In Chapter 2, "What is Your Style?," you'll have the opportunity to identify your own attachment style and gain self-awareness. I hope this book can help you find peace and security in your relationships.

CHAPTER ONE

An Overview of Attachment Theory

"Train up a child in the way he should go: and when he is old, he will not depart from it."

—Proverbs 22:6

When Ethan was born, he was immediately placed in a high-tech incubator due to a rare genetic disorder that involved a compromised immune system. The incubator was equipped with all the latest medical technology and allowed doctors to monitor Ethan's every vital sign remotely. His parents could only watch their newborn son through the glass of the incubator, longing to hold him but unable to do so for fear of spreading an infection to their child.

As Ethan grew older, he became more and more aware of the distance between himself and his parents. While they loved him deeply, the physical separation they were forced to maintain prevented them from forming a strong emotional bond. Ethan felt lonely and isolated, even in their presence.

One day, while browsing online, Ethan stumbled upon an article about attachment theory. He was fascinated by the idea that early childhood experiences could shape the way people form relationships throughout their lives. As he read more, he realized that his lack of physical touch and connection in his early years had left him with an insecure attachment style, making it difficult for him to form close relationships with others.

Determined to overcome his attachment challenges, Ethan began to experiment with ways to connect with others while still protecting his health. He started by asking his parents to hold his hand through the glove of his protective suit. As he grew more comfortable with physical touch, he started to expand his circle of trusted individuals to include his nurses and doctors, and eventually a small group of peers who also struggled with health challenges.

Through his determination and creativity, Ethan was able to build meaningful relationships with others, even in the face of adversity. While his genetic disorder would always present challenges, he found comfort in knowing that he could form deep and lasting connections with others and that his attachment style was not predetermined by his early experiences alone.

What Is Attachment Theory?

Attachment theory is a psychological concept that seeks to explain how humans form relationships and bonds with others, particularly with primary caregivers in early childhood. Several psychologists have developed this theory over the years, but the most notable contributors are John Bowlby and Mary Ainsworth. Attachment theory suggests that humans have an innate need to form close bonds with others, especially during infancy and childhood, for survival and emotional security. This bond is called an attachment and forms the foundation for future relationships.

Imagine a baby who is left in a room with a stranger. When the baby realizes their primary caregiver is absent, he or she will start crying and looking for them. The baby will continue to call and search for the caregiver until they return, providing comfort and security. This reaction exemplifies the attachment bond between the baby and the caregiver.

Mary Ainsworth further developed attachment theory by conducting the "Strange Situation" experiment, where she observed the behavior of children and their caregivers in a controlled environment (Ainsworth et al., 1978). A child with a secure attachment style has a healthy relationship with their caregiver and feels confident in their ability to seek comfort and security. They can also play and explore freely, knowing the caregiver is nearby. A classic example of a child with a secure attachment style is the character of Andy in the *Toy Story* movies. No matter what adventure Andy goes on, he knows that his toys (and, by extension, his caregiver) will always be there for him.

Insecure-avoidant attachment, on the other hand, is defined as a child being inconsistent in seeking comfort and security from their caregiver. They may avoid physical contact or seem indifferent to their caregiver's presence. This type of attachment can result from an unresponsive or neglectful caregiver. An example of a fictional character with an insecure-avoidant attachment is Nemo from the movie *Finding Nemo*. Despite his mother's love and protection, Nemo is brave and independent but distant from her sometimes.

Finally, insecure-ambivalent attachment is when a child constantly seeks comfort and security from their caregiver but also resists or becomes upset when they try to provide it. This type of attachment can result from a caregiver who is inconsistent in providing care or emotionally unavailable. An example of a fictional character with an insecure-ambivalent attachment is Simba from *The Lion King*. Despite his father's love and guidance, Simba is insecure about his abilities and frequently seeks his father's approval.

It is important to note that attachment styles are not set in stone and can change over time based on experiences and relationships with others. For example, a child with an insecure-avoidant attachment style may develop a more secure attachment style if they form a strong bond with a new caregiver.

Attachment theory helps us understand the foundation of human relationships and why we form bonds with others. It highlights the importance of early childhood relationships and their impact on our emotional security and future relationships. Whether it is Andy's unshakable confidence in his toys, Nemo's independence, or Simba's quest for approval, attachment theory can explain why we behave the way we do in our relationships. So, next time you watch your favorite movie or TV show, think about the attachment styles of the characters and how they relate to each other.

The concept of attachment also has implications for parenting. Parents can use attachment theory to understand their child's behavior and develop more effective parenting strategies. For instance, if a child has an insecure-avoidant attachment style, the parent needs to build trust and provide consistent comfort and security. If a child has an insecure-ambivalent attachment style, a parent may need to provide stability and support while giving the child space to explore and develop independence.

Attachment theory has been applied not only to parent-child relationships but also to adult romantic relationships, revealing that attachment styles can influence the quality of these relationships (Hazan & Shaver, 1987). A secure attachment style is associated with greater comfort with intimacy and trust in relationships, while individuals with insecure-avoidant attachment styles prefer to maintain emotional distance. Those with insecure-ambivalent attachment styles are more likely to struggle with jealousy and trust issues.

Attachment theory has also been applied to other fields, such as clinical psychology, education, and animal behavior (Shaver et al., 2016). In clinical psychology, attachment theory is often used to better understand and treat anxiety and depression rooted in childhood experiences and attachment patterns (Shaver et al., 2016).

In conclusion, attachment theory is a valuable framework for exploring the bonds and relationships that bring us together, whether we are considering the bond between a parent and child, romantic partners, or even our relationship with our pets. It is a rich and complex concept that continues to evolve and inform our understanding of human relationships (Shaver et al., 2016). Reflecting on the attachment styles and bonds in our relationships can provide insight into the forces that drive them.

Quick History

Early in the 20th century, British psychotherapist John Bowlby put forth the idea known as attachment theory. Bowlby held that a child's psychological development is significantly influenced by their interaction with their primary caregiver. He suggested that babies have a natural urge to create an emotional bond with their caregivers and that this need is crucial in developing a stable attachment.

Bowlby's theories were groundbreaking then, and his contributions laid the groundwork for attachment theory over the following several decades. Bowlby proposed that young children need an attachment to feel safe in their surroundings. His research mainly involved observations of young children and their caregivers. He also believed this parent-child relationship could significantly impact a child's psychological growth.

Following Bowlby's work, developmental psychologist Mary Ainsworth furthered the research on attachment theory. Ainsworth's studies led her to identify the various attachment styles that we touched on above. These attachment styles continue to serve as the foundation for understanding childhood attachment patterns today.

Another notable figure in the development of attachment theory is developmental psychologist and theorist Mary Main, who expanded the theory through her research on adult attachment patterns in the 1980s. According to Main, attachment styles formed throughout childhood may be observed in adulthood and can be used to predict how someone will behave in close relationships. Main's research confirms the significance of attachment for psychological growth and further established the importance of connection in psychological development.

Numerous theorists and researchers have continued to build and improve on attachment theory since the 1980s. The psychological community has now broadly accepted the legitimacy of attachment theory, which addresses many problems we face in our daily life, such as parenting practices, conflict in romantic relationships, anxiety, and depression. In clinical practice today, attachment theory is applied in several different ways. Psychologists use attachment theory to examine and comprehend relationships between adults in romantic relationships and between parents and children. Attachment theory is also used to understand and treat psychological disorders like anxiety and depression.

The theory has also been used to explore the impact of childhood adversity on psychological development. For example, a study by van IJzendoorn et al. (1995) found that children who experienced neglect or abuse had more difficulty in forming secure attachments than those who did not. Furthermore, a study by DeKlyen and Greenberg (2008) revealed that children who experienced early adversity had an increased risk of developing psychological problems, such as anxiety and depression, later in life. These findings suggest that attachment theory can be used to understand the effects of early childhood experiences on later psychological development.

In addition to its use in understanding the impact of early childhood experiences, attachment theory is also used to study adult romantic relationships. For example, a study by Feeney and Noller (1990) found that individuals with secure attachment styles were more likely to have successful and satisfying relationships. Furthermore,

Hazan and Shaver (1987) reveal that individuals with secure attachment are more likely to report higher levels of relationship satisfaction. These findings suggest that attachment theory can be used to understand the dynamics of adult romantic relationships.

Attachment theory has been a significant concept in psychology for over a century. From Bowlby's initial work to the further developments of Ainsworth, Main, and others, attachment theory has been developed and refined over the years and remains an important concept in many areas of psychology today.

Uses and Importance

Attachment theory has become one of the most essential and extensively researched theories in the field of psychology because it explores the relationship between a person and their attachment figure, usually their primary caregiver, as well as how these early connections affect our subsequent relationships and sense of self. However, we don't find attachment theory at work only in psychological research; since its beginnings, attachment theory has been used in a variety of professions and has significant implications for many areas of life, including relationships, mental health, and child development.

One of the main areas in which attachment theory can be applied is mental health. According to research, our attachment styles as children might significantly affect our mental health as adults. For example, individuals with secure attachments are more likely to be better adjusted psychologically, as well as having lower levels of anxiety and depression and higher levels of self-esteem and well-being compared to those with insecure attachments. With the development of attachment-based therapies to assist people in overcoming problems connected to attachment and trauma, attachment theory has also been applied to treating mental health concerns.

Another important use of attachment theory is in the field of child development. This theory helps us understand the importance of consistent, responsive caregiving in shaping a child's social, emotional, and cognitive development. Research has found that children with secure attachments are more likely to have better developmental outcomes, including better social skills, higher academic achievement, and improved overall health, than those with insecure attachments.

In addition, attachment theory can be applied more broadly in the study of interpersonal relationships. Individuals with a secure attachment style tend to form more fulfilling and satisfying relationships with their partners, family members, and friends (Ainsworth et al., 1978). They are also more likely to seek social support in times of stress and have more supportive social networks than those with insecure attachments.

Relationship experts have discovered that attachment theory provides a helpful foundation for comprehending how various attachment styles might affect the growth and success of partnerships. For instance, persons with secure attachments are more likely to develop happy, fulfilling love relationships and have more extensive social networks than those with insecure attachments. Researchers have also used attachment theory to examine parent-child interactions, examining how various attachment trajectories may affect the caliber of these relationships.

Attachment theory also has practical applications in the workplace. Research has shown that attachment style can impact an individual's ability to form positive relationships with coworkers and supervisors (Bowlby, 1969). This can affect job performance, satisfaction, and overall well-being. Employers and managers who understand attachment theory can use this knowledge to create a supportive work environment that promotes healthy relationships and improved job performance.

Attachment theory is also of great importance in the study of social support. Research has found that attachment style can predict the type of social support individuals are likely to seek and receive. Those with secure attachments are more likely to seek and receive emotional support than those with insecure attachments. Attachment theory has also been used to study the role of social help in coping with trauma and stress, with researchers exploring how different attachment styles can impact the effectiveness of social support in these situations.

Attachment theory has far-reaching implications for a range of disciplines beyond just psychology. It has been applied to education, social work, and even the workplace.

In education, attachment theory has been used to understand the impact of teachers and caregivers on the development of students. For example, teachers with a secure attachment style tend to form strong, supportive relationships with their students, leading to better academic outcomes and improved overall school performance (Bowlby, 1969). On the other hand, teachers with an insecure attachment style may struggle to form positive relationships with their students, leading to classroom disruptions and learning difficulties.

Attachment theory has been used in social work to understand and treat trauma. The attachment style of individuals who have experienced trauma can significantly affect their ability to cope and recover (Ainsworth et al., 1978). Social workers who understand attachment theory can use this knowledge to help individuals heal from past traumas and develop secure attachments in the future.

This theory is a rich and complex concept widely studied and applied in various fields. Whether you are a mental health professional, a teacher, a parent, or simply someone interested in human behavior, attachment theory has important implications for understanding how our early relationships shape our later lives. Attachment theory is essential to understand, focusing on the importance of consistent, responsive caregiving in shaping healthy development and relationships.

Attachment theory has wide-ranging implications for our understanding of human behavior and relationships. It offers valuable insights into how our early relationships shape our lives, from education and social work to the workplace and interpersonal relationships. By understanding attachment theory, we can work to promote secure attachments and positive outcomes in all areas of our lives.

Finally, attachment theory has important implications for our understanding of self. Research has found that our attachment style can impact our self-worth, self-esteem, and overall well-being (Bowlby, 1969). Individuals with a secure attachment style tend to have a positive self-image and a strong sense of self, while those with insecure attachments may struggle with self-doubt and low self-esteem.

Childhood Development and Attachment Theory

Childhood is a critical period of growth and development, during which children form the building blocks of their personality, behavior, and relationships (Hazan & Shaver, 1987). Understanding how children develop and the factors that shape their growth is essential to providing them with the support they need to become well-adjusted, confident adults. Childhood development refers to physical, cognitive, and emotional growth from birth to adolescence, during which children develop the skills to navigate the world around them and form relationships with others. The first five years of life is a crucial stage in childhood development as the child begins building the foundation of their personality and developing the skills they need to interact with others (van IJzendoorn, 2019).

Physical development is an essential aspect of childhood development. During the first five years of life, children experience rapid growth, learn to crawl, walk, run, and jump, develop fine motor skills, and gain the ability to use utensils and tools (Florida Tech Online, n.d.). As children grow, they become more agile and coordinated, further improving their motor skills.

Cognitive development is another critical aspect of childhood development. During the first five years of life, children's brains develop at an astonishing rate, and they learn to think, reason, and understand the world around them. They learn to recognize patterns, solve problems, and remember things, as well as develop their language skills and learn to communicate with others (NSPCC Learning, 2021).

Emotional development is the final aspect of childhood development. Children begin to recognize and express their emotions during the first five years of life, and they learn to understand their feelings and how to manage them. They develop empathy and the ability to understand and respond to others' emotions.

Childhood development is a complex process that involves physical, emotional, intellectual, social, and spiritual growth. It is a process that occurs over time, beginning from a child's birth and continuing through adulthood, and is heavily influenced by a child's environment, including their family, caretakers, and peers. Attachment is one of the most influential aspects of childhood development, as the child's relationships with their parents and other caregivers shape the child's future relationships (van IJzendoorn, 2019). Secure attachment relationships are particularly important for children's healthy development (Hazan & Shaver, 1987).

What Is Childhood Development?

Childhood development encompasses a child's growth and changes from birth until adulthood. This process is often divided into five main areas: physical, emotional, intellectual, social, and spiritual. Each of these areas of development is unique and important to a child's overall development. We have discussed the first three categories briefly in the previous section, but let us dive into them in more detail here.

Physical development includes various physical changes such as growth, motor skills, and coordination. A child's attachment style can significantly impact their physical development. For instance, a child with a secure attachment style may feel safe and confident enough to explore their environment, leading to better motor skills and coordination. On the other hand, a child with an insecure attachment style may have difficulty exploring and developing their physical abilities due to fear and anxiety.

Emotional development involves the ability to recognize and express emotions and form relationships with others. Attachment styles also play a significant role in a child's emotional development. Children with secure attachment styles tend to be more emotionally expressive and confident in forming relationships with others. In contrast, children with insecure attachment styles may struggle with regulating their emotions, leading to difficulty forming meaningful relationships.

Intellectual (or cognitive) development involves a child's ability to learn, reason, and solve problems. Children with secure attachment styles tend to have better cognitive skills, language development, and problem-solving abilities. By contrast, children with insecure attachment styles may struggle with learning and reasoning due to a lack of confidence in their abilities.

Social development is another important aspect of a child's growth, involving the ability to interact with others and form meaningful relationships. Children with secure attachment styles tend to have better social skills, communication, and conflict resolution skills. Children with insecure attachment styles, however, may struggle with social interactions, leading to difficulties in forming relationships and resolving conflicts.

Spiritual growth involves a child's understanding of the world and their beliefs and values. It forms the foundation of faith and thought patterns. A child's spiritual development ultimately forms their belief and perspective about God. It is a deeply personal and subjective aspect of development often shaped by a child's familial upbringing. However, research suggests a child's attachment style can also impact their spiritual development. Children with a secure attachment style tend to develop a deeper level of trust in their caregivers; this trust can be easily translated into trust in God, leading them to develop a stronger sense of faith or spirituality. On the other hand, children with insecure attachment styles may struggle with feelings of mistrust and disconnection, which can manifest as a negative spiritual outlook. They may feel disconnected from their faith or struggle to find meaning and purpose in life.

It is important to note that a child's attachment style is just one factor that can impact their spiritual development. Other factors, such as cultural background and exposure to different belief systems, can also play a significant role. Childhood development is a complex process; each child develops at their own pace. As a result, children must have a safe and supportive environment to reach their full potential.

Childhood development and attachment theory are two important concepts that explain how a child grows and develops. The childhood development lens focuses on the physical, emotional, intellectual, social, and spiritual aspects of a child's growth while attachment theory demonstrates the importance of a secure attachment relationship between a child and their primary caregiver. Parents and caregivers must provide a safe and supportive environment for children to reach their full potential.

The relationship between childhood development and attachment theory has been studied for decades and is still being researched.

Just as a secure attachment leads to positive outcomes, insecure attachments can lead to problems with self-confidence, self-esteem, and social skills. Insecure attachments can also lead to difficulty in regulating emotions and in forming relationships with others. Insecure attachments can also lead to problems in problem-solving and decision-making and increased stress and anxiety levels, impacting the child's physical, social, and emotional development.

One way to ensure secure attachments and healthy childhood development is through positive and supportive parenting. Positive parenting involves providing children with a safe and secure environment and opportunities to explore and learn. Parents should also provide children with consistent, loving, and non-judgmental guidance to develop trust and security in their relationships.

As parents, it's important to be there for your children in a supportive and non-judgmental way. This means creating an environment where your children feel safe to learn and explore without fear of criticism. It's also important to give consistent positive reinforcement and praise for their efforts and successes, helping them to build confidence and self-esteem.

Being an engaged parent is also crucial for your child's development. Take time to play and interact with your child, help with homework, and offer emotional support. Listening to your child and helping them process their emotions and experiences can help them to feel understood and supported, laying the foundation for healthy relationships in the future. Remember, your role as a parent is not just to provide for your child's basic needs but to actively participate in their growth and development.

In addition to the importance of secure attachments, early childhood development is influenced by a number of other factors. These include the child's physical health, nutrition, and environment. Parents must ensure their child receives adequate nutrition, regular health check-ups, and a safe and stimulating environment. This can help to support the child's physical, social, and emotional development.

As a parent, you want the best for your child. You want them to grow up happy, healthy, and successful. But have you ever thought about how your behavior toward and interactions with your child might impact their attachment style and, ultimately, their relationships later in life?

One of the most important things you can do for your child's development is to provide them with opportunities to explore and learn. This doesn't have to mean expensive toys or elaborate activities. It can be as simple as reading books together, going for a walk in the park, or playing a game of catch. By engaging with your child in these activities, you're not only helping them develop important skills, but you're also building a strong bond and attachment with them.

It's also important to be there for your child emotionally. Children need to feel safe and supported to develop a secure attachment style. This means listening to them when they talk, validating their feelings, and helping them process their experiences. By doing this, you're building trust and helping them to develop the skills necessary for healthy relationships later in life.

Of course, many other factors can impact childhood development, such as physical health and environment. But as a parent, you have a powerful influence on your child's early experiences. By providing a positive and supportive environment, you can help ensure that your child develops a secure attachment style and a healthy sense of self. And that can set them up for success in all areas of life.

Workbook One

1. What are the different attachment styles, and which one do you think you have? Take a few minutes to reflect on your relationships with close friends and family members, and consider how you typically respond to them.

2. Are there any negative patterns in your current relationships that you can trace back to childhood experiences? Try to identify the underlying attachment needs that might be driving these patterns.

3. Consider someone in your life who has a different attachment style than you. How does their behavior in relationships differ from your own, and how can you adapt your communication style to better understand and support them?

Chapter One Takeaway

By now, you should clearly understand attachment theory and its significance in childhood development. You have learned about the origins of attachment theory, its practical applications, and how it can help us better understand ourselves and others.

Remember, attachment theory is not just an academic concept. It has real-world implications for our relationships and emotional well-being. Whether you are struggling with an anxious attachment style or want to improve your relationships, attachment theory can be an invaluable tool.

As you continue reading this book, remember that self-awareness and compassion are key to overcoming an anxious attachment style. By understanding the root causes of our attachment patterns, we can begin to heal old wounds and form healthier, more fulfilling relationships.

Thank you for joining me on this journey. I hope you are as excited as I am to delve deeper into the topic of anxious attachment style and discover new ways to transform your relationships and your life.

CHAPTER TWO

What Is Your Style?

"The discerning heart seeks knowledge, but the mouth of a fool feeds on folly."

—Proverbs 15:14

Lilian found herself increasingly struggling in her relationships. She often felt anxious and insecure and had difficulty trusting her partner. As she and I began exploring her attachment style, we discovered that Lilian had an anxious attachment style, which meant she had a deep fear of rejection and abandonment.

Through the sessions, we worked on helping Lilian identify her attachment style and its impact on her relationships. She began to understand that her fears and anxieties were rooted in her early experiences with inconsistent caregiving and that these patterns were now affecting her adult relationships.

With this newfound awareness, Lilian was able to make significant progress in her relationships. She learned to communicate her needs and emotions more effectively and better understand her partner's behaviors and needs. By recognizing the patterns of her attachment style, Lilian was able to break free from her old habits and build healthier, more fulfilling relationships.

Lilian's story is a powerful example of why it is essential to identify your attachment style. Understanding how our early experiences shape our beliefs and relationship behaviors can give us a deeper insight into ourselves and others. With this insight, we can break free from harmful patterns and build healthier, more secure connections with those around us.

In this chapter, I will delve deeper into the different attachment styles and explore how they can affect our relationships and overall well-being. Understanding your attachment style can give you valuable insights into your behavior patterns, emotions, and thoughts in close relationships.

Through various assessments and exercises, I will help you identify your attachment style and guide you in navigating the challenges and opportunities that come with it. In addition to discussing the main three attachment styles (secure, avoidant, and anxious), I will also address the fourth style, disorganized, which is often overlooked but can significantly impact the lives of those who have this style.

This chapter offers you a roadmap to understanding yourself and others better. Join me as we explore the fascinating world of attachment theory and discover how it can transform relationships and lives.

Secure Attachment Style

Annie grew up with parents who were supportive and loving. They were always there for her when she needed emotional support but encouraged her to be independent and make her own decisions. As a result, Annie developed a strong sense of self-worth and high self-esteem and is comfortable expressing her emotions to others. She has close and supportive relationships with her friends and family and can offer support and comfort when they need it. When Annie is in a romantic relationship, she can trust her partner and is comfortable with emotional intimacy. She believes her partner will be there for her when she's in need, and she can offer the same support in return.

What does it mean to have a secure attachment style?

Having a secure attachment style means that an individual has developed a healthy sense of trust, emotional intimacy, and autonomy in their relationships with others. They have a strong sense of self-worth and their self-esteem is not overly dependent on other people's opinions. They are comfortable expressing their emotions and needs to others and are equally comfortable receiving emotional support from others.

People with a secure attachment style have a positive view of themselves and others. They believe that they are worthy of love and respect and that others are generally trustworthy and dependable. They can form close, intimate relationships without fear of abandonment or rejection.

Another thing to note about individuals with a secure attachment style is that they can maintain a healthy balance between intimacy and independence. They are comfortable being alone and pursuing their interests and goals, but they are also able to form strong bonds with others without feeling suffocated or overwhelmed.

Having a secure attachment style is characterized by a strong sense of self-worth, trust, emotional intimacy, autonomy, and a healthy balance between intimacy and independence in relationships. It is a valuable asset in creating and maintaining healthy, fulfilling relationships with others.

It is no surprise that people with a secure attachment style also tend to have good communication skills and can express their needs, feelings, and desires clearly and assertively. This allows them to navigate conflicts healthily and constructively, leading to more harmonious relationships with others. Moreover, individuals with a secure attachment style tend to have higher levels of emotional intelligence, which allows them to empathize with others and understand their emotions. This helps them build deeper connections with others and form more meaningful relationships.

What are the signs of a secure attachment style?

A strong sense of self-esteem and self-worth is one of the most telling signs of a secure attachment style. People with a secure attachment style are generally happy with themselves and their lives. They are comfortable with emotional intimacy and have close and supportive relationships with their partners, friends, and family. They can express their emotions openly and directly without fear of being rejected or judged. They are also comfortable with romantic partners expressing their feelings and can offer support and reassurance in times of need.

How does a secure attachment style develop?

Secure attachment develops when caregivers are responsive to an infant's needs and provide consistent and loving care. When the infant cries or expresses discomfort, the caregiver responds quickly and with warmth, soothing the infant's distress. Over time, this creates a strong bond between the infant and caregiver. As the child grows, the caregiver provides a safe and supportive environment, fostering independence while remaining emotionally available. This allows the child to develop a sense of security, which carries over into their relationships throughout their lives.

Avoidant Attachment Style

Miguel grew up with emotionally detached, distant parents. They did not offer him much emotional support or affection and often ignored his need for attention and validation. As a result, Miguel developed an avoidant attachment style, characterized by a reluctance to form close relationships and a tendency to emotionally distance himself from others.

The avoidant attachment style, also known as dismissive-avoidant attachment, is characterized by a tendency to distance oneself from others emotionally. Individuals with this attachment style tend to downplay the importance of close relationships and often avoid emotional intimacy. They may appear self-sufficient and independent, preferring to rely on themselves rather than others.

What does it mean to have an avoidant attachment style?

Having an avoidant attachment style means that an individual has difficulty forming close, intimate relationships with others. They may feel uncomfortable with emotional intimacy and tend to avoid or suppress their emotions to maintain a sense of independence and self-sufficiency. People with an avoidant attachment style may also have a negative view of themselves and others and may feel that relationships are not worth the effort or potential for hurt and disappointment.

What are the signs of an avoidant attachment style?

1. *A reluctance to form close relationships:* People with an avoidant attachment style may struggle to form intimate bonds with others. They may keep others at a distance or only engage in superficial relationships that do not require emotional intimacy or vulnerability.

2. *Difficulty expressing emotions:* People with an avoidant attachment style may avoid expressing their emotions, especially those related to

vulnerability or intimacy. They may feel uncomfortable with emotional displays or may suppress their own emotions to avoid feeling overwhelmed.

3. *A tendency to prioritize independence and self-sufficiency*: People with an avoidant attachment style may believe it is better to be independent than to form close relationships with others. They may feel that relying on others is a sign of weakness or may prefer to handle things on their own rather than seek support from others.

4. *A negative view of relationships*: People with an avoidant attachment style may view relationships as more trouble than they are worth. They may feel that relationships are likely to result in hurt or disappointment, and may avoid them altogether.

5. *Difficulty with trust*: People with an avoidant attachment style may struggle to trust others, especially in intimate or vulnerable situations. They may have difficulty relying on others for emotional support or may feel that others are not dependable or trustworthy.

How does an avoidant attachment style develop?

The avoidant attachment style typically develops in response to inconsistent or unresponsive caregiving in childhood. Children raised by emotionally distant parents who do not respond consistently to their needs may learn to suppress their emotions and rely on themselves for comfort and support. As a result, they may grow up believing that emotions are weak or dangerous and that self-sufficiency is the key to survival.

Imagine a child who cries for comfort when upset, but their caregiver consistently fails to respond in a nurturing or comforting way. Over time, the child may learn to stop seeking reassurance from others and suppress their emotions. They may develop a self-reliant attitude and learn to cope with their distress alone. As an adult, this child may exhibit an avoidant attachment style, avoiding emotional closeness and preferring to rely on themselves rather than on others.

Anxious Attachment Style

Despite her ardent devotion to the Christian faith and her fervent love for God, Sarah encountered difficulties in her relationships with others. Her tendency to develop overly strong bonds with romantic partners led her to constantly worry about their level of commitment and affection towards her in return.

Having previously experienced several failed relationships, Sarah became increasingly anxious, making it extremely difficult for her to trust others. Nevertheless, one fine day, Sarah met John at church. John's strengths were his compassionate nature, caring disposition, and unwavering faith in God. Sarah felt an immediate connection to him and began seeing him more frequently. However, as their relationship progressed, Sarah's anxious attachment style began to reemerge and take control. She would incessantly text John, inquiring about his whereabouts and activities, and soon became preoccupied with the idea that he may lose interest in her.

After noting Sarah's anxious tendencies, John attempted to console her by reaffirming his love and commitment to her. He expressed how much she meant to him and his dedication to their relationship. Nevertheless, Sarah's anxious thoughts persisted, making it difficult for her to believe John's assertions.

Eventually, Sarah's anxiety reached a boiling point. She had planned a special date with John, but he was running late. She began to worry excessively that he had abandoned her or found someone else. She tried calling and texting him but received no response. Her anxiety reached an unprecedented level, and she felt like she was spiraling out of control.

John finally arrived, bringing Sarah a sense of relief, but as they began to talk, she realized that her anxious attachment style had caused her to push him away. She knew she had to take responsibility, work on her trust issues, and learn to release her anxious thoughts.

Sarah turned to God for guidance and prayed for His help. With prayer and therapy, she was able to identify and reframe her anxious thoughts. She also developed trust in John and his love for her.

28

Gradually, Sarah's anxious attachment style began to dissipate. She learned to derive pleasure from her relationship with John without fretting over the future. She gained faith in God's plan and believed that everything would work out in the end. Above all, she regarded her relationship with John as a divine gift that she would always treasure.

What does it mean to have an anxious attachment style?

People with an anxious attachment style tend to experience high levels of anxiety and uncertainty in close relationships. They may worry that their partner will abandon them, feel neglected or unloved, or fear they are not good enough to be loved. This attachment style is often characterized by a strong desire for closeness and intimacy along with a fear of abandonment or rejection.

What are the signs of an anxious attachment style?

Anxious attachment is characterized by an intense need for closeness and intimacy in relationships. Some of the symptoms of an anxious attachment style include:

1. *Fear of abandonment*: Anxious individuals may be highly preoccupied with the fear of being abandoned or rejected by their partner. They may be overly clingy or needy, seeking constant reassurance that their partner loves and values them.

2. *Extreme sensitivity to rejection*: Anxious individuals tend to be highly sensitive to signals of rejection or disinterest from their partner. They may interpret even minor slights as evidence that their partner is losing interest in them, leading to intense anxiety and distress.

3. *Strong desire for intimacy and closeness*: Anxious individuals may feel a strong passion for intimacy and familiarity in their relationships. They may crave physical touch, emotional connection, and validation from their partner and become highly upset or anxious when these needs are unmet.

4. *Jealousy and possessiveness*: Anxious individuals may also experience intense jealousy or possessiveness, especially if they perceive that their

partner is becoming emotionally or physically close to someone else. This can lead to conflict and tension in the relationship.

5. *Difficulty trusting others*: Anxious individuals may struggle to trust others, especially in close relationships. They may be highly suspicious of their partner's motives or unable to believe that their partner truly cares for them, even in the face of evidence to the contrary.

Individuals with an anxious attachment style tend to experience intense emotional reactions to the ups and downs of their relationships. They may feel overwhelmed by emotions and struggle to regulate their responses to situations that trigger their attachment fears and anxieties. It is important to note that these behaviors and signs can vary in intensity and frequency and may not always be present in every person with an anxious attachment style.

How does an anxious attachment style develop?

Anxious attachment style can develop in childhood due to inconsistent or unpredictable caregiver responses. When a child's needs for comfort, reassurance, and validation are not met consistently, they can develop a sense of insecurity and anxiety in their attachment relationships.

For example, a child with an anxious attachment style may have a parent who is sometimes attentive and nurturing but other times dismissive or unavailable. The child may feel uncertain about when they will receive comfort and support, leading to a preoccupation with seeking reassurance and attention from their caregiver.

Over time, this can lead to a pattern of behavior in which the child becomes hypervigilant about their caregiver's availability, and they may become clingy, demanding, or emotionally reactive in response to any perceived threat to the relationship. This behavior can persist into adulthood and manifest in close relationships, leading to a pattern of seeking constant reassurance, feeling quickly rejected or abandoned, and experiencing heightened anxiety and stress in relationships.

Several other factors can contribute to developing an anxious attachment style, such as early trauma or disruptions in caregiving, inconsistent or unstable family environments, and genetics.

In adulthood, individuals with an anxious attachment style may struggle to form and maintain healthy relationships due to their fear of rejection and abandonment. They may find themselves in toxic or unhealthy relationships or struggle to communicate their needs effectively to their partner.

However, with awareness and support, individuals with an anxious attachment style can learn to manage their anxiety and form healthy, fulfilling relationships. Therapy, self-reflection, and building healthy communication skills can help you to work through anxious attachment patterns.

Disorganized Attachment Style

Samantha grew up in an environment where her caregivers were unpredictable and sometimes frightening. Her parents were often neglectful; when they were present, they were abusive and erratic. Samantha developed a disorganized attachment style. As a result, she lacks trust in others and has difficulty regulating her own emotions. In her relationships, Samantha struggles with fear, confusion, and disorientation, as her past experiences have left her without a clear framework for healthy attachment. She struggles with both avoidant and anxious behaviors in her relationships, finding it hard to set and maintain appropriate boundaries.

Despite these challenges, the good news is that with support and therapy, individuals with a disorganized attachment style can develop more secure and healthy attachment patterns.

What does it mean to have a disorganized attachment style?

A disorganized attachment style means that an individual has experienced significant and unresolved trauma or abuse during the early years of their development. This can result in conflicting feelings and behaviors in their relationships with others, as they may simultaneously seek and avoid emotional closeness. Individuals with a disorganized attachment style often struggle with

31

regulating their emotions and may exhibit unpredictable or even frightening behavior in their relationships. They may also have difficulty forming trusting relationships with others and struggle with a negative self-image.

What are the signs of a disorganized attachment style?

1. *Fear and confusion around attachment figures:* People with a disorganized attachment style may feel fearful or confused around their attachment figures. They may both want to be close to their attachment figures and want to avoid them at the same time.

2. *Inconsistent behavior:* People with a disorganized attachment style may display inconsistent behavior. They may alternate between seeking comfort from others and avoiding them.

3. *Difficulty regulating emotions:* Individuals with a disorganized attachment style may struggle to regulate their emotions. They may often feel overwhelmed by intense emotions and have difficulty calming down.

4. *Chaotic relationships:* People with a disorganized attachment style may have chaotic relationships characterized by intense emotional highs and lows. They may also struggle with maintaining long-term relationships.

5. *Tendency to dissociate:* People with a disorganized attachment style may dissociate when faced with stress or trauma. Dissociation is a state in which an individual feels detached from their thoughts, feelings, and surroundings.

6. *Poor boundaries:* Individuals with a disorganized attachment style may struggle with setting and maintaining healthy boundaries in their relationships. They may have difficulty expressing their needs and saying no to others.

7. *Trust issues:* People with a disorganized attachment style may struggle to trust others. They may have a deep-seated fear of being hurt or rejected by others and may struggle to form close, intimate relationships.

How does a disorganized attachment style develop?

A disorganized attachment style typically develops in response to significant trauma or abuse during early childhood. Children with disorganized attachment often have caregivers who are emotionally unstable, neglectful, or abusive. These caregivers may have difficulty regulating their emotions themselves or exhibit frightening or erratic behavior. As a result, the child learns to associate the caregiver with both comfort and fear, leading to confusion and disorientation.

Children with a disorganized attachment style may also experience a lack of a secure base, as they cannot rely on their caregiver for comfort or protection. This can lead to helplessness and a lack of trust in themselves and others.

Over time, these experiences can lead to the development of maladaptive coping strategies, such as dissociation, emotional numbing, or avoidance. These strategies may help the child to cope in the short term but can lead to difficulties in forming healthy relationships later in life.

It is important to note that not all children who experience trauma or abuse will develop a disorganized attachment style. However, the risk increases in those who have experienced multiple traumatic events, have caregivers with unresolved trauma or mental health issues, or lack support from other adults.

How to Identify Your Style

Knowing your attachment style might help you better understand how you interact with people and approach relationships. You can identify your attachment style in several ways, such as by reflecting on your early experiences, examining your current relationships, and going to counseling. By better understanding your attachment style, you can begin to make positive changes in your relationships and work towards *developing a more secure attachment style.* *

Ready to master communication? Dive into Worksheet #1 and unravel the intriguing differences between narcissists and codependents. Don't wait – download your BONUS #1 at the start of the book or check this QR code and transform your understanding today!

Here are some ways to identify your attachment style:

1. Take an attachment style quiz

One way to identify your attachment style is by taking a quiz. This can be beneficial if you already suspect you have a particular attachment style. Many online quizzes are available that can help you identify your style. These quizzes are usually based on well-researched questionnaires designed to evaluate your attachment patterns.

However, it is essential to note that online quizzes are not a substitute for professional therapy. A qualified therapist can provide a much more accurate assessment of your attachment style and help you understand how your attachment style affects your relationships and your life.

If you have identified your attachment style through a quiz or other means and you are concerned about how it may affect your life, it is essential to seek the help of a therapist. A therapist can help you explore your attachment patterns in a safe, supportive environment and help you identify ways to improve your relationships and increase your overall well-being.

Please note that therapy is not just for people struggling with severe mental health issues. It is a valuable tool that can help anyone who wants to improve their relationships, self-awareness, and overall quality of life. If you are ready to explore your attachment style and improve your relationships, consider seeing a therapist specializing in attachment theory. They can guide you in understanding your attachment style and developing healthy, secure attachment patterns that can lead to more fulfilling relationships.

2. Reflect on your childhood experiences

Our attachment style is often shaped by how we were cared for and responded to in childhood. Our caregivers' responsiveness and sensitivity to our needs can affect how we develop and maintain relationships. Therefore, reflecting on our childhood experiences can be a valuable tool in identifying our attachment style.

When reflecting on your childhood experiences, it is essential to consider the quality of your relationship with your caregivers. Did you feel secure and supported by them, or did you feel neglected and unimportant? Did they respond promptly and appropriately, or did you often feel that your needs were not addressed? These early experiences can have a lasting impact on your attachment style.

For example, if you grew up feeling like your needs were often ignored or dismissed, you may have developed an anxious attachment style. You may struggle with trust and feel insecure in your relationships, constantly seeking validation and reassurance from romantic partners. Alternatively, you may have developed a secure attachment style if you grew up feeling like your caregivers were consistently available and responsive to your needs. You will likely feel more confident in your relationships and trust that your partner will be there for you when you need them.

By reflecting on your childhood experiences, you can recognize patterns in your behavior and approach to relationships. You may identify specific triggers that cause you to feel anxious or insecure in your relationships, allowing you to work through these issues and develop a more secure attachment style.

3. Observe your current relationships

Your existing relationships can also explain your attachment style. Do you tend to feel anxious or insecure in your relationships? Do you find it difficult to trust others? Do you tend to avoid getting close to others? These patterns can be indicative of an insecure attachment style.

4. Seek therapy

As we touched on in the first point, a mental health professional can help you identify your attachment style and work through any issues contributing to it. Therapy can also provide a safe space to explore your relationships and learn new ways of relating to others. A therapist can help you identify negative patterns and help you develop a more secure attachment style. They can also help you develop strategies to address any challenges or difficulties you may be experiencing due to your attachment style.

5. Journal

Journaling can help you identify patterns in your behavior and emotions, as well as recognize triggers and situations that may be linked to your attachment style. It can also help you process difficult experiences and develop greater self-awareness.

While attachment styles are thought to be relatively stable across the lifespan, there is good news: it is possible to change one's attachment patterns with therapy, introspection, and a willingness to work on improving the quality of one's relationships. Remember, identifying your attachment style is the first step in creating more fulfilling and healthy relationships, as long as you take the time to develop greater self-awareness and are willing to explore and work on your attachment style.

Workbook Two

1. Which attachment style resonates with you the most, and why? Try to identify a past or current relationship that supports this attachment style.

_____

_____

_____

_____

2. Reflect on a recent disagreement or misunderstanding you had with someone close to you. Did your attachment style play a role in how you responded or reacted? If so, how?

_____

_____

_____

_____

Chapter Two Takeaway

By now, you should understand the four main attachment styles: secure, avoidant, anxious, and disorganized. You have learned how each style develops, the key traits associated with each style, and how to identify which attachment style you have.

Knowing your attachment style is the first step toward healing and growth. By understanding your own needs and tendencies, you can begin to identify the behaviors and thought patterns that may be holding you back. Whether you have an anxious, avoidant, or disorganized attachment style, there is hope for change.

Remember that God's love for us is unconditional, and He wants us to experience the joy and fulfillment that comes from healthy relationships. By relying on Him and His Word, we can begin to heal from our past hurts and develop a more secure attachment style that reflects the love and grace of our Heavenly Father.

PART TWO

UNDERSTANDING AND REWORKING YOUR STYLE

This part of the book is designed to provide you with a deeper understanding of your attachment style and how it impacts your relationships. This section is divided into three chapters, each tackling a specific aspect of attachment theory and offering practical advice for reworking one's attachment style.

In Chapter 3, "Attachment Style Interactions," you will learn how your attachment style affects your interactions with your partner (or with future partners). This chapter will help you identify how your attachment style might contribute to relationship problems and offer strategies for improving communication and resolving conflicts.

Chapter 4, "Changing Your Attachment Style," delves into the process of reworking one's attachment style. This chapter provides specific tools and techniques for changing your attachment style, including mindfulness practices.

Finally, Chapter 5, "Overcoming Jealousy and Insecurity in Your Relationships: Deal with Anxiety and Avoidance," focuses on two of the most common challenges faced by individuals with anxious attachment styles: jealousy and insecurity. This chapter will help you understand the root causes of these emotions and provide you with practical strategies for managing them and building healthier relationships.

Overall, Part 2 is an essential resource for anyone looking to improve their relationships and overcome attachment-related challenges.

CHAPTER THREE

Attachment Style Interactions

"Two are better than one because they have a good reward for their toil. For if they fall, one will lift up his fellow. But woe to him who is alone when he falls and has not another to lift him up!"

—Ecclesiastes 4:9-10

Mia and Sam seemed an unlikely pair. Mia was an introverted artist who spent most of her time alone in her studio, while Sam was an outgoing extrovert who loved being the life of the party.

Despite their differences, they found themselves drawn to each other and quickly fell in love. But as their relationship progressed, they started to notice some strange patterns in their interactions.

Mia would often become anxious when Sam was out with his friends, feeling like she wasn't important to him. Sam, on the other hand, would become distant and aloof when Mia needed emotional support.

While browsing online one day, Mia saw an article about attachment styles. After reading through it, she sent the article to Sam. They both then realized what was going on. Mia had a fearful-avoidant attachment style, which made her anxious and fearful in relationships. Sam had a disorganized attachment style, which made it difficult for him to form healthy emotional connections with others.

This unique pairing of attachment styles made their relationship a constant rollercoaster of emotions. Mia's fear of abandonment triggered Sam's fear of emotional intimacy, leading him to withdraw and shut down emotionally. Mia, in turn, would become even more anxious and fearful.

But despite these challenges, the couple were committed to making their relationship work. They started seeing a therapist, who helped them understand their attachment styles and learn healthier ways to communicate and support each other.

Through their journey, they learned that love isn't always easy, and that sometimes it takes hard work and commitment to build a healthy, secure relationship.

This unique story highlights the importance of understanding your attachment style and how it can impact your relationships in unexpected ways. In this chapter, we will explore each of the attachment styles and how they can interact with one another, even in the most uncommon and unique pairings.

Attachment Style Interactions

In Part 1 of this book, we laid the foundation for understanding attachment theory, including its history and development, the four attachment styles (secure, anxious, avoidant, and disorganized), and the role of attachment in shaping our emotions and behavior. As we discussed, attachment theory is a well-researched and widely accepted framework that helps explain how early childhood experiences shape the way we connect with others throughout our lives. Many studies have demonstrated how attachment styles can profoundly impact our social interactions and relationships.

This chapter, therefore, explores how our attachment styles influence our relationships with others. Whether you have an anxious, avoidant, secure, or disorganized attachment style, it affects how you approach relationships and respond to the people around you. By understanding the unique dynamics of each style, you can gain a greater awareness of your tendencies and patterns in relationships.

For example, individuals with an anxious attachment style tend to have a strong desire for intimacy and connection but also have a heightened fear of rejection or abandonment. This can lead to clinginess, jealousy, and emotional highs and lows in their relationships. On the other hand, individuals with an avoidant attachment style tend to prioritize independence and self-sufficiency but may struggle with vulnerability and emotional intimacy. This can result in behaviors such as emotional distancing, a fear of commitment, and avoidance of deeper emotional connections.

This section will explore the different attachment styles and how they manifest in our social interactions, including friendships, romantic relationships, and professional settings. We will also delve into the impact of attachment styles on relationship satisfaction, conflict resolution, and communication.

Importantly, this section will also focus on how to rework your attachment style to improve your relationships. While your attachment style is formed mainly in childhood, research has shown that it can be modified through intentional effort and practice. Whether you are struggling to find a fulfilling romantic partnership or experiencing difficulties in your friendships, developing a more secure attachment style can make all the difference.

I encourage you to continue reading and exploring the different attachment styles and their impact on your relationships. By understanding yourself and your interactions with others, you can take the necessary steps to create more fulfilling and healthy relationships.

Manifestations of Attachment Styles in Relationships

Humans have an innate need to form and maintain close relationships with others. Our attachment style largely influences the way we approach and experience these relationships. Over time, I have come to learn that understanding the manifestations of attachment styles in relationships is critical in helping individuals navigate their interpersonal connections. Understanding the role of attachment styles in relationships can help individuals develop more secure and satisfying connections with their partners, leading to greater emotional well-being and fulfillment (Shaver et al., 2016).

Attachment styles are manifested in relationships through various behaviors and attitudes that reflect an individual's feelings about intimacy, trust, and emotional connection. Here are some examples of how each attachment style may be manifested in relationships:

1. Avoidant attachment style

Individuals with an avoidant attachment style keep their partners at a distance, avoiding deep emotional connections and intimacy. They may prioritize independence and self-sufficiency over relationships and may feel uncomfortable with displays of vulnerability or neediness. Avoidant individuals may dismiss their partner's emotional needs and find engaging in emotional conversations difficult.

In romantic relationships, an avoidant attachment style can manifest in several ways. For example, an avoidant individual may withdraw emotionally or physically from their partner when they feel vulnerable or emotionally overwhelmed. They may also prioritize work or other activities over spending time with their partner, leading to feelings of neglect or abandonment on their partner's end. Other behaviors the person with avoidant attachment style may exhibit include:

- Being emotionally unavailable or detached from their partner
- Being reluctant to share personal information or feelings
- Avoiding physical affection, such as hugging or cuddling
- Feeling uncomfortable with emotional intimacy
- Pulling away from their partner when they feel emotionally overwhelmed

2. Secure attachment style

A secure attachment style is characterized by a comfortable sense of trust and safety in relationships. Individuals with this attachment style tend to be comfortable with emotional intimacy and can communicate their needs and emotions effectively to their partners. They are often able to balance their own needs with their partner's needs, creating a healthy and mutually satisfying relationship dynamic.

In romantic relationships, a secure attachment style can manifest in several ways. For example, a secure individual may prioritize spending time with their partner, actively listen to and validate their partner's emotions, and engage in healthy conflict resolution strategies. They may also be comfortable expressing their emotions and needs, creating a foundation of open and honest communication in the relationship. Individuals with a secure attachment style may exhibit the following behaviors:

- Being comfortable with closeness and emotional intimacy
- Feeling confident in their ability to communicate with their partner
- Being able to regulate their emotions during conflict

- Trusting their partner and feeling secure in the relationship
- Feeling comfortable expressing their needs and wants to their partner

3. Anxious attachment style

A fear of abandonment and a need for constant reassurance in relationships characterizes an anxious attachment style. Individuals with this attachment style may feel overwhelmed by their emotions and struggle to regulate them effectively. They may worry that their partner will leave or reject them, and they may engage in behaviors designed to elicit reassurance from their partner.

An anxious individual may become clingy or possessive of their partner, seeking constant contact or attention. They may also become easily upset or distressed when their partner is unavailable or unresponsive, leading to conflicts and misunderstandings. People with an anxious attachment style tend to exhibit these behavioral patterns:

- Seeking constant reassurance and validation from their partner
- Becoming overly sensitive to their partner's behaviors and moods
- Feeling anxious when their partner is not available or responsive
- Struggling with jealousy and insecurity in the relationship
- Becoming emotionally overwhelmed and easily upset during a conflict

4. Disorganized attachment style

A lack of consistency or coherence in attachment behaviors characterizes a disorganized attachment style. Individuals with this attachment style may struggle to regulate their emotions effectively, leading to erratic or unpredictable behaviors. They may have also experienced significant unresolved past relationship trauma, which impacts their current ability to form healthy relationships.

People with a disorganized attachment style may exhibit contradictory behaviors in romantic relationships, seeking emotional closeness and then distancing themselves from their partners. They may struggle with emotional regulation and fear being abandoned or engulfed by their partner. Individuals with a disorganized attachment style may exhibit the following behaviors:

- Engaging in erratic or unpredictable behavior

- Struggling with emotional regulation during a conflict

- Feeling torn between a desire for closeness and fear of abandonment

- Becoming overwhelmed by feelings of shame or guilt

- Feeling confused or uncertain about their own emotions and needs

Understanding how your attachment style manifests in your relationship is crucial in developing a healthier and more fulfilling connection with your partner. By recognizing and addressing negative behavior patterns, you can learn to communicate more effectively, regulate your emotions, and create more secure and satisfying relationships.

A Complex Mix

Attachment styles are not always clear-cut and can sometimes be a complex mix of different styles. This can be seen in individuals who have experienced childhood trauma or abuse and have struggled with multiple relationship challenges. In this context, it is vital to understand how these styles mix together in order to develop healthy relationships.

Anxious-Preoccupied Attachment Style

Anxious-preoccupied attachment style, also known as anxious-ambivalent, is characterized by a strong desire for intimacy and emotional connection. Individuals with this attachment style tend to seek out relationships and are often preoccupied with thoughts about said relationship and their partner's feelings toward them. They often fear rejection and abandonment and may exhibit clingy or needy behavior in their relationships.

Individuals with an anxious-preoccupied attachment style may have had inconsistent or unreliable caregivers during childhood, leading them to develop a deep sense of insecurity and distrust in relationships. As a result, they tend to be hypersensitive to changes in their partner's behavior, often interpreting them as a sign of rejection or abandonment. They may also struggle with low self-esteem, self-doubt, and anxiety in their relationships.

If you have an anxious-preoccupied attachment style, it is essential that you develop a sense of self-worth and confidence in your relationships. This may involve exploring past attachment experiences and working to reframe negative self-talk and beliefs about relationships. It is also essential to find a safe and supportive environment where you can express your emotions and fears without judgment or criticism. By building a secure base and promoting a sense of autonomy, you can learn to develop healthy relationships and feel more secure in your attachments.

Fearful-Avoidant Attachment Style

Fearful-avoidant attachment style can be a tricky one to understand. Picture a person who wants intimacy but at the same time is fearful of it. Sounds complicated, right? It's like wanting to swim in the ocean but being too scared to get in the water. It is indeed a complex mix of craving connection while also feeling the need to protect oneself from the vulnerability that comes with it.

People with a fearful-avoidant attachment style tend to have much internal conflict, oscillating between two opposing needs. On the one hand, they crave emotional intimacy, love, and closeness. On the other hand, they fear the hurt, disappointment, and rejection that often come with being in an intimate relationship. They may push people away, fearing they will inevitably leave if they let them get too close.

If you or someone you know identifies with a fearful-avoidant attachment style, it's important to remember that it does not have to be a life sentence. Through therapy, you can work to better understand and manage these unhealthy attachment patterns, ultimately leading to healthier and more fulfilling relationships.

Dismissive-Avoidant Attachment Style

Dismissive-avoidant attachment style is characterized by an emotional disconnection from others and a tendency to avoid close relationships. People with this attachment style prioritize independence and self-sufficiency over emotional intimacy, often viewing emotions as a sign of weakness.

As a therapist, I often see individuals with a dismissive-avoidant attachment style struggle to maintain intimate relationships—which they desire to have, despite their equal desire for independence. They may become distant or dismissive when their partner expresses a need for emotional connection, which can create feelings of rejection and frustration in the other person.

One of the challenges of working with individuals with a dismissive-avoidant attachment style is helping them recognize the importance of emotional connection in relationships. They may have learned to suppress their emotions as a coping mechanism, which can make it difficult for them to express themselves authentically in relationships.

I often work with clients to identify the underlying beliefs and fears contributing to their dismissive-avoidant attachment style. We may explore past experiences that have shaped their attachment styles, such as a history of emotional neglect or abandonment. Through this process, clients can begin to understand why they struggle with emotional intimacy and develop new strategies for building and maintaining healthy relationships.

It is important to note once again that a dismissive-avoidant attachment style is not necessarily a permanent trait. While it does present some unique challenges in relationships, with the proper support and self-awareness, you can learn to form more secure attachments and create fulfilling relationships.

Disorganized Attachment Style

We have discussed the disorganized attachment style at length in previous sections of this book, but I'd like to include it again here because it is considered the most complex and challenging to address in therapy due to its unpredictable and erratic behaviors. Individuals with disorganized attachment styles may exhibit both avoidant and anxious attachment patterns and often display inconsistent and contradictory behaviors. They may have experienced significant childhood trauma, including neglect, abuse, or exposure to domestic violence, resulting in an inability to develop coherent coping strategies and a lack of trust in others and the world around them.

Individuals with a disorganized attachment style require a safe and secure therapeutic environment to process their traumatic experiences and explore the root causes of their attachment difficulties. They may struggle with boundaries in their relationships, pushing others away one moment and then clinging to them the next, which leads to confusion and frustration for everyone involved. They may also struggle with emotional regulation, experiencing intense emotional reactions that can be overwhelming and difficult to manage.

If you have a disorganized attachment style, a therapist can work with you to develop healthy emotional regulation strategies, such as mindfulness and relaxation techniques. Your therapist may also help you develop a sense of safety and security in the therapeutic relationship by setting clear boundaries and consistently following through with them.

What Attachment Styles Are Attracted to Each Other?

Humans have a fundamental need to form connections with others, and these connections are formed through a complex interplay of emotions, behaviors, and beliefs. One of the most critical factors in forming and maintaining close relationships is, of course, attachment style, which is developed in early childhood and can profoundly impact adult relationships (Hoyt & Yates, 2011). Interestingly, research has shown that individuals with different attachment styles are often attracted to each other, even though their interactions can be fraught with tension and conflict. In this section, we will explore the dynamics of attraction between different attachment styles and provide examples to help you better understand these complex relationships.

While individuals with different attachment styles may be attracted to each other, their interactions can often be fraught with tension and conflict. By understanding the underlying factors that draw anxious and avoidant individuals to each other, we can begin to unpack the dynamics of these complex relationships and work towards more fulfilling, satisfying relationships.

Secure individuals tend to have positive views of themselves and their partners and feel comfortable with emotional intimacy. They value communication, trust, and mutual support in their relationships. They are attracted to partners who are also secure, as these relationships tend to be stable, satisfying, and mutually fulfilling. Secure individuals may also be attracted to anxious-preoccupied partners, who tend to be affectionate, expressive, and emotionally engaged. However, they may find dismissive-avoidant and fearful-avoidant partners challenging, as they tend to avoid intimacy and emotional vulnerability (Shaver et al., 2016).

Anxious-preoccupied individuals often crave emotional closeness and validation from their partners. They may worry about abandonment and may be anxious or jealous in relationships. They are often attracted to dismissive-avoidant partners, who may initially seem aloof or mysterious but later become distant or unresponsive. Anxious-preoccupied individuals may also be attracted to fearful-avoidant partners, who may display ambivalent or inconsistent behavior, which can trigger their attachment system. However, they may find secure partners less exciting, as they value stability and predictability over drama or intensity.

Dismissive-avoidant individuals often prioritize independence and self-sufficiency over emotional intimacy. They may feel uncomfortable with closeness or vulnerability and avoid commitment or relationship engagement. They are often attracted to anxious-preoccupied partners, who may seek reassurance or validation but may also become overly dependent or clingy. Dismissive-avoidant individuals may also be attracted to other dismissive-avoidant partners, as they share similar values and preferences for space and autonomy. However, they may find secure partners too demanding or intrusive, as these partners tend to prioritize emotional connection over individuality.

Fearful-avoidant individuals often struggle with ambivalence or confusion about their relationships. They may desire intimacy and connection but also fear rejection or abandonment. They are often attracted to partners who are emotionally intense or unpredictable, as this provides a sense of excitement or challenge. Fearful-avoidant individuals may also be attracted to other fearful-avoidant partners, as they share similar fears and insecurities. However, they may find secure partners to be too stable or boring, as these individuals often prioritize comfort and safety over novelty or risk-taking.

In summary, attachment styles play a critical role in the formation and maintenance of close relationships. While individuals with different attachment styles may be attracted to each other, their interactions can often be fraught with tension and conflict. Secure individuals tend to be attracted to partners who are also secure, while anxious-preoccupied individuals may be drawn to dismissive-avoidant and fearful-avoidant partners. Dismissive-avoidant individuals may be attracted to anxious-preoccupied partners, and fearful-avoidant individuals may be attracted to emotionally intense or unpredictable partners.

It is essential to note that these attraction patterns are not set in stone, and individuals may shift or adapt their attachment styles over time.

Moreover, individuals may also have a mix of attachment styles, which can complicate their attraction patterns. For example, someone with a fearful-avoidant style may initially be attracted to an anxious-preoccupied partner but become avoidant when their partner becomes too demanding or intrusive. Some people even have a mix of attachment styles, which can complicate their attraction patterns (Robinson et al., 2023).

Anxious and Avoidant Attachment Styles

Those with anxious and avoidant attachment styles are often attracted to each other, even though their behavior patterns are quite different. Anxiously attached people tend to be highly emotional and seek constant reassurance and validation from their partners. In contrast, avoidant individuals are often more reserved and distant, avoiding emotional intimacy and sometimes even physical contact. At first glance, these two attachment styles may seem incompatible, but some essential underlying factors draw them to each other.

For anxious individuals, pursuing an avoidant partner may stem from a deep-seated belief that they are unworthy of love and attention. They may feel that they must work hard to earn the affection of someone who seems emotionally unavailable or uninterested. On the other hand, avoidant individuals may be drawn to anxious partners because they feel a sense of power and control in the relationship—this allows them to feel important and needed.

Understanding the attraction patterns between different attachment styles can help individuals navigate their relationships more effectively. By recognizing your attachment style and your partner's attachment style, you can identify potential sources of conflict or misunderstanding and work on building stronger bonds of emotional intimacy and trust. With awareness, communication, and a willingness to learn and grow, you can create healthy, fulfilling, and long-lasting relationships, regardless of your attachment style.

Attachment Styles and Broader Social Networks

Each style has been linked to various aspects of social networks and social functioning. We will further explore how attachment styles can affect broader social networks and how understanding them can help people better navigate their relationships.

Avoidant attachment styles are characterized by a lack of trust in others, a reluctance to rely on others, and a tendency to keep relationships at arm's length. People with avoidant attachment styles often have difficulty forming and maintaining close relationships and may have difficulty engaging with potential partners and friends. As a result, they may find themselves with a limited social network.

Anxious attachment styles are characterized by a fear of abandonment, a need for constant reassurance, and an inability to let go of relationships. People with anxious attachment styles often struggle to trust others and may fear being rejected by those they care about. This can lead to difficulty forming new relationships and an unhealthy dependence on existing relationships. As a result, people with anxious attachment styles may have a smaller social network than those with other attachment styles.

Secure attachment styles are characterized by trust and security in relationships, maintaining independence while forming close relationships, and a willingness to rely on others in times of need. People with secure attachment styles often have extensive and diverse social networks. They are also more likely to form healthy long-term relationships.

Disorganized attachment styles are characterized by an inability to form secure relationships, a fear of being overwhelmed by closeness, and a tendency to avoid relationships altogether. People with disorganized attachment styles often have difficulty forming and maintaining relationships and may find themselves without much of a social network whatsoever.

Understanding your attachment style can help you understand your broader social network. For example, if you have an avoidant attachment style, you may struggle to form and maintain relationships due to your fear of abandonment and difficulty trusting others. If you have an anxious attachment style, you may experience fear of rejection and thus have difficulty letting go of existing relationships. Of course, if you have a secure attachment style, you likely have a large and diverse social network because you're generally able to form and maintain healthy relationships. Finally, if you have a disorganized attachment style, you may severely struggle to form a social network due to your current inability to form secure relationships.

It is important to note once again that attachment styles are not immutable and that people can learn to form healthier relationships and more extensive social networks with time and effort. Understanding your attachment style is a useful starting point for making changes, and it can also help you navigate your broader social networks. Recognizing unhealthy patterns and building healthy relationships can help people with any attachment style expand their social networks and build a more fulfilling social life.

Attachment styles can also affect the type and quality of your relationships within your social network. For example, those with avoidant attachment styles may find themselves in superficial relationships characterized by distance and insecurity. An anxious attachment style may lead to over-dependence on others and unhealthy emotional intensity. Secure attachment styles lead to relationships characterized by trust, respect, and mutual support. Finally, disorganized attachment styles can result in a lack of relationships altogether.

Finally, your attachment style affects how you interact with your broader social network. Those with avoidant attachment styles, for example, may find themselves withdrawing from social situations and avoiding contact with potential partners and friends. Those with anxious attachment styles may have difficulty engaging in conversations and forming new relationships.

Studies suggest that individuals with a secure attachment style are more likely to form and maintain social connections outside of their closest relationships. For example, they are typically more comfortable meeting new people, engaging in social activities, and seeking social support when needed. On the other hand, individuals with an insecure attachment style, such as avoidant or anxious, may struggle to form and maintain broader social connections. They are less likely to seek new social opportunities or find it challenging to trust others and form deep connections.

Understanding the relationship between attachment styles and broader social networks has crucial mental health and well-being implications. Individuals with a solid social support network have been shown to have better mental health outcomes, such as reduced rates of depression and anxiety. Additionally, social isolation has been linked to various adverse health outcomes, including cardiovascular disease and increased mortality rates. By recognizing how your attachment style impacts your broader social network, you can begin to develop healthy, trusting relationships with a variety of people in your life.

Secure Attachment Style

Individuals with a secure attachment style tend to view themselves and others positively, which can lead to a greater willingness to form social connections outside of their immediate social circle. They feel comfortable with intimacy, which translates to a greater likelihood of seeking out social connections.

Those with a secure attachment style may also be more open and receptive to new experiences and social opportunities. They are likely to have a strong sense of community and may participate in group activities, clubs, or organizations.

Anxious Attachment Style

Individuals with an anxious attachment style tend to have negative views of themselves but positive views of others. They crave intimacy and closeness but feel anxious or uncertain about their ability to maintain these connections. This anxiety can translate into difficulty forming and maintaining broader social connections.

Those with an anxious attachment style may be hesitant to seek new social opportunities and struggle to form trusting relationships with others. They may worry about rejection or abandonment by those close to them, which can lead to clingy behavior or pushing others away. As a result, they have a smaller and less diverse social network and may rely heavily on a few close relationships for support.

Avoidant Attachment Style

Individuals with an avoidant attachment style prioritize independence and self-reliance over relationships. They struggle to form and maintain social connections outside of their inner circle. They may be more selective about the types of social connections they form and less likely to seek out new social opportunities.

Those with an avoidant attachment style may be perceived as aloof or uninterested in social connections, which makes forming new relationships difficult. They may also struggle with asking for or accepting social support, which can further limit the size and diversity of their social network.

Disorganized Attachment Style

Individuals with a disorganized attachment style often have conflicting feelings about intimacy and a fear of vulnerability. This can translate into difficulty forming and maintaining social connections. They may hesitate to seek new social opportunities and struggle to form trusting relationships with others.

These individuals therefore typically have a smaller and less diverse social network. They struggle to form close relationships due to their fear of vulnerability or tendency to push others away. They may also have difficulty with boundaries and be unsure how to navigate different social connections.

It is important to remember that these descriptions are generalizations. Your social network depends on a wide variety of factors beyond your attachment style, including your personality, life experiences, and cultural context. Just remember that understanding how your attachment style influences your ability to create a social network can provide insights into how you can create and maintain healthy, valuable relationships.

Workbook Three

1. Take a moment to reflect on your attachment style and identify at least one way it has influenced your interactions with others.

2. Think of a past relationship or friendship that didn't work out. How did your attachment style contribute to the dynamic of the relationship?

3. Identify a positive characteristic of someone with a different attachment style than yours. How can you appreciate and learn from their approach to relationships?

Chapter Three Takeaway

As you close the final pages of Chapter 3, take a deep breath and reflect on the journey of self-discovery you've just embarked on. The insights and revelations you've gained about your attachment style and the styles of those around you are powerful tools for building meaningful relationships.

Perhaps you've recognized the patterns of avoidant behavior that have caused you to push away potential partners or the anxious tendencies that have left you feeling insecure and clingy. Hopefully, you have also identified the secure attachment style you strive for and can now work towards cultivating those characteristics in yourself.

But the knowledge gained from this chapter goes beyond just personal growth. By understanding attachment styles, you'll be better equipped to navigate the complexities of human interaction. You'll recognize the behaviors and needs of those around you and be able to respond in a way that builds connection and intimacy.

So, take this newfound understanding and put it into practice. Use it to deepen your existing relationships and forge new ones with confidence and intention. Remember, self-discovery is never truly over, but with each step, you'll find yourself better equipped to face life's challenges with grace and resilience.

Hey! Before you go the next chapter, may I ask you a favor? Honest reviews from wonderful customers like you help other readers in their personal development. Sharing your thoughts on this book would be greatly appreciated. Thank you!

CHAPTER FOUR

Fixing Your Attachment Style

"He heals the brokenhearted and binds up their wounds."

—Psalms 147:3

"When we are no longer able to change a situation, we are challenged to change ourselves."

—Viktor E. Frankl

Have you ever found yourself repeating the same unhealthy patterns in your relationships, despite your best efforts to break free? Maybe you're always attracting partners who seem to confirm your deepest fears or insecurities. Or perhaps you struggle to open up and trust others, even when you know building a robust and healthy relationship is necessary.

If any of this sounds familiar, you may be stuck in an attachment style that's no longer serving you. Attachment style usually stems from our childhood experiences. But the good news is that you can change your attachment style and create more fulfilling, satisfying relationships.

Let's consider Chad's story. Chad had always had an anxious attachment style, constantly seeking validation and reassurance from his partners. He would obsess over his partner's every move, constantly questioning whether they truly loved him or not. This led to a pattern of continually seeking out new relationships and never genuinely feeling secure in any of them.

But Chad knew he wanted more out of his relationships. He sought out therapy and began to work on changing his attachment style. Through therapy and self-reflection, he was able to identify the root causes of his anxiety and learn new skills for managing his emotions and building trust with his partners. As a result, Chad entered into a new relationship with a sense of confidence and security that he had never experienced before.

If Chad can change his attachment style, so can you. In this chapter, we'll explore why changing your attachment style is essential and how you can go about doing it. We'll discuss the different attachment styles and their impact on our relationships, as well as strategies for identifying and changing your attachment style. By the end of this chapter, you'll be equipped with the tools you need to create more fulfilling, satisfying relationships. So let's get started.

Can My Style Change?

Attachment styles are deeply ingrained patterns of relating to others that develop early in life, often in response to how we were cared for by our parents or primary caregivers. These patterns can be difficult to change because they are deeply embedded in our beliefs and behaviors. However, shifting toward a more secure attachment style is possible with effort, insight, and willingness to challenge old patterns.

So, if you're wondering whether it's possible to change your attachment style, the answer is yes. Attachment styles are not set in stone, and it is possible to shift from one style to another. However, it's important to note that changing your attachment style is a complex process and may require significant effort and self-reflection.

Research supports the idea that attachment styles can change, particularly in response to new relationship experiences (Shaver et al., 2016). For example, a person who has always had an anxious attachment style may develop a more secure attachment style after being in a long-term, stable relationship with a consistently supportive and responsive partner. On the other hand, a person who has always had a secure attachment style may develop an anxious or avoidant attachment style after experiencing a traumatic event or going through a difficult breakup (Hazan & Shaver, 1994).

It's important to note that changing your attachment style is a challenging fix, and it may not be possible to completely eliminate certain old behavior patterns. However, learning new skills and developing a greater sense of self-awareness can lead to a more secure attachment style. For example, if you have an anxious attachment style, you can learn to recognize when you're seeking reassurance from your partner and develop alternative coping strategies for managing anxiety. If you have an avoidant attachment style, you can learn to recognize when you are withdrawing from your partner and develop new communication skills for expressing your needs and feelings.

We should also recognize that attachment style change may only be desirable in some contexts, as each style has strengths and weaknesses depending on the context. For example, a person with an avoidant attachment style may be highly successful in their career due to their independence and self-reliance. However, this same attachment style may cause problems in their relationships, as they may need help forming close emotional connections with others. In this case, developing new skills for managing intimacy while maintaining independence could be helpful.

Ultimately, whether or not you can change your attachment style depends on a multitude of factors, including your personal history, current relationship experiences, and willingness to engage in self-reflection and therapy. While attachment style change is not easy, it is possible, and it can lead to more fulfilling relationships and a greater sense of emotional well-being. By cultivating self-awareness, learning new skills, and seeking support when needed, you can develop a more secure attachment style and create the close, fulfilling relationships you desire.

One of the first steps towards changing your attachment style is becoming aware of your current one. You can do this by reflecting on your past relationships, identifying patterns, and exploring how you respond emotionally to certain situations. This process can be challenging, requiring vulnerability and self-reflection, but it is crucial for personal growth.

Once you have identified your attachment style, you can explore new ways of relating to others. This might involve seeking new experiences, practicing healthy communication skills, and developing self-awareness. Working with a therapist or counselor specializing in attachment theory can also be helpful in this process, as they can provide guidance and support.

Another critical factor in changing your attachment style is developing a sense of security within yourself. This means building self-esteem, practicing self-compassion, and learning to regulate your emotions. When you feel more secure, you can better navigate relationships in a healthy manner.

Attachment style change may also occur in response to therapy or other forms of intervention. For example, cognitive-behavioral therapy (CBT) is effective in helping people with anxiety disorders, including those with an anxious attachment style. CBT can help people learn new coping skills for managing anxiety and building relationship trust.

Another form of therapy that may help change attachment styles is attachment-based therapy. This approach emphasizes identifying and addressing the underlying emotions and beliefs driving attachment patterns. Attachment-based therapy can help individuals develop new skills for managing emotions and building healthy relationships.

It is also essential to be patient with yourself throughout this process. Changing your attachment style is a gradual process that takes time and effort. There may be setbacks along the way, but it is crucial to stay committed to the process and not give up.

While changing your attachment style may seem daunting, it is possible with effort and the right tools. Developing awareness of your current attachment style, exploring new ways of relating, building a sense of security within yourself, and being patient throughout the process can all help you shift towards a more secure attachment style. Remember that changing your attachment style is a personal decision, and it is important to approach the process with self-compassion and self-awareness.

How Your Attachment Style Impacts Your Self-Esteem

Have you ever stopped to consider how your attachment style affects your self-esteem? The way we formed attachments in childhood can profoundly impact how we view ourselves as adults.

Self-esteem is a critical component of our emotional and mental well-being. Our attachment style plays a vital role in determining our self-esteem. An individual with a secure attachment style tends to have a higher sense of self-worth, confidence, and overall mental health. On the other hand, those with insecure attachment styles may struggle with low self-esteem, self-doubt, and negative self-image.

Secure Attachment and Self-Esteem

Individuals with a secure attachment style tend to have a favorable view of themselves and others. They feel comfortable expressing their needs and emotions and believe they deserve love and care. This positive self-perception can lead to higher levels of self-esteem.

In childhood, securely attached individuals typically had caregivers who were responsive to their needs, provided comfort when they were distressed, and created a safe and predictable environment. These experiences help us to develop a secure sense of self and confidence in forming healthy relationships.

Anxious-Preoccupied Attachment and Self-Esteem

Individuals with an anxious-preoccupied attachment style tend to have a negative view of themselves and a positive view of others. They often feel anxious or worried about their relationships, seeking reassurance and approval from their partners. Their low self-esteem may stem from a fear of rejection or abandonment.

In childhood, anxious-preoccupied individuals' caregivers were often inconsistent in their responsiveness, sometimes meeting their needs and at other times neglecting them. These experiences can lead to a lack of trust in ourselves and others, as well as lower self-esteem.

Dismissive-Avoidant Attachment and Self-Esteem

Those with a dismissive-avoidant attachment style tend to have a favorable view of themselves and a negative view of others. They often feel independent and self-reliant, avoiding emotional intimacy with others. Their high self-esteem may stem from a sense of control and autonomy.

In childhood, dismissive-avoidant individuals typically had caregivers who were emotionally unavailable or unresponsive, forcing them to learn to rely on themselves for emotional regulation. These experiences can lead to a lack of trust in others and difficulty forming close relationships, contributing to lower self-esteem in the long term.

Fearful-Avoidant Attachment and Self-Esteem

People with a fearful-avoidant attachment style tend to view both themselves and others negatively. They may struggle with emotional regulation and often feel overwhelmed by intense emotions. Their low self-esteem may stem from a fear of rejection or abandonment and a lack of trust in themselves and others.

In childhood, fearful-avoidant individuals' caregivers were generally inconsistent in their responsiveness, sometimes meeting their needs and at other times neglecting them. These experiences can lead to feelings of helplessness and insecurity, contributing to lower self-esteem.

Impact of Attachment Style on Self-Esteem

It should be clear by now that those with a secure attachment style tend to have higher self-esteem than those with insecure attachment styles. This is because securely attached individuals have had positive early experiences with caregivers, contributing to their positive sense of self-worth and confidence in relationships, whereas people with insecure attachment styles did not have those positive early experiences. Anxious-preoccupied individuals may have difficulty trusting themselves and others, leading to feelings of inadequacy and a fear of rejection. Dismissive-avoidant individuals may have trouble forming close relationships, leading to a lack of emotional support and feelings of isolation. Fearful-avoidant individuals may struggle with emotional regulation, leading to helplessness and insecurity.

Improving Self-Esteem with Different Attachment Styles

While the impact of your attachment style on your self-esteem is significant, it is not the only factor contributing to your self-worth. Other factors, such as personality traits, childhood experiences, and cultural influences, also play a crucial role. Therefore, understanding your attachment style's impact on self-esteem is just one piece of the puzzle.

However, having a secure attachment style can positively impact self-esteem in many ways. A secure attachment style can lead to a more positive self-image, increased confidence, and an improved sense of self-worth. People with secure attachment styles are often better at regulating their emotions, leading to a more positive outlook on life and greater resilience in the face of stress and adversity.

On the other hand, those with insecure attachment styles may struggle with low self-esteem and self-doubt. People with an anxious attachment style may be more likely to seek validation and approval from others, leading to a reliance on external sources for their self-worth. Meanwhile, those with an avoidant attachment style may struggle with intimacy and emotional vulnerability, leading to isolation and disconnection.

However, please remember that attachment styles are not set in stone; they can be changed with conscious effort and therapy. This process involves recognizing and understanding your attachment style, identifying how it impacts your self-esteem, and learning healthier ways of relating to yourself and to the people around you.

In conclusion, attachment styles do, indeed, significantly impact self-esteem, but they are not the only factor contributing to one's self-worth. While a secure attachment style can positively impact self-esteem, those with insecure attachment styles may struggle with low self-esteem and self-doubt. However, if you put in the work, it is possible to change your attachment style and improve your self-esteem.

How to Change Your Attachment Style – Full Guide

So, now that we know that it's possible to change our attachment style, thereby improving our self-esteem and our relationships, how exactly do we do that? This guide will provide practical steps to help you develop a more secure attachment style and strengthen your relationships.

1. Identify your current attachment style

The first step in changing your attachment style is understanding what it is. To identify your attachment style, you can take an attachment style quiz or reflect on your past relationships to see what patterns emerge. Once you understand your attachment style, you can start to work on changing it.

2. Identify your triggers

Our attachment styles are often triggered by specific situations or the behaviors of others. For example, if you have an anxious-preoccupied attachment style, you may become anxious when your partner doesn't respond to your texts immediately. If you have a dismissive-avoidant attachment style, you may withdraw emotionally when overwhelmed. By identifying what triggers your attachment style, you can bring these situations to your conscious awareness and work on responding differently.

3. Practice self-compassion

Changing your attachment style is a process that takes time and effort. It's important to be kind and patient with yourself throughout this journey. It's also important to recognize that your attachment style developed as a way to help you cope with childhood experiences. It's not a reflection of your worth as a person. Practice self-compassion by speaking kindly to yourself and acknowledging that changing your attachment style will take time.

4. Develop a positive self-image

People with a secure attachment style tend to have a positive self-image. They believe they are worthy of love and that others will be there for them when they need support. You may struggle with low self-esteem or self-worth if you have an insecure attachment style. Work on developing a positive self-image by identifying your strengths and accomplishments. You can also practice self-care and do things that make you feel good about yourself.

5. Practice healthy communication

Communication is vital to building healthy relationships. If you have an anxious-preoccupied attachment style, you may be prone to over-communicating or being passive-aggressive. If you have a dismissive-avoidant attachment style, you may avoid discussing your feelings altogether. To change your attachment style, practice healthy communication by expressing your needs and boundaries clearly and respectfully. Listen to the other person's perspective and be open to compromise.

6. Seek therapy

Changing your attachment style can be challenging, especially if you've had traumatic past experiences that have shaped your attachment style. Seeking therapy can be a helpful tool in understanding and changing your attachment style. A therapist can help you identify and process those past experiences that may be impacting your approach to relationships. They can also teach you healthy coping mechanisms and communication skills.

7. Practice healthy attachment behaviors

To develop a more secure attachment style, practice healthy attachment behaviors. These include being reliable, showing affection, and practicing empathy. People with a secure attachment style tend to be comfortable with intimacy and can balance independence and closeness in their relationships. Work on developing these skills by practicing them in your daily life.

Keep in mind that changing your attachment style is a process that takes time and effort. It requires self-awareness, self-compassion, and a willingness to change. By identifying your attachment style, understanding your triggers, and practicing healthy communication and attachment behaviors, you can develop a more secure attachment style and build more beneficial relationships. Remember to be patient and kind to yourself throughout this journey (more on that in the next section).

The Role of Self-Compassion in Rewiring Your Attachment Style

Do you ever feel insecure or anxious in your relationships? Do you avoid emotional intimacy with your partner? Do you constantly seek validation from your partner, fear abandonment, or struggle to trust others fully? These are all signs of attachment issues, which can wreak havoc on your romantic life. But don't despair! There's hope for transforming your attachment style, and the critical ingredient that might surprise you? Self-compassion. That's right, showing kindness and understanding to yourself is not just a feel-good practice; it can rewire your brain and transform your attachment patterns.

Research has shown that self-compassion is a mediator between attachment anxiety and body appreciation, which means that when you're more compassionate towards yourself, you're less likely to experience attachment-related anxiety and more likely to appreciate your body and its needs. In addition, practicing self-compassion has been shown to increase feelings of security and decrease anxiety and avoidance, both of which are associated with insecure attachment styles.

What exactly is self-compassion? Self-compassion is the practice of treating oneself with kindness, understanding, and care, especially during times of stress, failure, or inadequacy. It involves acknowledging one's imperfections and shortcomings without judgment, and recognizing that all humans struggle and make mistakes.

When we lack self-compassion, we often struggle to form healthy relationships. People with insecure attachment styles tend to be overly critical of themselves, have difficulty accepting love and affection from others, and often struggle with emotional regulation. However, practicing self-compassion can help individuals develop more secure attachment styles by increasing feelings of self-worth and self-acceptance (Sbarra & Hazan, 2008).

So how can you develop self-compassion? It starts with treating yourself the way you would treat a good friend. When you make a mistake, offer encouragement and support instead of berating yourself. When you're feeling down, practice self-care and permit yourself to take a break. And when you're feeling overwhelmed by attachment-related emotions, remind yourself that it's okay to feel what you're feeling and that you're not alone in your struggles.

By developing a more compassionate relationship with yourself, you can rewire your brain and your attachment style, leading to happier, healthier, and more secure relationships. So go ahead, give yourself a break, and watch your attachment style transform before your very eyes.

Self-compassion also helps individuals become more attuned to their emotions and needs, which is crucial for developing healthy relationships. When we are compassionate towards ourselves, we can better recognize and respond to our emotional states, which helps us communicate more effectively with our partners. This, in turn, fosters a more secure attachment style.

In addition, self-compassion promotes a more positive self-image, which can enhance one's ability to form secure attachments. People who lack self-compassion often believe that they are unworthy of love and affection. This belief can be a self-fulfilling prophecy, as it can cause individuals to push away potential partners and engage in self-sabotaging behaviors. However, practicing self-compassion can help you develop a positive view of yourself, which can enhance your ability to form secure attachments (Sbarra & Hazan, 2008).

Kind self-talk is one practice that will help you develop self-compassion. It involves treating yourself with the same kindness you offer to your loved ones. The idea of being kind to oneself is not new, and it has been studied in the context of mindfulness-based interventions for many years. When we speak kindly to ourselves, we create a safe and secure inner environment that can foster a sense of security and trust in our relationships with others. This, in turn, can help us develop a secure attachment style. When we feel secure, we are less likely to seek validation from others and more likely to form authentic connections with people who share our values and interests.

Additionally, kind self-talk can help us develop greater empathy and understanding toward others. When we are kind to ourselves, we become more attuned to our own emotions and needs, and we can better recognize these same emotions and needs in others. This can help us form deeper and more meaningful relationships with others, as we can better understand and respond to their needs.

In summary, being kind to ourselves through the practice of self-talk can transform our relationships and help us develop a secure attachment style. When we are gentle with ourselves, we create a safe and secure inner environment that fosters trust and security within ourselves and our relationships with others. So, the next time you find yourself being self-critical or harsh, try practicing kind self-talk* and see how it can improve your relationships.

⁎ Wave goodbye to guilt and hello to self-care! Jump into Worksheet #3 from BONUS #1 at the start of the book or check this QR code and let the fun-filled self-discovery begin!

Workbook Four

1. What are some of the practical steps you can take to transition from an insecure to a secure attachment style?

2. Think about a specific relationship in your life. How might changing your attachment style positively impact that relationship?

Chapter Four Takeaway

The knowledge and tools provided in this chapter are designed to help you transition from an insecure attachment style to a more secure one. While changing your attachment style may seem daunting, it is important to remember that it is a marathon, not a sprint. It will require commitment and time on your part. But the benefits of making this change are immeasurable. You will begin to form deeper, more fulfilling relationships with those around you and experience greater emotional stability and overall well-being.

This chapter has offered you practical steps and exercises to incorporate into your daily life to reprogram your brain and start building healthier relationship patterns. By committing to these exercises and working through the challenges, you will begin to see the positive impact on your life and relationships.

Remember, changing your attachment style is possible for any of us who are willing to put in the effort. It is a worthwhile endeavor that can profoundly impact your life. So, take the knowledge and tools in this chapter, and begin your journey towards a more secure attachment style today.

Overcoming Jealousy and Insecurity in Your Relationships – Dealing with Anxiety and Avoidance

"A heart at peace gives life to the body, but envy rots the bones."

—Proverbs 14:30

"Jealousy is a disease, love is a healthy condition. The immature mind often mistakes one for the other, or assumes that the greater the love, the greater the jealousy—in fact, they are almost incompatible; one emotion hardly leaves room for the other."

—Robert A. Heinlein

Maggie had always struggled with feelings of jealousy and insecurity in her relationship with her partner, Alex. She knew that Alex loved her deeply, but whenever he spent time with other women, even though it was just as friends, Maggie's mind would race with thoughts of betrayal and abandonment.

As her jealousy and anxiety continued to escalate, Maggie decided to seek help. She began working with a therapist and learned that her jealousy and fear were rooted in her insecurities and past traumas.

Together, Maggie and her therapist developed a set of tools for managing these anxieties. They worked on identifying and challenging negative thought patterns, practicing relaxation techniques to reduce anxiety, and improving communication skills to express her feelings and needs to Alex in a healthy way.

One of the key takeaways for Maggie was the importance of self-compassion. She learned to be kind and understanding towards herself when she felt jealous or insecure and to permit herself to feel her emotions without judgment.

Over time, Maggie's relationship with Alex began to improve. She felt more confident and secure in their bond and was able to trust him more deeply. Her newfound sense of self-compassion and emotional regulation also helped her to become a better partner, able to communicate more effectively and empathize with Alex's feelings and needs.

Maggie's journey demonstrates to us that with the right tools and support, it is absolutely possible to overcome even the most intense feelings of jealousy and insecurity in your relationship. By practicing self-compassion, improving your communication skills, and working to challenge negative thought patterns, you, too, can create a more loving and fulfilling partnership and find greater peace and happiness in your life.

This chapter will examine practical strategies and tools to help you overcome the issues you may be dealing with in your relationship as a result of your attachment style, whether that's jealousy, insecurity, anxiety, or avoidance of emotional intimacy. We will explore how to trace the root cause these issues, deal with lack of trust in your relationship, and handle overthinking and negative thoughts. So, let's dive in.

Tracing the Root Cause of Your Jealousy and Insecurity

Jealousy and insecurity can be destructive emotions in any relationship. They can create mistrust and resentment, leading to a breakdown of intimacy and communication. If you're struggling with jealousy and insecurity in your relationship, you must trace the root cause of these feelings and work on them with your partner. Here are some suggestions on how to trace that root cause:

1. Look at your past experiences

These experiences can shape your current reactions to certain situations. Consider whether you have experienced past traumas or betrayals that may be influencing your current feelings of jealousy and insecurity. Past traumas or betrayals can create a strong emotional response to situations that remind us of those past experiences.

For example, suppose you were cheated on in a past relationship. In that case, you may feel jealousy or insecurity in your current relationship, even if your partner has given you no reason to doubt their fidelity. This is because the pain and betrayal from your experience can make it difficult to trust again and may cause you to be more sensitive to certain behaviors or situations that trigger those painful memories.

Tracing the root cause of your jealousy and insecurity can be difficult and emotional, but it's an essential step in finding ways to address and overcome these feelings. By recognizing how your past experiences are affecting your current reactions, you can begin to work through those emotions and develop healthier coping mechanisms.

Talking to a therapist or counselor can be a helpful way to work through past traumas and develop strategies for addressing the jealousy and insecurity you're feeling. A therapist can help you identify patterns in your behavior and provide tools for communication and building trust with your partner.

Ultimately, by looking at your past experiences and addressing any unresolved emotional wounds, you can move towards a more secure and confident place in your relationships.

2. Identify your triggers

Identifying your triggers is vital in managing jealousy and insecurity in relationships. These triggers can be specific actions or situations that evoke feelings of jealousy and insecurity, such as when your partner spends time with someone else or receives a text message from an unknown number, or when you're not included in plans with your partner's friends or family.

It is essential to identify your triggers because they can help you become more self-aware and recognize when you are experiencing jealousy and insecurity. Once you are aware of your triggers, you can take steps to manage your emotions and respond more healthily.

For example, if seeing your partner talk to someone of the opposite sex triggers jealousy, you can work on acknowledging those feelings and using coping strategies to manage them. This might include taking deep breaths, distracting yourself with an activity you enjoy, or talking to a trusted friend or therapist about your feelings.

It's important to note that triggers can differ for everyone and may evolve. Regularly reflecting on what triggers your jealousy and insecurity can help you stay attuned to your emotions and continue to grow and develop healthier coping mechanisms.

3. Evaluate your attachment style

As we have explored throughout this book, attachment theory posits that our early experiences with caregivers shape our attachment style, affecting how we form and maintain relationships with others throughout our lives.

If you suspect you have an anxious or insecure attachment style, exploring this further with a therapist or counselor may be helpful. They can help you understand how your attachment style affects your relationships and provide strategies to help you develop more secure attachment patterns. Additionally, it can be beneficial to practice self-care and focus on building your self-esteem, which can help to reduce feelings of insecurity and jealousy.

4. Examine your self-worth

Examining your sense of self-worth is another essential aspect here. It is common for individuals to struggle with feelings of inadequacy or self-doubt, which can lead to doubts about their partner's love and fidelity. Consider if you have any beliefs or insecurities about yourself contributing to these feelings.

For example, if you have a deep-seated fear of abandonment or rejection, you may be more prone to feelings of jealousy and insecurity in your relationship. Alternatively, suppose you have a negative self-image or a tendency to compare yourself to others. In that case, you may feel jealous or insecure when your partner interacts with others or appears to show interest in someone else.

5. Communicate with your partner

Communicating with your partner is also crucial in addressing jealousy and insecurity. By sharing your feelings with your partner, you can work together to identify the root cause of these emotions and develop strategies to manage them. It is essential to approach these conversations with openness and honesty without placing blame or making accusations.

Your partner can also provide support and reassurance, which can help to alleviate the negative feelings you're having. Together, you can build trust and strengthen your relationship, which can help reduce feelings of jealousy and insecurity over time.

Dealing with Trust Issues

Trust issues can significantly impact our relationships, causing anxiety, fear, and insecurity. Whether they stem from past betrayals or negative self-beliefs, trust issues can be challenging to overcome. However, by identifying the root cause of these issues, building self-trust, and working on communication skills, it is possible to develop healthier and more fulfilling relationships. Here are some suggestions on how to deal with trust issues:

· Identify the root cause

Understanding the root cause of your trust issues is the first step in addressing them. It could be related to past experiences of betrayal or a general lack of trust in people. As mentioned earlier, trust issues can stem from various sources, such as past experiences, childhood trauma, and cultural or societal conditioning. It's essential to identify the root in order to address these issues effectively. This process typically involves introspection and possibly even therapy or counseling to help you unpack and process your past experiences.

· Work on building self-trust

It may surprise you to learn that building trust in yourself can actually help you to overcome trust issues with a partner. One way to build self-trust is by keeping promises to yourself and setting boundaries. Developing a solid sense of self-trust can help you feel more secure in your relationships. Start by setting small, achievable goals for yourself and following through with them. Keep track of your accomplishments and be sure to celebrate them. Be honest with yourself about your feelings, needs, and boundaries, and communicate them clearly to others.

· Communicate with your partner

Open and honest communication with your partner can help to build trust in the relationship. It is essential to express your concerns and fears and work together to find solutions.

· Practice vulnerability

Being vulnerable and opening up to others can help to build trust as well. Start small and gradually build up to sharing more personal information. Holding on to grudges and resentments can erode trust, so practice forgiveness—not just for others but also for yourself. Recognize that everyone makes mistakes and that forgiving doesn't necessarily mean forgetting; it means letting go of anger and resentment and moving forward with compassion and understanding.

· Challenge negative beliefs

Trust issues can be perpetuated by negative beliefs you may hold about yourself or others. It is important to challenge these beliefs and replace them with positive and realistic ones.

· Set boundaries

Healthy boundaries can help build trust by establishing clear expectations for behavior in a relationship. Be clear about what behaviors you will and will not tolerate and communicate them to your partner. Respect your partner's boundaries and work together to compromise when necessary.

Remember that building trust takes time and effort, and setbacks are normal. Be patient and kind to yourself as you work through your trust issues, and celebrate your progress along the way.

Dealing with Anxiety Issues in Your Relationship

Anxiety is a fairly common issue in relationships, causing stress and tension that can strain even the deepest connections. However, understanding the root causes of your anxiety can help you and your partner navigate and manage this challenging emotion. Attachment theory is a valuable framework for understanding the underlying causes of anxiety in relationships and developing strategies for managing it (Choosing Therapy, n.d.; Meek, 2022; Cherry, 2023).

Anxiety in relationships can stem from an insecure attachment style, particularly an anxious one since anxious attachment involves a deep fear of rejection and abandonment and can cause intense anxiety when a partner appears distant or disinterested. Those with anxious attachment styles may struggle with insecurity and may be more likely to experience feelings of jealousy and possessiveness towards their partner (Meek, 2022; Cherry, 2023).

If you or your partner is struggling with anxiety in your relationship, it can be helpful to understand attachment theory and work to identify your attachment styles. This can help you better understand your own and each other's emotions and behaviors, leading to more effective communication and support. Here are some valuable tips to help you handle anxiety in your relationship:

Communicate openly and honestly

Communication is crucial in any relationship, but it's even more critical when dealing with anxiety. When anxiety strikes, it's easy to shut down and keep your feelings bottled up. However, this can lead to misunderstandings and make the situation worse. So, it's essential to communicate openly and honestly with your partner about how you're feeling. Let them know what triggers your anxiety and what they can do to help you feel better. This way, they can better understand you and offer support when needed.

Practice self-care

Taking care of yourself is essential, especially when dealing with anxiety. Practicing self-care can help you manage your anxiety and reduce stress. Find activities that make you feel good and incorporate them into your daily routine. It could be something as simple as taking a warm bath or going for a peaceful walk. Prioritize your mental health by practicing mindfulness or meditation. The more you care for yourself, the more resilient you'll become and the better equipped you will be to manage your anxiety.

Set boundaries

Setting boundaries is crucial to any relationship, but it's absolutely key when dealing with anxiety issues. Anxiety can make you feel like you need constant reassurance from your partner, but this can quickly become overwhelming. Setting boundaries around how much support you need and when you need it can help you feel more in control. You should also consider taking a break from social media or limiting the number of times you check your phone, as social media is an anxiety trigger for many. Whatever the case may be for you, communicate your needs to your partner and work together to establish healthy boundaries.

Seek professional help

Sometimes, anxiety can be too much to handle alone, even if your partner is trying to support you. Seeking professional help can be beneficial when dealing with anxiety issues in your relationship. A therapist can help you identify the root causes of your anxiety and teach you coping strategies to manage it. They can also help you communicate better with your partner and develop healthy habits to improve your relationship. Don't be afraid to seek help if you need it. Remember that it's okay to ask for support.

Focus on the present moment

Anxiety can make you worry about the future, leading to catastrophic thinking. This type of thinking causes unnecessary stress and anxiety and can affect your relationship. Focusing on the present moment can help you manage your anxiety and stay grounded. Mindfulness and meditation are helpful tools for this. Focus on your breath or your senses, and try to stay in the moment. This can help you feel more centered and reduce your anxiety.

Dealing with Overthinking and Negative Thoughts in Your Relationship

Overthinking and negative thoughts can be a real buzzkill in any relationship. They can cause unnecessary stress and anxiety and even lead to conflict. While it's natural to have doubts and worries about your partner from time to time, constantly dwelling on them can harm your mental health and your relationship (Lusinski, 2018).

One common scenario in which negative thoughts may arise is when a partner takes longer than usual to respond to a text or call. The ensuing rumination can lead to misunderstandings, and the resulting anxiety can be damaging to the relationship (MindWell NYC, n.d.). Similarly, feeling threatened or jealous when a partner mentions hanging out with friends can stem from past experiences or insecurities, but it can still be harmful if left unchecked (Serai, n.d.).

Fortunately, there are ways to stop overthinking and negative thoughts and maintain a healthy and happy partnership with your significant other. So, how exactly can you go about doing that? Here are some tips:

1. Recognize the thought patterns: The first step in stopping negative thoughts is recognizing when they arise. Pay attention to the situations that trigger these thought patterns. Are you catastrophizing or jumping to conclusions without evidence? Once you identify these patterns, you can challenge and reframe them.

2. Practice mindfulness: Mindfulness is a useful tool in stopping overthinking and negative thoughts. It involves being present in the moment and observing your thoughts without judgment. This practice can help you become more aware of your thought patterns and prevent them from spiraling out of control.

3. Communicate with your partner: If you're feeling anxious or having negative thoughts about your relationship, it's essential to communicate this with your partner. Be honest and open about how you're feeling, and don't be afraid to ask for reassurance. Talking things out can help alleviate your worries and strengthen your bond.

4. Challenge your thoughts: When you have negative thoughts, challenge them with evidence-based reasoning. Ask yourself, "Is this thought based on fact or assumption?" "What evidence supports or refutes this thought?" "What's the worst-case scenario, and how likely is it?" By challenging your thoughts, you can avoid unnecessary worry and stress.

5. Focus on the positive: Instead of dwelling on negative thoughts, focus on the positive aspects of your relationship. What do you appreciate about your partner? What are some of the good times you've shared? Shifting your focus to the positive can cultivate a more optimistic outlook and strengthen your connection with your partner.

6. Reframe negative thoughts: Instead of getting caught up in negative thoughts and assumptions about your partner or your relationship, try to reframe those thoughts in a more positive light. For example, if you think, "My partner doesn't care about me," try reframing that thought to, "My partner has been busy lately, but they've shown me they care in other ways."

7. Set boundaries: If you find yourself overthinking or obsessing over your partner's behavior, it may be helpful to set some boundaries for yourself. This could mean limiting the amount of time you spend checking your partner's social media or setting aside specific times to talk about your relationship rather than constantly analyzing it.

Workbook Five

1. Which of the specific strategies outlined in this chapter for overcoming jealousy and insecurity in relationships do you think would work best for you?

2. Have you ever experienced anxiety or avoidance in a relationship? How did you handle it, and what could you have done differently with the knowledge from this chapter?

3. Think about a relationship in your life that you would like to improve. How might the tools and exercises in this chapter help you work towards that goal?

Chapter Five Takeaway

Overthinking and negative thoughts can harm your relationship. By recognizing your thought patterns, practicing mindfulness, communicating with your partner, challenging your thoughts, and focusing on the positive, you can stop this negativity and cultivate a healthier, happier relationship.

By following the practical advice and exercises outlined in this chapter, you can begin to build stronger, more trusting relationships with those around you. Remember, although it's not easy to overcome jealousy and insecurity, it is possible, and with persistence and effort, you can find greater peace and fulfillment in your relationships.

PART THREE

FURTHER HEALTHY PRACTICES

Emma had been struggling with toxic relationships for a long time. She had always felt she needed someone else to make her happy and never learned to be independent. But one day, something changed.

Emma decided to take up a new hobby: painting. She started going to a local art class and practicing regularly and soon found that she loved the sense of creative expression it gave her. She also found that painting was helping her overcome her codependent tendencies and improve her relationships with others.

As she continued her new hobby, Emma realized that cultivating healthy relationships starts with cultivating a healthy sense of self.

In this third and final part of the book, we will dive into some further practices that will help you cultivate a healthy relationship.

Chapter 6 explores how to overcome codependency and improve interdependence. By learning to be more self-sufficient and setting healthy boundaries, you can build stronger, more fulfilling connections with others.

But healthy relationships aren't just about being independent. In Chapter 7, we look at building and maintaining positive connections with others. From effective communication to active listening, empathy to forgiveness, this chapter is packed with practical tips and insights for anyone looking to create more meaningful relationships.

Emma's story is a powerful reminder that it's never too late to start cultivating healthy habits and building stronger relationships with others. Whether through painting, therapy, or other forms of self-care, we all have the power to transform our lives and create the connections we desire.

CHAPTER SIX

Overcoming Codependency and Improving Interdependence

"Two are better than one, because they have a good reward for their toil. For if they fall, one will lift up the other; but woe to one who is alone and falls and does not have another to help."

—Ecclesiastes 4:9-10

Lila had always been an independent and self-reliant person. Growing up, she was taught to take care of herself and not rely on anyone else for her happiness. But as she entered her twenties, she found herself in a relationship with a man named Max, who needed her to take care of him. Max was charming and loving but struggled with addiction and often relied on Lila to bail him out of difficult situations. At first, Lila didn't mind. She saw herself as Max's savior, and she enjoyed feeling needed.

However, as time passed, Lila realized she had become enmeshed in Max's life. She constantly worried about him, trying to fix his problems and sacrificing her needs to meet his. She had become codependent, a pattern of behavior in which someone excessively relies on another person for their emotional or physical well-being.

Lila's attachment style was also affected by her codependency. Lila had always considered herself securely attached, but she now began exhibiting anxious attachment behaviors. She was clingy, needy, and fearful of losing Max. She had become so intertwined with Max's life that she didn't know who she was without him.

It wasn't until Max hit rock bottom and was forced to enter rehab that Lila began to see the negative impact of her codependency. She had been so focused on saving

Max that she'd neglected her needs and desires. While Max was in rehab, Lila began to explore her interests and hobbies. She started seeing a therapist to work on her codependency and attachment issues. Over time, she learned to be more interdependent—striking a healthy balance between relying on others and caring for oneself.

In the end, Lila and Max's relationship survived. Lila emerged from the experience more robust and more self-assured than ever before. She had reached the understanding that true love and attachment can only exist when both partners can take care of themselves and rely on each other in a healthy, interdependent way.

As human beings, we are wired for connection. We crave closeness, affection, and to be understood and accepted. Attachment theory, as we know, explains the biological and emotional basis of this need for connection; however, it also helps us understand how we relate to ourselves. This is where the concepts of codependency and interdependence come into play. Codependency is a term that has been used for decades to describe a pattern of behavior in which one person becomes overly enmeshed in the life of another. This can happen in romantic relationships, friendships, or even in families.

A codependent person will often sacrifice their own needs and wants to keep their partner or loved one happy, and they may feel a deep sense of responsibility for that person's emotions and well-being.

On the other hand, interdependence refers to a healthy pattern of behavior in which two people rely on each other for emotional support and care while maintaining their sense of identity and autonomy. In an interdependent relationship, both parties can express their own needs and desires while respecting the other person's needs and wishes.

So, what does all of this have to do with attachment theory? If we have a secure attachment style, we're more likely to form healthy, interdependent relationships as adults. However, an insecure attachment style may lead us to struggle with codependency or other unhealthy relationship patterns. This chapter will explore the connection between attachment theory and codependency / interdependence. We will delve into the signs and symptoms of codependency, its impact on our relationships and mental health, and strategies for moving towards a more interdependent way of relating to others.

To better understand this connection, let's examine the story of Rachel and her boyfriend, Jake. Rachel and Jake had been together for three years and were deeply in love. Rachel had always been there for Jake through thick and thin. She would drop everything to be by his side whenever he needed her, and she felt a sense of pride in being his rock. However, at some point she noticed that she was losing herself in the relationship. She had stopped pursuing her hobbies and interests and had begun relying solely on Jake for emotional support. She felt guilty whenever she expressed her needs or desires and constantly put Jake's needs ahead of her own.

As time went on, Rachel began to feel increasingly anxious and overwhelmed. She had lost touch with who she was as an individual, and she didn't know how to break free from this pattern of codependency. She realized she needed to change to save her relationship and, more importantly, her sense of self. Through therapy, Rachel began to understand how her early experiences with her parents had influenced her attachment style. She had grown up in a family where her needs were often overlooked, and she had learned to prioritize the needs of others above her own.

This led to a pattern of codependency in her adult relationships, which was now taking a toll on her mental health. With the help of her therapist, Rachel began to set boundaries in her relationship with Jake. She started prioritizing her needs and desires and learned to communicate them to Jake healthily and assertively. At first, Jake was taken aback by this change in Rachel's behavior, but he eventually came to appreciate her newfound sense of independence and self-confidence.

Over time, Rachel and Jake developed a more interdependent way of relating to each other. They maintained their identities and interests but relied on each other for emotional support and care. Rachel felt more fulfilled in the relationship and knew she had made a positive change for herself and their future together.

As you read this chapter, you will learn, just as Rachel did, how to identify and address codependency and unhealthy patterns in your relationship.

What Is Codependency?

Codependency is a behavioral and emotional pattern that is prevalent in many types of relationships (Meek, 2022). It is characterized by a person's excessive reliance on others to meet their emotional and physical needs. Codependent individuals often feel a strong need to take care of others, often to the detriment of their own well-being (Gilbert, 2020).

One of the primary indicators of codependency is the tendency to become enmeshed in another person's life, often assuming roles such as caregiver, rescuer, or fixer. This behavior stems from the codependent individual feeling responsible for managing the other person's emotions, decisions, and behaviors (Psych Central, n.d.). As a result, codependent individuals may experience feelings of overwhelm, anxiety, and burnout as they struggle to maintain control over a situation that is ultimately beyond their control (WebMD Editorial Contributors, 2022).

Let's examine the two following stories to understand codependency better. The first story is about Liam. Liam had always been the responsible one in his family. As the oldest sibling, he felt he had to care for his younger sister, Maya, and for his parents, who had a tumultuous relationship. Maya was constantly getting into trouble, and his parents were always fighting. Liam felt like it was his job to keep everything together.

As he got older, Liam started dating a girl named Sophie. She was kind, thoughtful, and fun, but Liam became increasingly obsessed with her. He would cancel plans with friends, skip work, and lie to his family about where he was just to be with her.

Sophie, on the other hand, was more independent. She had her own hobbies and interests, and while she loved spending time with Liam, she didn't want to be with him all the time. This made Liam anxious and insecure. He couldn't stand the thought of not being with Sophie, and he would become jealous and possessive if she spent time with other people.

As Liam's behavior became more and more extreme, Sophie started to feel suffocated. She loved Liam but couldn't handle the constant neediness and control. Eventually, she ended the relationship, leaving Liam heartbroken and lost.

This is a classic example of codependency, where one person becomes overly enmeshed in the life of another, sacrificing their own needs and wants to keep the other person happy. Liam's need to control Sophie's time and attention stemmed from his childhood experiences of feeling responsible for his family's well-being. He had never learned how to form healthy, interdependent relationships and instead relied on others to feel a sense of purpose and identity.

Liam has given us one example of what codependency can look like; now let's look at Josh's heartbreaking story. Josh had always been the breadwinner in his family, working long hours to provide for his wife and children. He felt proud of his ability to support his family financially, but over time, he noticed that his wife, Lisa, was becoming increasingly dependent on him to manage their finances.

Lisa had never been interested in handling money or paying bills and relied on Josh to take care of everything. At first, Josh was fine with this arrangement, but as their family grew and their expenses increased, he began to feel overwhelmed and stressed.

Despite his concerns, Lisa would become upset and anxious whenever Josh suggested she take a more active role in managing their finances. She would say things like, "I just don't understand it like you do," or "I'm too busy with the kids to worry about money."

Josh began to feel trapped and resentful. He felt like he was carrying the weight of the entire family on his shoulders, and he didn't know how to talk to Lisa about his concerns without causing a fight.

He started withdrawing from his family as the stress of managing the finances mounted. He stopped participating in family activities and began working even longer hours, hoping that he could make up for the financial strain he was feeling.

One day, Josh's stress reached a breaking point when he was unexpectedly laid off from his job. He didn't know how to support his family without his steady income and felt like a failure. Josh went to see a therapist as he struggled to cope with the sudden loss of his job and the mounting stress of his financial situation. During the sessions, they uncovered that Josh had been enabling Lisa to rely on him for everything, including their finances, which had created a cycle of codependency that was hard to break.

Together, they worked on identifying the underlying issues that had led to his codependency and discussed ways for him to set boundaries with his wife while still being supportive. They also worked on building his self-esteem and finding ways for him to manage his stress and anxiety.

Over time, Josh began communicating more openly with Lisa about their finances and found ways to involve her without overwhelming her. He also found new ways to cope with his stress, including meditating and practicing self-care.

Through the therapy sessions, Josh was able to break free from his codependent patterns and establish a healthier relationship with his wife. He felt more empowered and in control of his life, even when facing financial challenges.

In the end, Josh found a new job and felt confident in supporting his family while prioritizing his well-being. With Lisa's support and understanding, they were able to create and stick to a budget, which helped ease their financial stress and improve their communication about money. As their relationship strengthened, Josh and Lisa began to work on their long-term financial goals together, such as saving for their children's education and planning for retirement. They continued to attend therapy sessions periodically to check in and address any new challenges that arose. Josh learned the importance of setting boundaries and effectively communicating his needs through this journey. He also recognized the value of self-reflection and taking proactive steps to improve his mental health. Overall, Josh and Lisa's relationship was significantly enhanced, and they began to build a stable and fulfilling life together.

Codependency vs. Interdependence

Codependency and interdependence are two distinct relationship types that are often confused with one another. Codependency is an unequal relationship where one person is overly dependent on the other, while interdependence is a mutually beneficial and balanced relationship where both parties rely on each other for support (Avalon Recovery Society, 2021).

Here's a table highlighting some of the critical differences between codependency and interdependence:

Codependency	Interdependence
One person takes on responsibility for the other person's happiness and well-being	Both partners take responsibility for their happiness and well-being
One person sacrifices their own needs and wants to please the other person	Both partners communicate their needs and wants openly and honestly
Feeling guilty or ashamed if one doesn't live up to the other person's expectations	Both partners can compromise and find solutions that work for both of them
An unequal balance of power, with one person being overly dependent on the other	A healthy balance of power, with both partners supporting each other
Difficulty setting and maintaining boundaries	Clear boundaries are set and respected by both partners
A lack of individuality, with both partners losing sight of their own needs and wants	Recognition of each partner's individuality, with both partners maintaining their sense of self
Fear of abandonment or rejection	Trust and respect for each other's independence
Trying to fix or rescue the other person	Supporting the other person without trying to fix them
Constantly seeking validation and approval from the other person	Feeling secure in oneself and the relationship without needing constant validation
A lack of emotional intimacy and vulnerability	Open communication and a willingness to be vulnerable with each other
Difficulty expressing emotions and needs	Both partners feel safe and comfortable expressing their emotions and needs
An emphasis on external validation and material possessions	A focus on shared experiences and emotional connection
A tendency to ignore or minimize one's feelings and needs	Both partners prioritize their self-care and well-being
Enabling the other person's unhealthy behaviors or habits	Encouraging each other to make healthy choices and grow together

A lack of personal boundaries and a tendency to overstep or violate the other person's boundaries	Respect for each other's boundaries and a commitment to healthy communication

By understanding the difference between codependency and interdependence, you can work towards building a healthier, more balanced relationship that allows both you and your partner to thrive. Remember, it's not about being completely independent or dependent—it's about finding a healthy balance.

Checklist: Are You Codependent or Interdependent?

I've created a simple checklist to help you determine whether you're exhibiting signs of codependency or interdependence in your relationships. This checklist is designed to be a tool for self-reflection, allowing you to identify areas where you might need to work on building healthier, more balanced relationships. So if you're ready to take a closer look, read on!

Checklist: Are You Codependent or Interdependent?		
Instructions: Answer each question honestly and check the appropriate box. Add up your total score for each column at the end.		
Questions	Yes (Codependent)	No (Interdependent)
1. Do you find it difficult to make decisions independently, without seeking approval or advice from others?	[ ]	[ ]
2. Do you feel responsible for other people's feelings, actions, and well-being, even when they are not your responsibility?	[ ]	[ ]
3. Do you have trouble setting boundaries with others and saying "no" to requests or demands?	[ ]	[ ]
4. Do you feel guilty or anxious when you prioritize your needs and wants over others'?	[ ]	[ ]
5. Do you have difficulty expressing your feelings and needs in relationships?	[ ]	[ ]
6. Do you rely on others for validation and self-worth?	[ ]	[ ]

7. Do you often feel resentful or angry when others don't meet your expectations or needs?	[ ]	[ ]
8. Do you need to "fix" or rescue others from their problems, or do you take responsibility for their actions?	[ ]	[ ]
9. Do you have difficulty saying "I'm sorry" or admitting you are wrong?	[ ]	[ ]
10. Do you feel uncomfortable asking for help and support when needed?	[ ]	[ ]

Once you have completed the checklist, add up your total score for each column to determine whether you lean more toward codependency or interdependence.

Attachment Styles and Codependency

Codependency has been linked to attachment styles in several ways. Individuals with an anxious attachment style may be more susceptible to codependency due to their need for validation and approval from others in their relationships. This may lead to unhealthy reliance on others for emotional well-being when their partner is unavailable or their needs are not being met. Avoidant attachment style individuals may also struggle with codependency, albeit in a different way. Such individuals tend to fear intimacy or vulnerability, leading them to avoid emotional closeness with others. Nevertheless, they may rely on others for practical or logistical support, such as financial or household help, leading to a form of codependency (Guenther, n.d.).

Individuals with a secure attachment style, on the other hand, are less likely to struggle with codependency since they possess a healthy sense of self-worth and are comfortable with both emotional and physical intimacy. However, those with a secure attachment style can still fall into codependent patterns if they are in a relationship with someone who has an unhealthy attachment style.

Understanding your own attachment style can help identify tendencies towards codependency and allow you to work towards healthier relationships. Through self-awareness and prioritizing your emotional well-being, you can break free from codependent patterns and build interdependent relationships based on mutual respect and healthy boundaries (Meek, 2022).

How to Overcome Codependency for Good

If you think you might be struggling with codependency, you're not alone. Many people struggle with this issue, but the good news is that it's possible to overcome it. Codependency can have a devastating effect on our lives, relationships, and mental health. It's a pattern of behavior where we prioritize other people's needs over our own to the point where it becomes unhealthy and harmful.

We can become so enmeshed with our partner that we lose our sense of self and identity. Fortunately, we can overcome codependency with time, effort, and the right tools.

Here are some effective ways to overcome codependency for good:

1. Understand what codependency is

To overcome codependency, you need to start by understanding it. Codependency is a pattern of behavior where you rely on others for your sense of self-worth, validation, and identity. It often stems from childhood experiences, such as growing up with a parent with addiction or mental health problems. When you're codependent, you're more concerned with caring for others than yourself. You may feel guilty when you prioritize your own needs, or you may feel responsible for other people's problems. This can lead to insecurity and the belief that others' needs are more important than yours.

2. Set boundaries

Codependency often involves blurring boundaries between yourself and others. You may feel responsible for other people's emotions and actions, even when they're not your fault. This can lead to a cycle of putting others' needs before your own and neglecting your own well-being. To overcome codependency, it's important to set healthy boundaries and stick to them.

Setting boundaries means learning to say no when you need to, expressing your needs clearly and assertively, and taking responsibility only for your own emotions and behaviors. This can be a challenging process, especially if you're used to putting others' needs first. However, it's essential for your own well-being and to establish healthy relationships. Remember, setting boundaries doesn't mean you don't care about others or their needs. It simply means that you're prioritizing your own well-being and establishing healthy limits.

3. Develop your own sense of self

Codependency often involves losing yourself and your own identity in the needs and wants of others. This means that you may have lost touch with your own interests, passions, and values. You may also rely on others for validation and self-worth, rather than learning to love and accept yourself for who you are.

Developing a strong sense of self can involve exploring your own interests and passions, whether that means trying out new hobbies or rediscovering ones you used to enjoy. It also means taking time to reflect on your values and beliefs, and figuring out what's truly important to you. Learning to love and accept yourself can involve practicing self-care, such as taking care of your physical and emotional health, setting boundaries, and speaking kindly to yourself. With time and effort, you can cultivate a stronger sense of self and overcome codependency.

4. Focus on personal growth

To start on the journey of overcoming codependency, one must make a commitment to personal growth. This involves taking ownership of your thoughts, feelings, and behaviors, and actively working towards positive change. It's important to develop healthy coping mechanisms that work for you, build up your self-esteem, and create a sense of independence.

Focusing on personal growth can be challenging, but it's a critical part of overcoming codependency. You can start by identifying areas in which you'd like to improve and setting realistic goals for yourself. This might involve seeking therapy or support groups, practicing self-care, or pursuing new hobbies and interests. Whatever approach you choose, remember to be patient with yourself and celebrate your progress along the way. With time and effort, you can break free from codependency and create a healthier, more fulfilling life.

5. Challenge negative thought patterns

When you're deep in a codependent relationship, chances are your mental health isn't where it should be. You might find yourself experiencing a lot of negative thoughts, overthinking small incidents, and feeling anxious or worried. It's important that you challenge these negative thoughts when they arise. Allowing the negativity to continue to spiral will make it much more difficult for you to overcome your codependency.

6. Celebrate progress, not perfection

Remember that progress is a process. Striving for perfection can be counterproductive and lead to feelings of failure and inadequacy. Instead, focus on making small changes and celebrate each step towards a healthier, more fulfilling life. Recognize the progress you have made, even if it seems small, and take pride in the positive changes you have implemented in your life.

It's also important to keep in mind that setbacks and challenges are a natural part of the process of personal growth and healing. When you experience a setback, be kind and compassionate to yourself rather than beating yourself up. Recognize that setbacks are an opportunity for learning and growth and use them as a chance to recommit to your goals and make positive changes moving forward. By celebrating progress and being gentle with yourself, you can create a positive and empowering mindset that will support you in your journey toward overcoming codependency.

Workbook Six

1. What are some of the warning signs of codependency, and how can you identify these patterns in your own behavior?

2. Think about a relationship in your life that feels imbalanced or codependent. How might setting boundaries and practicing self-care help to improve this dynamic?

3. How might embracing interdependence benefit your relationships and overall well-being? What steps can you take to move towards a more interdependent mindset?

Chapter Six Takeaway

The focus of this chapter was on overcoming codependency and developing a more interdependent approach to relationships. Through applying the strategies outlined here, you can learn to set healthy boundaries, prioritize self-care, and cultivate a sense of self-worth that is independent of external validation. By breaking free from codependent patterns, you can build a healthier, more balanced relationship with your significant other that support mutual growth and well-being.

CHAPTER SEVEN

Tips for Cultivating Healthy Relationships

"A friend loves at all times, and a brother is born for a time of adversity."

—Proverbs 17:17

When Anna was in college, she struggled to maintain healthy relationships with her friends and romantic partners. She often found herself feeling anxious and unsure of how to communicate her needs and boundaries effectively. One day, she stumbled upon a quote that stuck with her: "You can't pour from an empty cup." This simple phrase reminded Anna that taking care of herself was essential for building strong, fulfilling relationships with others. From that day on, she made a conscious effort to prioritize her own self-care and communicate her needs assertively. As a result, she noticed a significant improvement in her relationships and felt more confident and fulfilled in her connections with others.

Have you ever wondered why some people always seem to attract positive, healthy relationships into their lives while others struggle to find the right kind of people? Your attachment style plays a big role in determining the kind of people you attract.

These patterns can influence how you behave in relationships as an adult, including whom you choose to be with and how you interact with them. So, if you find yourself attracting the wrong kind of people into your life, it might be time to take a closer look at your attachment style and see if there are any changes you can make. Here are some tips that can help you attract the right people.

Tips for Attracting the Right People

When it comes to finding the right people to surround yourself with, whether it be in your personal or professional life, it can often feel like a daunting task. You want to attract individuals who share your values, goals, and interests—but how? The answer lies in understanding what qualities and traits you should look for in people and projecting those qualities and traits yourself. So, whether you're looking for friends, business partners, or a romantic relationship, here are some tips to consider:

1. Be yourself

The first and most important step in attracting the right people is just being yourself. People are naturally drawn to authenticity, and when you're genuine and true to yourself, you'll attract others who appreciate and respect you for who you are. This means embracing your quirks, strengths, and weaknesses and being comfortable in your own skin.

It can be easy to fall into the trap of trying to be someone you're not to fit in or impress others. However, this often backfires and leads to superficial relationships that lack depth and meaning. Instead, focus on being the best version of yourself and trusting that the right people will be drawn to you.

2. Identify your values

Knowing your values is key to attracting the right people. Your values are the guiding principles that shape your beliefs, priorities, and decisions. When you're clear on your values, you'll naturally gravitate toward others who share your beliefs and outlook on life.

To identify your values, take some time to reflect on what matters most to you. Ask yourself questions like: What do I stand for? What brings me joy and fulfillment? What do I want to contribute to the world? Once you clearly understand your values, seek out communities, groups, and activities that align with them.

3. Pursue your interests

One of the best ways to attract the right people is to pursue what you love. When you engage in activities that align with your passions, you'll naturally meet others who share your enthusiasm and zest for life. Whether it's joining a book club, taking a cooking class, or volunteering for a cause you care about, engaging in activities you enjoy can lead to meaningful connections.

When pursuing your interests, you're more likely to be in a state of flow and positivity, which can be attractive to others. This doesn't mean you need to be an extroverted social butterfly, though—introverts can achieve the same goal by participating in activities that align with their interests and values. Over time, relationships with people who share those interests will begin to develop naturally.

4. Practice positivity

Positive energy is contagious, and cultivating a positive attitude can be a magnet for attracting the right people. When you approach life with gratitude, optimism, and hope, you'll naturally attract others who share your positive outlook.

This doesn't mean ignoring or denying the challenges and struggles of life; it simply means focusing on the good rather than the negative and finding joy in the little things. When you radiate positivity, you'll naturally draw in others who are similarly optimistic and hopeful.

5. Be open-minded

When meeting new people, it's important to keep an open mind. Don't be too quick to judge or dismiss someone based on first impressions, and be open to new experiences and perspectives. This means being willing to step outside of your comfort zone and try new things.

Being open-minded also means embracing diversity and seeking opportunities to learn from people different from you. When you approach life with curiosity and a willingness to learn, you'll attract others who share your open-mindedness and thirst for knowledge.

6. Communicate effectively

Effective communication is crucial in building healthy relationships. This means being clear and honest about your intentions and expectations and actively listening to what others say. Communicating effectively makes you more likely to build trust, respect, and understanding with others.

Effective communication also means being assertive and setting boundaries when necessary. When you're clear about your needs and limits, you'll attract people who respect and value your boundaries (see Tip #7).

7. Set boundaries

Knowing your limits and setting boundaries can help attract people who respect and value your needs. This means being clear about what you will and won't tolerate and being willing to say no or speak up when someone crosses your boundaries. When you set boundaries, you communicate to others that you value and respect yourself, and you're more likely to attract people who share those values.

Setting boundaries also means being aware of red flags and warning signs in your relationships. Suppose someone constantly disrespects your boundaries, ignores your feelings, or behaves in a way that makes you uncomfortable. In that case, it may be time to re-evaluate the relationship and consider ending it.

Attracting the right people starts with being true to yourself, identifying your values, and pursuing your interests. It also involves practicing positivity, being open-minded, communicating effectively, and setting boundaries. Cultivating these habits and attitudes will naturally attract others who share your values and outlook. Remember that relationships take time and effort to build, so be patient, stay true to yourself, and trust that the right people will come into your life at the right time.

Drawing and Maintaining Healthy Boundaries

Our last tip in the previous section was about boundaries. It turns out this is such a key aspect of attracting good people into your life that it bears closer examination.

As human beings, we all have different preferences, personalities, and needs. These differences make us unique but can also cause conflicts, especially when we fail to set boundaries. Drawing and maintaining healthy boundaries can be challenging, but it's crucial for our emotional, mental, and physical well-being.

Let's consider the story of Sarah, a people-pleaser. She went to a therapist feeling overwhelmed and stressed out. She had difficulty saying no, so she constantly took on more than she could handle. She felt like she was always putting other people's needs before her own, which was taking a toll on her mental health.

As they talked more, it became clear that Sarah had difficulty setting boundaries because she feared disappointing people or being seen as selfish. She had a strong desire to be liked and accepted by everyone, making it difficult to prioritize her needs.

The therapist worked with Sarah to help her understand that setting boundaries wasn't about being selfish but about caring for herself so she could be there for others in a healthy way. They discussed strategies she could use to draw and maintain healthy boundaries, such as saying no when needed, communicating her needs clearly, and setting limits on her time and energy.

At first, Sarah found it difficult to put these strategies into practice. She was used to saying yes to everything, and it felt uncomfortable to start setting limits. But as she started to see the positive impact on her mental health, she became more confident in her ability to set boundaries.

One day, Sarah had an experience that really highlighted the importance of drawing healthy boundaries. A friend asked to borrow some money, and Sarah felt torn. On the one hand, she wanted to help her friend, but on the other hand, she knew that lending money would strain her finances.

Instead of immediately agreeing to lend the money, Sarah took a step back and thought about what would be best for her own well-being. She realized she needed to draw a boundary and clearly communicate her decision to her friend. She explained that while she wanted to help, she couldn't lend the money.

To Sarah's surprise, her friend was understanding and grateful for her honesty. Sarah felt relieved and empowered by the experience, and it reinforced the importance of setting healthy boundaries in all areas of her life.

Through working with her therapist, Sarah learned that drawing and maintaining healthy boundaries was essential for her well-being and her relationships with others. She gained the confidence to prioritize her needs and communicate them clearly, which ultimately helped her lead a more fulfilling life.

This story gives us a valuable lesson about the importance of setting boundaries. If you don't set boundaries, it's all too easy to become emotionally burnt out.

Now, let's dive even deeper into maintaining healthy boundaries.

Once you've established clear boundaries, it's important to maintain them. This can be challenging, especially if you're used to putting other people's needs before yours. However, maintaining boundaries is essential to building healthy relationships.

One effective way to maintain boundaries is to communicate them clearly and consistently. This can be as simple as saying no when someone asks you to do something that makes you uncomfortable, or firmly reminding people of your boundaries if they try to push past them (Lifehack, 2021). It's also important to hold yourself accountable for maintaining your own boundaries. If you find yourself slipping, step back and reassess the situation.

Another key aspect of maintaining healthy boundaries is letting go of people who don't respect them. This can be difficult, especially if you care about the person or have a long history with them. However, if someone constantly ignores or disrespects your boundaries, it's important to recognize that it may not be healthy to have them in your life (Mark Manson, n.d.). You deserve to surround yourself with people who treat you with respect and kindness.

By learning to communicate your needs clearly and holding yourself and others accountable, you can create a supportive and nurturing social network that brings joy and fulfillment to your life. So don't be afraid to say no, speak up for yourself, and let go of those who don't have your best interests at heart.

As you learn to set and maintain healthy boundaries, you'll also begin to recognize when others aren't respecting them. You might encounter people who push your boundaries or try to cross them altogether. It's important to remember that you have the right to enforce your boundaries (Psych Central, 2022). It can be tough to say no to friends or family members, but if someone continually disrespects your boundaries, it may be necessary to distance yourself from that person.

Setting and maintaining healthy boundaries takes practice, but it's a critical skill for developing healthy relationships. Being clear about your needs, communicating effectively, and enforcing your boundaries will create an environment where you feel respected, heard, and valued. And that's the foundation for healthy and fulfilling relationships.

Remember, setting boundaries isn't about controlling others or being selfish. It's about taking charge of your life and creating a healthy environment for everyone involved. When you prioritize your own well-being, you can show up as your best self in your relationships and your life. So don't be afraid to set those boundaries and stick to them. Your relationships (and your mental health) will thank you for it.

The Importance of Empathy

I once heard a story that perfectly illustrates the importance of empathy. It's about a woman named Julie who worked at a software company in San Francisco. One day, Julie's colleague, Joe, approached her and requested to take over one of her projects. Julie felt a twinge of annoyance, as she had been working on this project for weeks and felt proud of the progress she had made. She was about to say no when she noticed that Joe seemed visibly upset. His hands were shaking, and he looked like he had not slept in days.

Julie decided to put herself in Joe's shoes and asked him what was going on. He explained that his mother had recently been diagnosed with cancer and that he was struggling to cope with the news. Julie could see the pain in his eyes, and she realized that her project was not as important as she had thought.

She took a deep breath and told Joe that she would be happy to hand over the project to him. She assured him that she would be there to support him in any way she could. Joe's face lit up, and he thanked her profusely. Over the next few weeks, Julie helped Joe with his workload and offered emotional support. She could see the weight lifting from his shoulders, and he started to smile more often.

Joe's mother passed away a few months later, and he was understandably devastated. Julie was there for him, offering a listening ear and a shoulder to cry on. She knew that nothing could take away the pain of losing a loved one, but she hoped that her presence could offer some comfort.

I am sure that after that experience, Julie realized the importance of empathy. She learned that sometimes, the needs of others outweigh our own desires. By putting ourselves in someone else's shoes and showing compassion, we can make a difference in their lives. And in doing so, we may also find a deeper sense of purpose and fulfillment.

As you navigate through life and interact with others, it's important to remember the power of empathy. Trying to understand someone else's perspective can create stronger relationships, build trust, and foster a more supportive and inclusive environment.

To truly empathize with someone, you must actively listen to what they say without judgment or interruption. Being fully present and engaged shows that you care about their feelings and experiences. This allows you to better understand their needs, respond appropriately to their emotions, resolve conflicts effectively, and foster a stronger relationship.

So how can you cultivate empathy in yourself and others? It starts with active listening, curiosity, and an open mind. Be willing to step outside your own experiences and try to understand the experiences of others, and in this way you can create a more inclusive and supportive environment. You can also ask questions, share your own feelings, and express genuine interest and concern.

Another way to cultivate empathy is to practice active listening. When you actively listen to someone, you give them your full attention and show that you care about what they're saying. This means putting away distractions like your phone or computer, making eye contact, and nodding or responding appropriately to show that you're engaged in the conversation.

It's also important to approach conversations with an open mind and curiosity. Instead of assuming you know how someone feels or what they're going through, try asking questions and seeking to understand their perspective. You might be surprised by what you learn and how it can deepen your connection.

Finally, remember to express genuine interest and concern for others. Let them know that you care about their feelings and experiences and that you're there to support them. This can be as simple as offering a kind word or a listening ear when someone needs it.

Empathy is a powerful tool to help you connect with others and create a more compassionate world. Practicing empathy can create a more supportive and inclusive environment in all areas of your life. It can help you build stronger relationships, foster trust, and create a more compassionate world, whether at work, with friends, or at home with family. So why not give it a try? You might be surprised by how much of a difference it can make.

Using the 3 C's: Communication, Compromise, and Commitment

Communication, compromise, and commitment are key when it comes to maintaining a healthy and happy relationship. These three C's can make all the difference in whether a relationship thrives or falls apart. Let's examine how these principles can help you build a strong and fulfilling connection with your partner.

Communication is at the heart of any successful relationship. It's important to be open and honest with your partner, expressing your thoughts and feelings respectfully and constructively. This includes not just talking but actively listening as well. When your partner shares something with you, take the time to really hear them out and understand where they're coming from. Use "I" statements instead of "you" statements, which can be perceived as accusatory. For example, saying, "I feel hurt when you do X," is more productive than "You always do X, and it's annoying." And remember, communication is a two-way street, so make sure you're also receptive to your partner's feedback and willing to work together to find solutions to any issues that arise.

Compromise is another crucial aspect of a healthy relationship. No two people are exactly the same, so there will inevitably be times when you don't see eye-to-eye with your partner. In these situations, finding a middle ground that works for both of you is important. This might mean making small sacrifices or finding creative solutions that allow you both to get what you want. It's important to remember that compromise isn't about giving in or giving up but about finding a way to meet each other halfway.

Finally, commitment is the glue that holds a relationship together. It's not just about being faithful, although that's certainly important. Commitment means being there for your partner through thick and thin, supporting each other through the ups and downs of life. It means prioritizing your relationship and trying to show your partner they're loved and valued. And it means being willing to work through any challenges that come your way rather than giving up at the first sign of trouble.

By incorporating these three C's into your relationship, you can build a strong foundation that will stand the test of time. Remember that communication, compromise, and commitment are ongoing processes, so make a conscious effort to practice them daily. You and your partner can create a happy and fulfilling life together with time and effort.

How Knowing the Attachment Styles and Building a Secure Attachment Can Help You Stop Overthinking

If you have an anxious or insecure attachment style, you may have a tendency to overthink your relationship. You may be concerned about your partner's affection for you and be on the lookout for indicators that they will leave you. This can cause a great deal of tension and stress, making it difficult to enjoy your relationship.

Understanding your attachment style will help you begin to recognize the thoughts and actions that contribute to your anxiety. This will also help you to begin learning how to develop a more stable connection style.

In addition to learning about attachment styles, you can do a few other things to build a secure attachment and stop overthinking:

1. Concentrate on the current moment. Bring your focus back to the current moment when you begin to overthink. Take notice of your environment, your body, and your breathing.

2. Get adequate rest. When you're well-rested, you can deal with stress and worry better.

3. Get 7-8 hours of sleep every night, and exercise regularly. Exercise is an excellent approach to relieve tension and anxiety. On most days of the week, aim for at least 30 minutes of moderate-intensity exercise.

4. Create a support system. A solid network of friends and family might make you feel safer and less worried. Discuss your feelings with your loved ones and tell them how they can help.

5. Maintain a healthy diet. Eating a balanced diet provides you with the energy you require to deal with stress and worry. Consume plenty of fruits, veggies, and whole grains.

6. Spend time with family and friends. Spending time with family and friends will help you feel supported and connected. Make time for activities with friends and family that you enjoy.

Workbook Seven

1. Which of the specific tips offered in this chapter for cultivating healthy relationships are most useful to you? How might you implement these strategies in your own life?

2. Think about a relationship in your life that could benefit from improved communication or trust. What steps can you take to work towards a stronger, more fulfilling connection?

3. In what ways might prioritizing self-awareness and self-care benefit your relationships with others? How can you balance the needs of both yourself and others in your relationships?

Chapter Seven Takeaway

The tips outlined in this chapter can be applied to various types of relationships, including romantic partnerships, friendships, and professional connections. Whether you are looking to improve existing relationships or build new ones, after reading this chapter, you now have several practical strategies for fostering deeper connections and greater intimacy.

Conclusion

Dear reader,

As I conclude the writing of this book on fixing your anxious attachment style, my heart is full of emotion. I feel empathy for the pain you may have experienced in your relationships, and I hope that the tools and strategies outlined in this book will help you on your journey toward healing and growth.

Attachment theory is a powerful framework that can help us understand the patterns of behavior we bring into our relationships. For those with an anxious attachment style, these patterns often stem from a deep-seated fear of abandonment and a need for constant reassurance and validation. These patterns can lead to toxic jealousy, insecurity, and anxiety in our relationships, making it difficult to form deep, meaningful connections with others.

But, as this book has shown, there is hope. We can break free from these patterns through prayer, reflection, and intentional action and build healthier, more fulfilling relationships. We can learn to communicate our needs and boundaries in healthy ways and work on building our self-esteem and self-worth so that we do not rely on others to fill those needs.

As you embark on this journey of healing and growth, it's essential to acknowledge that it won't happen overnight. Breaking free from anxious attachment patterns is a process, and it takes time and effort to build new, healthier habits. But the good news is that it is possible.

Through prayer, you can tap into the power of God to guide you and strengthen you on your journey. You can ask for the wisdom and insight you need to recognize your patterns of behavior and the courage to confront them head-on. With God's help, you can learn to trust in His love and plan for your life and release your fears and anxieties.

Reflection is another important tool in your journey toward healing. You must be willing to look honestly at yourself and your relationships and ask yourself tough questions. What are your triggers? What are the negative patterns of behavior that you need to break free from? What are the core beliefs that drive your anxious attachment style? By answering these questions, you can better understand yourself and your relationships.

Intentional action is the final piece of the puzzle. You must be willing to take concrete steps toward change, even when it's uncomfortable or difficult. This means setting healthy boundaries, communicating your needs clearly and respectfully, and caring for yourself physically, mentally, and spiritually. It also means being open to feedback and adjusting as you go along.

As you put these tools into practice, you will begin to see changes in yourself and your relationships. You will feel more secure in your connections with others and more confident in yourself. You will be better equipped to handle the ups and downs of life and more resilient in the face of challenges.

We are called to love others as ourselves and to seek to build healthy, life-giving relationships. This means confronting our issues and working towards healing and growth. It means recognizing that true love is not based on fear or control but trust and respect.

So, dear friend, I want to encourage you to take heart. There is hope for healing and growth, no matter how entrenched your behavior patterns may seem. Through prayer, reflection, and intentional action, we can break free from the toxic patterns of anxious attachment and build healthier, more fulfilling relationships. And as we do, may we find peace, joy, and love in our connections.

I want to encourage you, dear friend, to take the lessons of this book to heart and begin your journey of healing and growth. It may not be easy, but it is worth it. As you work towards a healthier attachment style, you will find that your relationships become more fulfilling, joyful, and life-giving.

Finally, I want to remind you that you are not alone. There are people in your life who love and support you, and there is a God who loves you unconditionally. Lean on these sources of support as you work through your attachment issues, and remember that you are worthy of love and belonging.

Let us pray together:

Dear Heavenly Father,

As we come before you today, we bring the pain and struggles of our relationships. We confess that our anxious attachment styles have caused us to feel insecure, jealous, and fearful, and we ask for your forgiveness and help in overcoming these patterns.

We pray for the wisdom and insight we need to recognize our negative patterns of behavior and the courage to confront them. Please help us communicate our needs and boundaries healthily and build our self-esteem and self-worth so that we do not rely on others to fill those needs.

We ask that you guide us as we reflect on our relationships and behavior. Please help us to be honest and see ourselves as you visit us. We pray that you would reveal any core beliefs or fears driving our anxious attachment style and help us release them into your loving care.

We pray for the strength and perseverance to take intentional action toward change. Help us to set healthy boundaries, communicate with love and respect, and to take care of ourselves physically, mentally, and spiritually. We ask for your guidance and your presence with us every step of the way.

And finally, we pray for your peace, joy, and love to fill our relationships. May we learn to trust in your love and plan for our lives and find security and fulfillment in our connections with others. We thank you for your grace and mercy and ask for your continued blessings on our journey toward healing and growth.

In Jesus' name, we pray,

Amen.

BOOK #2

Setting Boundaries to Find Peace with Narcissists & Codependents

How to Communicate with Toxic People to Free Yourself
From Manipulation and Gaslighting Without Feeling Guilty

Introduction

You are strong,
You are firm,
You are stable.

To start this book, I'd like to share this story with you.

I first heard about the concept of setting up boundaries a couple of days after my 23rd birthday. I was having issues with my friends, as they were intent on dictating every aspect of my life. I needed to keep them away from me but I didn't know how. Someone spoke to me about setting boundaries, and I was genuinely shocked that something like that existed.

You must understand why. I grew up with no notion of privacy and was taught that I was responsible for the happiness of my siblings. I was cast in this role and I had no choice but to act as though I liked it, even though I was often disrespected in the process. I lived with this discontentment all my life till I became an adult, and one day, I snapped. I wasn't going to take it anymore, and I let everyone know.

Somehow, I believed my declaration would be met with approval, with encouragement. (I know, I was painfully naive.) Eventually, my enforcement of my boundaries led to being ostracized by my family and having my reputation *massacred. But it paid off. Slowly, I started learning how to respect myself and ensure I behaved in a way that was kind to others, yet not disrespectful to myself. Boundaries won me my life back and gave me the foundation to create the kind of life I desired for myself.*

—Sam

So you're stuck with a toxic person in your life, or you've had an encounter (or maybe five) with a narcissist and you're tired of being cannon fodder for their manipulative behavior? Or maybe you're not really even sure if you're being manipulated. You've heard the words "narcissism" and "codependency" so often that you're more than a little confused about what they really mean. You may not even be sure about what a "toxic person" is or how to identify them. Well, reading this book is the best decision you could've made, and I'll show you why.

I find that the first step to effective learning and eventual transformation is to demystify misconceptions and shatter illusions. In the first part of this book, we'll be looking at what narcissism means. We'll examine the typical characteristics of the average narcissist and how you can identify one. You'll learn how to tell the difference between someone who's a narcissist and someone who's abusive (they're not necessarily mutually exclusive). We'll bust all the myths you may be harboring about narcissism, too.

Next, we'll look at what codependency is, how it's different from being narcissistic, and the connections between narcissism and codependency. What does psychology have to say about these two terms? How can you tell if you're in a codependent relationship? Is a narcissist better than a codependent person?

Then you'll find out if it's really possible to be free of manipulation and toxic gaslighting. We'll see how to prevent yourself from falling for the same narcissistic tactics over and over again. You'll learn how to respond to those behaviors in a way that leaves you with your dignity and self-respect intact.

Next up, have you ever tried taking a look at all your social connections to identify the toxic people in your life? I think this is necessary because for most of us, family and friends are a very big blind spot when it comes to identifying toxicity. How can you handle narcissistic family members? What's the best way to deal with codependent parents and siblings? We'll look at real-life examples and scenarios.

You'll learn how to identify these traits in your family members, coworkers, and close friends. You'll learn how to mentally condition yourself to handle them and the best time to let go, if necessary.

Armed with the knowledge you've gained from the earlier parts of the book, we'll dive into the last section and seek to teach you the importance of setting boundaries and the most practical ways to do it. You'll learn how to create boundaries at work, with your family, and even with your significant other. You'll learn how to avoid unnecessary arguments and bickering by expressing your boundaries and reinforcing them. You'll see how to handle toxic people that you can't walk away from (without losing your mind) and how to say no without falling for the guilt trap.

Perhaps the most important thing you'll learn in this book is the need to love and prioritize yourself because that's anathema to a narcissist who's trying to manipulate someone. You'll discover how to stop blaming yourself and get rid of the effects of toxicity in your life. You'll get to use practical exercises and worksheets to apply the things you've learned and replicate your results with every relationship you have.

Many people can't stop talking about what they call "the Great Disparity." If you're wondering what that is, it's simply the fact that while a lot of emphasis is placed on people going to school to get educated, most of the truly important stuff you need to learn isn't taught in school—topics like emotional intelligence, setting boundaries, financial intelligence, and simple things like making relationships work. The most unfortunate aspect here is that most people don't even *know* what they don't know. They don't know what they need, and even if they do, they're not motivated enough to learn about it and diligently apply that knowledge, just like they would in school.

That's why I can boldly say that you deserve great praise for choosing to buy this book and learn this essential life skill. I'm not one to patronize people; the truth is, the fact that you're motivated enough to be here shows that you're programmed to be successful at this. It shows that you have the grit and tenacity to do what needs to be done. Even if you don't feel like it, there's a deep well of courage and strength available within you to guide you to where you need to be.

I'm not going to deceive you or sugarcoat the facts: there's a lot of work to be done. There's a lot of soul-searching and brutal honesty needed here. You'll have to be willing to dig deep into hurtful memories and come to terms with unpleasant truths about yourself. You'll have to abandon previously held conceptions about yourself and the people you love. You'll have to break yourself down and build your real self back up. You may cry in the process, or even feel tempted to set this book aside and give up at some point. But I'm more than confident that you can handle it. I also know that this book will be a turning point for you.

Finally, throughout the book, I have applied a biblical approach to addressing these issues, and at the end of each chapter, you'll find a quick workbook to help you integrate what you've learned.

Now, without spending any more time introducing the topic — let's delve right into it, shall we?

—Robert

PART ONE

Explaining Codependency and Narcissism

The great thing about the age of social media is the fact that information spreads faster than wildfire. This has a lot of advantages, primarily that people who need essential knowledge can get access to it with a snap of their fingers. Unfortunately, this comes with disadvantages too. I think the greatest drawback is the spread of incomplete and untrue information, which, as we all know, can have debilitating effects (Menczer & Hills, 2020).

The same holds true for the concepts of toxicity, narcissism, and codependency. You don't have to scroll too far on any social media before you come across someone teaching you stuff (which is untrue most of the time) and leading you to draw erroneous conclusions about yourself and other people.

Instead of playing at guessing or harboring any sort of uncertainty about this important issue, this first part will be about how to recognize narcissism and codependency. We'll examine if all abusive people are narcissistic and even how to tell if you're being abused by a narcissist. We'll look at the nitty-gritty of codependency and we'll check if other buzzwords, like "obsession," "dependency," and "trauma," are actually relevant in this scenario.

A fair number of people I've interacted with couldn't tell if they were codependent or even if they were in a codependent relationship. You may be in the same boat: you could be mistaking an unhealthy, codependent partnership for "true love" or a codependent friendship for a loyal one. We'll see the truth about that once and for all here.

Oh, and what about people that are both narcissistic and codependent? Is that really a thing and is that important to know? Yes, it's important to find out as much about the narcissistic person in your life as possible. You need to know why you should address the narcissistic codependent cycle in your life, even if it feels good some of the time.

By the end of this part, you'll be clear on the inner workings of narcissism and codependency. You'll stop throwing those buzzwords around carelessly and you'll be able to speak and act with confidence. We take a lot of time to break things down here so you'll have a clear understanding of what you're dealing with. I daresay that by the end of this part, you'll be able to predict the next move the narcissist or toxic person in your life will make, and you'll even have an idea of how to stop them in their tracks. This part is all about enlightenment, which is a vital step for empowerment.

CHAPTER ONE

The Overused Labels

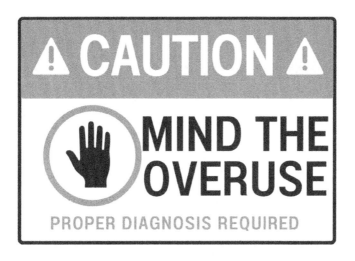

"Thorns and snares are in the way of the crooked; whoever guards his soul will keep far from them."

—Proverbs 22:5 ESV

"When I look at narcissism through the vulnerability lens, I see the shame-based fear of being ordinary. I see the fear of never feeling extraordinary enough to be noticed, to be lovable, to belong, or to cultivate a sense of purpose."

—Brené Brown

I*t was a sunny afternoon and I was out on the porch, having a glass of iced tea and trying to decide if I wanted to go for a walk because it was a particularly beautiful day. I remember this day because I had my sunglasses on and I looked at the sky through them. Of course, because of how opaque the glasses were, I*

115

didn't get to see the clear, pretty blue of the sky, nor the blindingly white fluffy clouds clearly.

It was at this point that I got a call from Sally, a young woman who was distressed because she claimed that her husband was a narcissist and an abuser. I quickly calmed her down and we scheduled a meeting. When we met, she told me that she'd been unhappy in her marriage and she just realized that her husband was a narcissist, thanks to a helpful TikTok video she saw. When we examined his behavior, her behavior, and what narcissism truly was, she had to reluctantly admit that she was wrong on a few counts.

I got together with Sally and her husband, and thankfully, they were able to clear up their issues because they were both invested in their marriage. I sat out on the porch after my last meeting with them and realized that Sally had been the victim of misinformation. She couldn't see her husband for who he really was, or his faults for what they were, because her vision was blocked by false perceptions, much like when I observed the sky through my sunglasses.

—Olivia

Are you in the same situation as Sally in the story above? Let's find out.

How to Know If Someone Is a Narcissist or Just Plain Abusive

Did you know that narcissism can and should be officially diagnosed by a mental health expert? (Cleveland Clinic, 2020). Have you ever heard of narcissistic personality disorder? Yes, it's a whole thing and there's a specific guideline for its diagnosis.

I'd like to ask you a question, if you don't mind. How many people have you labeled as a "narcissist" just because you didn't like a particular behavior or attitude? Did you know that even the average, "normal" person is manipulative to an extent? Did you know that even innocent children can be manipulative too? So, where do you draw the line? How can you clearly detect an abusive person or tell if they're narcissistic or even codependent?

The fact is that while we admit that abuse can occur in various ways and affect various aspects of one's life, not every abusive person is a narcissist. Don't get me wrong, being abused is detrimental, no matter what form it takes—but it's important for us to be specific about the personality of the abuser and the type of abuse. This is because each abusive personality has different effects on their victim and a thorough knowledge is needed for healing to be effective.

Another interesting tidbit is that, according to clinical therapist Dr. Alyssa Mancao (2020), people with narcissistic behaviors do not automatically have narcissistic personality disorder. This means that even though the people in our lives may exhibit some narcissistic behaviors, we can't just diagnose them with a disorder.

Narcissistic abuse is centered on the abuser and is a reflection of the fact that they lack empathy, have an inflated sense of self-importance, and need to be admired. All their narcissistic behaviors stem from these major roots, and any abuse that's perpetrated for reasons outside these can't be qualified as narcissistic abuse.

Understanding What NPD Is All About

Narcissistic Personality Disorder (NPD) is a mental health disorder characterized by a need for special treatment or admiration, a sense of self-importance or grandiosity, and a consistent fantasy of exaggerated power (Kacel et al., 2017). According to the 5th edition of the Diagnostic and Statistical Manual of Mental Disorders (DSM-5), NPD is classified as a "Cluster B" personality disorder. This class of disorders involves dramatic, emotional, and erratic behavior. NPD one of the personality disorders that is diagnosed least often (Pies, 2011).

A lack of empathy in addition to a need for special attention and feelings of grandiosity are hallmarks of NPD (Ronningstam & Weinberg, 2013). It is interesting to note that people with NPD often have an air of confidence or arrogance and may be described as condescending. However, in actuality, these individuals usually struggle with low self-esteem and feelings of inadequacy.

I've already mentioned that a lot of people may exhibit narcissist traits, but there's a particular set of criteria that has to be met before NPD is diagnosed. Of course, people that have NPD are greatly affected when it comes to their interpersonal relationships and their life in general. More often than not, they try to control and manipulate those around them even when it's harmful to others.

According to the American Psychiatric Association, NPD usually starts when the narcissist is in early adulthood (APA, 2013), and it is more common in men than women (Ronningstam & Weinberg, 2013). So when can we definitively say that someone has NPD?

Well, Dr. Zach Rosenthal (as cited by Biggers, 2022) believes that NPD can be diagnosed when someone exhibits any five of these nine characteristics:

1. A desire and a tendency to oppress others

2. A lack of empathy

3. An exaggerated sense of self-importance

4. An obsession with fantasies of fame and brilliance

5. A resentment of others or a belief that other people are resentful of them

6. A thirst for undue attention and admiration

7. A belief that they are extraordinary or special and can only be understood by other special people and they should only associate with other special people

8. A sense of entitlement

9. A tendency to exhibit conceited or egotistical behaviors

Of course, this diagnosis is best made by a mental health expert, but I believe it's easy to put two and two together by yourself, especially if you've taken the pains to do the proper research. If you have a narcissist in your life, you may believe that it's easier for you to just go with the flow and put up with their excessive behaviors, especially because they don't know how to handle criticism or disagreement.

Unfortunately, you'll find that doing this will only stretch you till you break. And the narcissist will still demand that you stretch further. Isn't it better to find out how to handle them once and for all without losing (any more of) yourself?

Traits of a Person with NPD

According to the American Psychological Association's dictionary, a trait is "*an enduring personality characteristic that describes or determines an individual's behavior across a wide range of situations*" (APA, n.d.).

Furthermore, Encyclopedia Britannica defines personality as "a characteristic way of thinking, feeling, and behaving." That means a person's personality is their habitual or default way of being in the world. It affects their attitude, mood, and even their opinions, and it's how we each make our mark on the world (Holzman, 2023). If we follow this line of thought, a trait is also a person's habitual behaviors, thought patterns, and feelings. People with a particular trait are naturally inclined to behave in that particular way the vast majority of the time, all things being equal.

It's extremely important to highlight these differences here so that you have a clear understanding of the condition and you'll be able to assess someone's behavior and thought patterns before you slap the narcissist label on them. Let's take a deeper look at the habitual behaviors, thoughts, and feelings (the traits) of someone with NPD:

Lack of empathy

Narcissists often do not have the capacity, or have a limited capacity, to understand or care about anyone else's feelings. They have a hard time apologizing and can't view matters from another person's perspective. A narcissistic partner or friend can't truly validate your feelings or understand you because of this trait.

Frequent attempts to monopolize conversations and gatherings

Talking over others, interrupting them, and directing the conversation back to themselves or to their achievements is a common narcissistic trait that may be easy to spot. The typical narcissist believes that they deserve to be in the spotlight no matter where they are and will stop at nothing to achieve that. This feeds into their need for special attention and their desire to be recognized and also pacifies their internal struggle with low self-esteem.

Overblown sense of self-importance

The average narcissist is convinced that they're the best thing since sliced bread—and they don't keep that to themselves. They feel that they are special, superior, or set apart from everyone else and that they deserve to only mingle with other special people like them. To top it all off, they also have grand fantasies about gaining massive power, admiration, fame, or even love.

Shallow relationships

Most narcissists are not capable of showing empathy, and this is reflected in the quality of relationships they have with others. No matter how intense or committed they may seem to someone, they view relationships as transactional and they only participate when they have a lot to gain.

They never want to take the blame, are convinced that other people are jealous of them, are jealous of everyone, and they have no qualms about pretending to love you just to get you attached to them. They love to have control over their relationships and will do anything to retain said control, no matter how dramatic. They are also very vengeful and do not like being criticized, corrected, or disagreed with.

Gaslighting

This is another popular buzzword that refers to the situation when someone says or does something to you and later denies the words or actions in such an expert manner that you're convinced you hallucinated those events. They do this to make you discredit your own senses and rely on their judgment rather than your own.

There are a lot of narcissistic traits apart from these popular ones which come up in different forms in response to certain social behaviors. A narcissist's traits also depend on what kind of narcissist they are.

Types of Narcissists and What They Do

Something a lot of people struggle with is acknowledging that their partner, parent, or any other loved one is a narcissist, especially after they've done a lot of research on NPD. Even though they may identify one or two traits, they simply refuse to believe that someone they love lacks empathy or is manipulative. This is mostly because narcissists are great at pretending. They will pretend to be friendly, warm, loving, or generous—whatever it takes to keep you on their hook!

There are various types of narcissists, and you may recognize someone you know in one of these subtypes:

1. The overt or obvious narcissist

This is also known as grandiose narcissism or agentic narcissism. They fit the typical description of a narc: they are arrogant, confident, assertive, competitive, aggressive, and they always strive to be the center of attention. They are most likely selfish, overbearing, and stubborn. They have an exaggerated sense of their intelligence and capabilities.

2. The covert or closet narcissist

They can also be called vulnerable narcissists because they don't fit the regular pattern of the typical narc. They are more passive-aggressive and can experience anxiety, depression, and low self-esteem. This makes them unable to receive criticism; they would rather avoid that scenario than be told off.

They may not exhibit the typical traits of narcissism, but they definitely possess the major narc characteristics. They can seem like saints, and they often associate with people that they admire. They also feel like they've been constantly victimized, and they're convinced that others are out to get them. They almost seem to feed off of the empathy and attention.

3. The toxic narcissist

This group of narcs can be described as "narcissism on steroids." They exist on the more severe end of the spectrum of toxicity and may exhibit other strongly negative traits like sadism, paranoia, and hostility. They have been described as the most dangerous type of narcissists because they will stop at nothing to achieve their goals even if it hurts the other person physically, mentally, emotionally, or financially.

4. The communal narcissist

This type of narc is all about being good and fair to others. They often have a high moral standard and are quick to fight against what they perceive to be injustice. The big problem here is that these types of narcissists are doing this for the social recognition and power that come with being a "freedom fighter." Another obvious discrepancy is the fact that their behavior often doesn't match up to their ideals under close scrutiny.

Which of these narcissists have you encountered before? Take a moment to examine your various relationships and evaluate them.

Codependent or Obsessive?

We all agree that humans need other humans and that "no man is an island." In fact, some level of vulnerability and dependence is encouraged when done in a healthy manner.

On the other hand, codependency comes into the picture when there is an unhealthy reliance on someone else. This behavior is born of low self-esteem, where the person who suffers from it comes to rely on an external source for validation.

This goes a step further than being a "people person" or being madly in love. A codependent individual has a hard time delineating their identity from the other person's. They don't know how to think for themselves or even what to feel about themselves, other people, and other situations. This comes about as a result of being raised in a dysfunctional environment with a lot of neglect and ignorance at play.

This lack of a strong sense of identity and an absence of self-love may translate into feelings of anxiety for the codependent individual, which makes them fixated on their relationships to distract themselves from the internal chaos.

The answer to the question above is that codependency and obsession often go hand-in-hand.

Am I Codependent?

The main theme of codependency is that the codependent individual puts other people's needs above their own. Now, it's essential to find out if you're a true romantic or if you're actually codependent.

Here are a few signs that may indicate you're codependent:

- You find it difficult to make decisions in your relationship.
- You don't trust yourself and you have low self-esteem.
- You're afraid of being abandoned.
- You don't pay any attention to your own needs or desires.
- You're always apologizing or taking the blame to avoid any drama.
- You're excessively worried about the other person's behaviors.
- You feel guilty whenever you do something for yourself alone.
- You always prefer to avoid conflict.
- You find yourself craving approval from other people.
- Your mood reflects other people's moods, not your own emotions.
- You try to control the other person's life or make decisions for them.
- You entertain fantasies about the other person and the state of your relationship with them, even if you're not fulfilled in the relationship.

When you find that your desire for your partner or loved one's wellbeing begins to cross the boundary into the unhealthy zone, then you need to step back and take a good look at what's happening.

Traits of Dependent Personality Disorder

Dependent personality disorder (DPD) is a mental health disorder that was first published in the Diagnostic and Statistical Manual of Mental Disorders, 3rd edition (DSM-III) in 1980. It was revised in 1987 (Ramsay & Jolayemi, 2020).

In the codependent individual, DPD causes a need for constant reassurance and an inability to have independent thoughts or make independent decisions without input from others. It's not unusual for this individual to feel helpless or even submissive to others. This behavior pattern is characterized by a lack of self confidence and fear of being alone.

According to the DSM-IV, a diagnosis of DPD can only be made when there is an overwhelming need to be cared for and if five of the following criteria are met (Ramsay & Jolayemi, 2020):

1. The individual cannot start projects by themselves because they lack self-confidence.
2. They agree with others even if they don't think they're right.
3. They do stuff that they don't like just so others will approve of them.
4. They don't like being alone and feel helpless when they're alone.
5. They allow other people to make important decisions for them.
6. They cannot make routine decisions without getting some form of reassurance from other people.
7. They are very afraid of being abandoned and are obsessed with preventing that outcome.
8. They are distressed when their intimate relationships come to an end and they quickly find someone to replace it.

If five of these eight criteria are satisfied, then we can boldly diagnose DPD. People with this condition are prone to self-criticism and may even stay away from big projects or commitments to avoid disappointing other people.

Signs You're in a Codependent Relationship

No matter how we may try to justify it—even if your partner indulges you or you're willing and able to indulge their tendencies and entertain their codependent needs—it's not a healthy state for any relationship to be in. While things may look rosy on the surface, the underlying issues that encompass low self-esteem, self-doubt, and fear of abandonment need to be worked on.

Guess what? Your codependent partner may be easy to live with now, but where does it stop? Can you guarantee that there won't be resentment and disappointment at some point? Can you truly promise to keep giving in to their demands and let them smother you?

Before we continue, let's look at some signs that you're in a codependent relationship:

Low self-esteem

The typical codependent often feels left out. It's possible that both people in this kind of relationship may suffer from poor self-esteem. Needing the other person's input and approval for basic decisions is a warning sign.

Absence of boundaries

There are bound to be problems with recognizing, acknowledging, and reinforcing boundaries in a codependent relationship. By their very definition, boundaries absolve you from being responsible for other people's happiness, which is what the codependent person needs to be. It's clear to see how boundaries will be shattered in such a relationship.

Tendency to people-please

Being a people-pleaser or being in a relationship with one can be quite frustrating. Most times, they don't even like what they're doing, but they feel obliged to continue so that they'll get the approval they seek. If your partner has this tendency or if you've been accused of this habit, you may need to pause and do some deep reflection.

More reactive than proactive to situations

Feeling obliged to take care of and please everyone else will cause a disconnect with your true wants and needs. This will hamper your ability to proactively navigate situations in a genuine manner and may keep you constantly on the defensive and even damage your self-esteem. It also doesn't help that you're not able to set proper boundaries as well.

Poor communication

Being a codependent person means that you're quick to disregard your own wants, and you may not express them even when you're aware of them. You may think that expressing yourself will just upset the other person and make them leave. On the flipside, a codependent person may not really understand their partner and may even enjoy the control they have, without taking time to listen to the other person.

It may be hard to identify a codependency cycle,* break out of it, and stay out of it. However, it's important that you step away as soon as you can to examine the possible damage it has left on you as well as prevent future wounds.

Unravel the mysteries of toxic relationships and codependency! Dive into Worksheet #4 by grabbing your BONUS #1 now or check this QR code.

Your Quick Workbook

This exercise aims to help you practice self-awareness, understand yourself better, and start making changes towards a healthier and happier life.

1. Write down 10 things you did for others within the past few days, both big and small.

_____

_____

_____

2. Identify which of these actions were motivated by a desire to help the person, and which were motivated by a fear of rejection or abandonment.

_____

_____

_____

3. Identify in which of these actions you prioritized others above yourself.

_____

_____

_____

4. Write down 10 things that others have done for you within the last few days.

_____

_____

_____

5. Identify which of these actions are helpful and healthy, and which enable your codependency.

_____

_____

_____

6. Identify a specific relationship or situation in which you struggle with codependency.

_____

_____

_____

7. Describe your feelings, thoughts, and behaviors in this situation.

_____

_____

_____

8. What do you think are your underlying needs or fears in this situation?

_____

_____

_____

9. How does your codependent behavior serve you in the short term?

_____

_____

_____

10. How does it harm you in the long term?

_____

_____

_____

11. Write down what you want to change about your codependent behaviors.

_____

_____

_____

12. Write down a list of positive traits and values that you want to cultivate in yourself (e.g., self-care, self-respect, assertiveness, independence).

_____

_____

_____

13. Consider how you can start to develop and embody these positive traits and values in your life. This may include seeking therapy, engaging in self-reflection, setting boundaries with others, and seeking support from friends and family.

_____

_____

_____

Chapter 1 Takeaway

There are all sorts of humans on earth, and the fact is that a lot of us are not very good people. The narcissist is one of those not-really-good people, and identifying them isn't all that difficult. Dealing with them, however, is hard, and you must be ready for this.

Interdependence is the code of humanity. We can't do anything alone and will always need the help of others. But, just like with anything else in the world, abusing this principle even a bit will lead to a relationship where one person literally cannot do anything without the other (i.e., codependency). This is obviously not the best scenario, and things can get really dicey.

CHAPTER TWO

Narcissism-Codependency Dynamics

"Speaking the truth in love, may grow up in all things into Him who is the head—Christ."

—Ephesians 4:15 NKJV

"The narcissist devours people, consumes their output, and casts the empty, writhing shells aside."

— Sam Vaknin

Are narcissists drawn to codependent people? Is there a strange mechanism by which they connect? What's the big deal about narcissism and codependency anyways? Let's jump right in!

The Dance Between the Narcissist and the Codependent

Thus far we've taken a close look at the traits that accompany narcissism as well as those that are prominent in codependency.

In a nutshell, we could conclude that the codependent person is the giver in a relationship, willing to sacrifice their own happiness just so that their partner is happy. They're always taking care of others and seeing to other people's needs while ensuring that they get attention and reassurance from those people.

On the other side of the curtain, we have the narcissists, who I liken to black holes, ready to devour any and every crumb of attention and affection from others.

Both of these personality types have a few things in common, such as:

- They both need to stay in control.
- They both need attention and approval from other people.
- They both have poor self-esteem.
- They neither recognize nor respect boundaries set in relationships.

One major difference between the two is that narcs are very entitled and often lack empathy while codependents are not. The next big question is: Why are narcissists and codependents attracted to each other?

Great question. You see, the narcissist has what the codependent wants and vice versa. The narc is drawn to the codependent person because of their tendency and willingness to give everything they have and sacrifice all for their partner's pleasure. The narc enjoys this codependent personality because it's acceptable for them to dominate and control to their heart's desire. They are content being the center of the relationship and eat up every bit of attention from the codependent while asking for more.

The needy codependent is drawn to the first version of the narcissist they met. That version is usually very charming and affectionate. The narc showers them with both physical and emotional signs of love, fulfilling all the codependent individual's deepest desires. They also feel needed and are always available to stroke the narcissist's ego and serve as a sounding board for their grand plans and great fantasies. We can even go so far as to say that the narc's bad behavior is equally perfect for the codependent—it makes them feel even more secure and loved.

When these two start the dance, they're eager and excited because they seem to complement each other perfectly, and it's like they're a match made in heaven. As the dance progresses, however, their true nature begins to shine forth and the loving version of the narcissist goes away. This makes the codependent anxious, and they try harder to win back that first version, which feeds the narcissist more and encourages them to misbehave even more. Eventually, they both realize that they're not exactly happy in the relationship.

But because both of their needs are being met, they could be stuck in that toxic cycle for a long time until someone tries to get help. Yikes.

A Narcissist vs. a Codependent: Is One Better Than the Other?

If you had to pick a relationship with one, which would you pick? I bet you'd say a codependent person because they're said to be warm, loyal, and selfless. If we looked closer, though, we'd find that they hide their weak traits by trying to meet other people's needs as a means of gaining approval and acceptance. They also believe that they are ultimately responsible for whatever their partner says and does. They even downplay their own needs by pretending not to have any if asked.

The truth remains that narcissism and codependency have the same core problem, but they express their needs in different ways. They both have a damaged sense of self, and this is the fuel behind most of their actions. This means that, on average, they rely on others to create their identities and they really value other people's opinions.

Narcissists are focused entirely on themselves and may only care about others when it benefits them. So they need a regular source of praise, admiration, and attention to attend to their egos. This is the narcissistic supply, and it's what the average narcissist thrives on.

Codependents are so focused on other people that serving others soon becomes their identity. They may go as far as controlling other people because they're convinced that they know best for that person. Instead of praise, admiration, and attention, the codependent needs to be needed and loves to be thanked. In a way, you could say they're just as bad as narcs because they're focused on achieving their own goals and satisfying their needs at every point in time. It gets worse as time goes by because the codependent individual starts to believe they're the only one special or powerful enough to truly help the other people in their life.

The whole point I'm trying to make here is that it's not necessary to view narcissism and codependency as opposite sides of the scale. Instead, it's in our best interest to realize that both types of personalities are operating from a similar motivation and are trying to achieve the same thing, albeit through different methods.

This is why it's extremely possible to probe a codependent individual's behavior and find that they have some narcissistic traits and expectations that they simply express in a different manner. Instead of trying to consider which personality type is "better," think of their driving force and willingness to achieve their aims using different methods for a clearer view on the issue.

Can a Person Be Both Codependent and a Narcissist?

Since we've already established that narcissism and codependency have a common root and that they both depend on others for validation, it's not far fetched to wonder if narcissists can be codependents or if codependents can have a narcissistic personality (or, at the very least, narcissistic traits) too.

In life, I think you'll find that things are hardly ever clearly delineated in black and white. Most times, there are so many shades of gray that you may find yourself getting lost amidst all the grays. One thing that narcs and codependents often have in common is having experienced some form of abuse or trauma while growing up. Of course, having parents with NPD or who were codependent themselves also plays a huge role. Some might say they're two sides of the same coin, but sometimes the boundaries between the two conditions can get blurred and you find traits from one condition in the other.

It's not surprising to find that, in a relationship between a narc and a codependent person, the narcissist may try to manipulate their codependent partner into thinking that they're a narcissist themselves, just to control them. It's also not out of place to see codependent people exhibiting narcissistic traits from time to time.

A young lady I worked with, Kaley, once told me that she knew she was definitely codependent. In a stunning burst of insight, she also admitted that she had some narcissistic tendencies which came into play quite often. "I knowingly manipulated people into staying with me even though I made it look like I was vulnerable. Every time I went above and beyond to take care of them, I deliberately made sure they'd stay with me. It was a form of control for me and I got high off the fact that I could really make them do whatever I wanted."

- Thomas

Kaley was clearly codependent, with narcissistic traits she'd probably learned as a child.

It's also entirely possible for a narcissist to have codependent traits, but this doesn't mean they suddenly become nicer. Nope, this simply means they're more consumed with being admired, respected, and/or feared.

If you're having a hard time deciding whether someone you know is codependent or narcissistic, there is a likelihood that they are either codependent with narcissistic traits or a narcissist that is also codependent.

Behavioral Patterns and Characteristics of Codependency

Everyone is interdependent to a certain extent, and that's to be expected and even encouraged. It's hard to strictly define the specific behaviors that indicate codependency, but the main operating principle here is the law of reciprocity. This means that there's a form of healthy exchange, a give and take, that makes a relationship healthy. The burden of giving doesn't solely lie with one person; both partners give and receive based on who's in the most need at that particular time. This type of exchange exemplifies a healthy interdependent relationship.

There's no one-size-fits-all approach to identifying codependency because a codependent person may exhibit various patterns in response to their environment and their interactions with others. Here are some common patterns you need to be aware of:

They like to take control

This urge to control others is born from the belief that other people are simply not as capable of taking care of themselves. You'll find a codependent with this pattern trying to tell others what to do, or even how to think. They often offer unsolicited advice and can feel resentful if their offer of help isn't accepted.

They're not above giving extravagant gifts or doing people favors to influence them or gain approval. As is typical of most codependents, they need to feel needed by others. They may try to charm their way into being seen as caring, but sometimes they can be stubborn and uncooperative.

They exhibit avoidance patterns

They may be evasive in their communication just to avoid conflict. They may avoid people who might reject or shame them for their actions. They are prone to judging others harshly and will go as far as avoiding physical and emotional contact just to maintain distance. They pull others toward them only to push them away because they don't want to have intimate relationships. These types of codependents believe that expressing emotions is weak, and they never show appreciation.

They may be in denial

At this point, they can't really identify their feelings or they'd rather minimize their feelings. They are very conscious of the fact that they see themselves as generous and committed to other people's wellbeing. Most of them do not have empathy for other people's feelings, and they never see that the person to whom they're attached is not available or healthy for them.

They have poor self-esteem

Most codependents struggle with self-esteem, and this makes it difficult for them to make a decision on their own. They are quick to judge anything they say or do as inferior and do not think they deserve love or are special.

They also have a need to always appear to be correct and will go as far as lying to look good to others. They think they are better than others and may not easily admit to their mistakes. Of course, they aren't able to set proper boundaries and often run to other people for a sense of safety and security.

They may be extremely compliant

They are very loyal and don't mind staying in situations that aren't safe for them just to be close to others. They will easily compromise their own personal values and even their integrity as long as it's for others. They are also hyperaware of other people's feelings and can assume those feelings. They are quick to make decisions without thinking about the consequences, and they will accept special attention in place of love.

Which of these patterns are familiar to you?

Why You Should Deal with Narcissistic-Codependent Relationships Quickly

Narcissistic-codependent relationships can be incredibly damaging and toxic, and it's important to recognize when you're in one and take steps to address the issue. True, if you're codependent it may seem better to just stay put and manage your partner's harmful behaviors, but sooner or later you'll realize that this partnership is damaging you mentally, and you need to sit up and address this situation.

Another major thing to keep in mind is the fact that you're not really meeting the narcissist's needs. They aren't truly happy. So even if you feel like you're giving them your all and you're being appreciated for it, it'll get to the point where nothing you do will seem to be enough and they will never be happy. You must know that this isn't your fault because no one is capable of truly meeting their needs anyway. I compared a narcissist to a black hole earlier; that's because black holes are yawning abysses that devour everything without being affected—even whole planets and galaxies. Narcissists do the same to the people in their lives.

When these two types of people come together in a relationship, we already know that the narcissist is able to exploit the codependent's need to be needed, while the codependent is able to feed the narcissist's need for admiration and attention. This creates a cycle of manipulation and exploitation, with the codependent being constantly hurt and used, and the narcissist never getting their true needs met.

Recognizing the signs of a narcissistic-codependent relationship, such as feeling like you're constantly walking on eggshells, being constantly criticized and put down, and feeling like you're always giving more than you're getting in return, is essential.

I know it can be incredibly difficult to leave a codependent relationship with a narcissist. Narcissists can be charming and alluring at first, but their true colors often reveal themselves over time. They can be controlling, manipulative, and emotionally abusive. Apart from the damage to your self-esteem and mental health when they make you feel like you are not good enough, and their constant criticism and belittling of you, they will also gaslight you, making you question your own reality. This can lead to feelings of worthlessness, anxiety, and depression.

Of course, being codependent can prevent you from asserting your own needs and desires and can make it difficult for you to make decisions or to leave the relationship. Codependency can also lead to a lack of boundaries, which can further enable the narcissist's toxic behavior.

The first step in managing a narcissistic-codependent relationship is to recognize that you deserve better. You deserve to be in a relationship where you feel respected, valued, and loved. You deserve to be in a relationship where your needs are met and your feelings are taken into account. It's important to remind yourself that you are worthy of love and respect, and that you don't have to put up with being treated poorly.

The next step is to set boundaries with your partner. This means standing up for yourself and refusing to accept negative or abusive behavior. It also means setting limits on what you will tolerate in the relationship and communicating these boundaries clearly to your partner. This can be difficult, especially if you're used to putting the needs of your partner above your own, but it's important to remember that you deserve to be treated with respect and kindness.

It's also important to seek out support during this process. This can come in the form of friends, family, or a therapist. It's important to have people in your life who can support you and remind you of your worth, and who can help you navigate the difficult process.

Don't forget to focus on yourself and your own wellbeing. Take care of yourself physically, emotionally, and mentally. Engage in activities that make you happy and fulfilled, and surround yourself with positive and supportive people. It's also important to work on any personal issues that may have contributed to the relationship, such as low self-esteem or a need to be needed.

Your Quick Workbook

This exercise focuses on helping you reflect on the negative impacts of being in a narcissistic-codependent relationship and gain a clearer understanding of how harmful the relationship is.

1. Write down a list of behaviors and thoughts that are common in codependents as we discussed above, such as putting others' needs before their own, feeling responsible for others' emotions, difficulty setting boundaries, low self-esteem, and constantly seeking validation from others.

_____

_____

_____

2. Reflect on which of these behaviors and thoughts you recognize in yourself.

_____

_____

_____

3. Consider how these behaviors and thoughts have affected your own life, relationships, and wellbeing. For example, have you given up your own goals and desires in order to please others? Have you neglected your own emotional and physical needs?

_____

_____

_____

4. Identify patterns in your relationship: Take note of the behavioral patterns and dynamics in your relationship. How does your partner treat you and how do you respond?

_____

_____

5. Write down all of the negative thoughts, feelings, and behaviors that you experience in the relationship. This can include things like low self-esteem, self-doubt, anger, anxiety, and depression.

_____

_____

_____

6. Reflect on how these negative experiences impact your life outside of the relationship. For example, do they interfere with your work, your relationships with friends and family, or your ability to engage in hobbies and activities you enjoy?

_____

_____

_____

7. Write down all of the positive things about yourself that you have lost or given up in the relationship. This can include things like your self-worth, your confidence, your independence, and your ability to make decisions for yourself.

_____

_____

_____

Chapter Two Takeaway

Narcissistic-codependent relationships are very complicated, and finding yourself in the midst of such a relationship can be a bit disorienting. While the codependent might seem more of a mellow personality than the narcissist, both are toxic traits to have, and having relationships with such people will drain you more than it fills you.

CHAPTER THREE

Building Immunity Against the Weapons of a Narcissist

"For the grace of God has appeared, bringing salvation for all people, training us to renounce ungodliness and worldly passions, and to live self-controlled, upright, and godly lives in the present age."

—Titus 2:11-12 ESV

"When I look at narcissism through the vulnerability lens, I see the shame-based fear of being ordinary. I see the fear of never feeling extraordinary enough to be noticed, to be lovable, to belong, or to cultivate a sense of purpose."

—Brené Brown

One of the greatest Chinese generals to ever walk the earth, Sun Tzu, compiled his war strategies in a book titled *The Art of War*. Those war strategies have been modified into principles to arm readers in all fields with the required insight to be victorious in life. We all need strategies to subdue anything that threatens our peace and prosperity.

Well, consider the things I'm about to share with you to be the strategies you'll need to emerge victorious against the toxicity of a narcissist threatening your wellbeing. You're not literally in a war situation, but when you're in a toxic relationship with a narcissist, there will be more conflicts going on in your mind than there would be taking place on a literal battlefield.

Here are your strategies to win:

Understand How a Narcissist Thinks

Narcissists may use their physical appearance, charm, or intelligence to manipulate those around them. They usually target a specific group of people: empathetic, kind, and easily manipulated people. Narcissists can also be very persuasive, but their main goal is to maintain control and gain power over others.

The online resource *Abuse Warrior* explains that manipulation (a frequent tactic of narcissists) can be emotional or psychological. The goal of emotional manipulation is to make the victim lose their emotional stability. Psychological manipulation, on the other hand, affects the victim's mental capability to the point that the victim's beliefs or behaviors align with exactly what the manipulator wants.

These are a few ways narcissists manipulate:

Lying

Making a false statement and making it look like it's the truth. This could toy with the victim's mind and create confusion. The narcissist can make their victim look like a liar with a false statement.

Deflecting

When a narcissist is caught lying, they try to deflect the accusation to their victim; they make their victim look like the real culprit. They rarely take responsibility for their deceptive actions.

Stalking

A narcissist will make the extra effort to monitor their victim's movements, transactions, activities, etc., with the aim of knowing everything possible about their victim. This give them information with which to manipulate the person even more.

Other tactics include playing the victim, gaslighting, shifting the goalposts, projecting, and more. Next up, we'll dive into a few of these in depth and show you how to handle them.

Handling Guilt Tripping

A narcissist will do their best to make their victim doubt their ability to care, love, or show compassion for anyone. A narcissist does this by making statements that make their victim feel guilty about not being caring or loving enough, or for not showing enough compassion.

Threatening

This is one of the most potent weapons narcissists use. They use the tool of fear to subdue their victim by threatening them into submission.

Blaming

When the spotlight eventually shines on victims of any form of manipulation, they're made to look like they're responsible for what has been happening to them. A narcissist manipulates their victim in such a way that the victim will have defend their actions, thereby protecting the narc.

Know this: whenever someone tries to influence your feelings or your behavior to align with what they want, it's narcissistic. But how do you respond to this?

Your Strategy:

Dislodge fear

Fear is a terrible place to be. Once a narcissist manipulates you into a place of fear, it becomes easy for them to bend your mind and emotions to their will. The first step to combat this is to note down the things your manipulator does to instill fear in you. It's usually not the same for everyone. Identify yours.

Get the facts straight

Narcissists threaten their victims with false statements that could be used against the victim. What could be better as a way to prevent this than knowing the truth and being confident about it? There's a sense of security that comes with knowing the truth about something.

Set clear boundaries

This is what this book is about. You need to learn to set limits to how far you can allow a narcissist partner, colleague, or relative to intrude into your space.

Communicate your views assertively

Stay calm and composed. Don't be jittery or defensive. Just make your point and wait or move on as the occasion demands.

Handling Gaslighting

Interestingly, Merriam-Webster Dictionary voted the word "gaslighting" as 2022 Word of the Year because it was the most searched word. Wondering why lots of people searched for this word? Well, in my view, people were curious about the word due to the increase in its usage and, more importantly, increase in the experience.

According to research group YouGov, about 75% of adults in the U.S. knew nothing about this term in 2017, even though it has been in use since the 1930s (Bame, 2017). However, the experience has always been there. Sweet (2021) describes the gaslighting experience as a form of psychological abuse that makes victims feel they're crazy.

One of the victims of gaslighting Sweet interviewed explained that during her 12-year marriage, her ex-husband regularly cheated. But he would defend himself by calling her crazy and paranoid despite the evidence of his affairs she produced. She worked diligently to provide all the care her children needed on her own, but her ex-husband convinced her that she still needed him. One of the ways he did this was by delaying the payment of the electricity bills, and then waiting till the power was shut off. He would then blame her. The goal was to make her seem dependent on him despite her best efforts.

In other words, a narcissist tries to make you disbelieve what you know to be truth, thereby making you doubt your ability to know what truth is. When a narcissist wants to manipulate their victim, they make them question their sanity, memory, or perception of events. This can be done through lying, denying, or contradicting the victim's reality.

Ultimately, it'll cause the victim to doubt themselves and the people around them. The victim can become battered emotionally because it's a form of emotional abuse.

Your Strategy:

Acknowledge it

The first strategy to overcoming any form of abuse is to admit that it is happening to you. Failure to do this will mask the truth and, thus, the solution that could liberate you.

Stop doubting yourself

The whole point of gaslighting is to get you to distrust yourself and doubt your sanity. But the truth is that you're not insane. What you know about the issue is the truth. What you see isn't an illusion, and you aren't just making it up. It's true.

Detach yourself from other people's opinions

One of the ways you can stop doubting yourself is to detach yourself from other people's opinions about what is true. Don't argue with them. Just independently hold on to your truth and let it be the light that guides your action. You have the right to have your own thoughts and feelings. As a matter of fact, you're not insane. Don't let anyone drive you crazy regardless of the place they hold in your life. Your mental health is your priority.

Handling Love Bombing

Loving someone is a great thing, isn't it? It's certainly not a bad thing to demonstrate to someone how much you love them. However, there's a point when this demonstration of love is taken to the extreme. That's when it becomes manipulative. That's the point when love becomes love bombing. Don't get me wrong; people can show love excessively for genuine reasons too. However, there are those whose motive is to manipulate the recipient of their love.

Love bombing is a manipulative tactic that can be employed in romantic and non-romantic relationships. The strategy is the same in both contexts. A narcissist "bombs" someone with love to win over and control the other person. They achieve this by showering them with excessive attention, affection, and gifts.

The goal is to create a sense of dependency and make it difficult for the other person to see the need to set boundaries. Peykar (cited by Lamothe, 2019) notes that a narcissist who showers you with excessive love typically has a goal. Once they win your trust and affection, they can carry on with their plan.

Love bombing could be mistaken for genuine love because the signs are similar, but pay attention to these love bombing signals:

- They lavish you with gifts that you cannot decline because you'll be in their black book if you do.

- They give you extravagant compliments that make your head spin.

- They demand all your attention and time to the point that you may be isolated from your family and friends. When your supposed lover gets angry that you made plans to spend time with someone else instead of with them, that's a love bombing red flag.

145

- They persuade you to make an early commitment to a long-term relationship.

- *Your Strategy:*

- Don't neglect the inner feelings of sadness when you're isolated from other people besides your lover. Or the feeling that something's wrong when you constantly get unnecessary gifts, or when they suggest starting a committed relationship very early on.

- Don't be sentimental. Go in with your eyes open. Don't make rash decisions based on how you feel at that moment. Give it time. It's easier to opt out when you've not made a long-term commitment than when you've gone all-in.

- Note the red flag if you feel suffocated by your partner's fast-paced demands to be in a committed relationship almost immediately, or that you always be available whenever they need you without consideration for your needs.

Handling Triangulation

One of the things you should always remember about a narcissist is that they're toxic players who derive joy from watching other people get frustrated and disoriented. One of the strategies they employ to achieve this is triangulation.

This is a manipulative tactic that a narcissist may use to control and manipulate their relationships. The narcissist involves a third person in the relationship in order to make the other person jealous or to create a sense of competition. The narcissist may use triangulation to create feelings of insecurity in their partner, to control their partner's behavior, or to create a sense of dependence on the narcissist. Narcissistic triangulation can be emotionally damaging to all parties involved and can lead to the breakdown of relationships.

Here's a good example of triangulation:

Will and Anna had been seeing each other for a few months. Will showered Anna with lots of affection, attention, and gifts (love bombing). That was enough for Anna to fall madly in love with Will. After all, that's exactly what he wanted. They began to talk about marriage and babies. Will kept assuring her that he loved her and she was perfect for him.

At some point, Anna started noticing that the loads of texts from Will were no longer flooding her phone as usual. He kept evading her questions. He started finding fault with her over trivial issues.

Before long, Anna found out that Will was seeing another girl, Lindsay. Will started comparing Anna with Lindsay. It hurt her feelings. She expressed this to Will, but he said she was just being jealous and that there was nothing to worry about. Yet he was doing this deliberately to stir up jealousy in Anna—and he was doing the same thing to Lindsay.

As a result, the two women began to envy each other. Will was enjoying the little show he had set up and the attention he was getting from it. The entire scenario fueled his need to control the situation.

Your Strategy:

Recognize triangulation

If you've not noticed it yet in your relationship, you might need to take a closer look and assess the pattern of interaction. If you discover that you're being pulled into a triangle dynamic, you must begin to handle the situation maturely. Use the following strategies:

- Review your interactions with people who triangulate you.
- Don't get stuck in the circle of manipulation.
- Don't get drawn into silly competitions with anyone. Focus on yourself and your life.
- Don't get carried away with positive compliments that compare you with another person.
- Safeguard your emotional wellbeing by hanging around a network of healthy friends.
- Stop sharing personal details with anyone that draws you into a triangle dynamic.

Handling Playing the Victim

Playing the victim is another strategy narcissists employ to manipulate their victim. No one would expect a narcissist to play the victim card because they're egoistic and love to be in control. But if playing the victim card gives them an opportunity to manipulate their victim, why wouldn't they?

Playing the victim card is nothing new to most of us, though. At times, non-narcissists do this too. When someone wants to get sympathy and make other people feel like they're responsible for their predicament, that's playing the victim card. People who play the victim card don't ever want to take responsibility for the negative things that happen to them. They cry and indulge in self-pity to make other people feel like they're the reason for it.

It might not be an intentional or regular thing for a non-narcissist, but a narcissist uses it as a weapon against their victim. This is manipulative. It pushes the victim into a position of helplessness, where they feel mentally stressed and unable to fight back against the layers of lies cast on them.

Casabianca (2021) suggests that a narcissist feels attacked when you don't agree with them or when you point out their mistake. Their inability to introspect and their inflated self-worth prevents them from seeing the situation as they ought to. Therefore, they resort to playing the victim card in some scenarios.

Why should you feel guilty for the mistakes of someone else?

Your Strategy:

- Don't ever doubt yourself.
- Don't take a narcissist's words to heart. Try not to pay attention to them.
- When you see the sign, don't take the bait. Control your need to respond or defend yourself and just walk away.
- Don't go along with their pity party. It only boosts their ego.

Handling Projections

If you've ever had a relationship with a narcissist, you'll know that generally they lack self-awareness. They derive their sense of self-esteem and self-worth from other people's perceptions of them. They don't believe they have any flaws, and they never accept they are wrong about anything. When fingers are pointed at them, they blame it on other people.

Their shortcomings, mistakes, and misfortunes never seem to be their fault. There is always someone to blame for it. This is a manipulative strategy called projection.

Cikanavicius (2019) identifies a few ways narcissists project and attack their victim. These include:

1. Calling you things that you are not

When they're the real culprit, they tend to loudly accuse you of the things they are guilty of. For instance, they may say you're cheating on them when, in actuality, they're the one cheating on you. They may accuse you of only ever thinking about yourself while in the meantime they're the truly selfish person in the relationship, never showing empathy for anyone else. It's just always about them.

2. Grandiosity, mimicking, and exaggeration

Here's how a narcissist thinks: "I'm special and deserve exceptional treatment. Everyone else must see how special I am and treat me specially. No one else matters here more than I do." This is the type of thinking that makes them feel entitled and better than everyone else.

They have a distorted perception of the world and themselves. Therefore, when they manipulate other people through lies, gaslighting, projection, exploitation, and other manipulative tactics to boost their self-esteem and satisfy their egoistic needs, they see it as a normal thing.

At other times, to make themselves seen and recognized by everyone, they take on other people's traits and achievements out of envy. They can mimic, defame, and belittle others, and/or destroy other people's credibility, to assert themselves.

According to Cikanavicius (2019), narcissists also play the victim in projecting.

How can you respond to this?

Just as with other manipulative strategies, don't ever doubt yourself and don't let your emotions get the best of you.

Handling Smear Campaigns

Another dangerous manipulative trick of a narcissist is a smear campaign. It's a step further from playing the victim card. When a narcissist discovers that they've been exposed, they go on a campaign to put their victim on the spot by damaging their victim's reputation among their friends and family. The narcissist acts fast to make themselves appear to be the victim rather than a vicious monster.

When a narcissist goes on a smear campaign, they're out to paint their victim as insane, an addict, an alcoholic, unstable, a thief, a cheater, or a poor parent. They achieve this by falsifying and exaggerating their victim's conduct. The goal is to destroy the victim's credibility and sanity.

How will this turn out for the victim? The victim will have no one to run to since their image has been tarnished among their support system. They'll feel isolated, unsure about their sanity, and helpless.

Your Strategy:

- Don't respond to the accusations with an outburst of anger. Try to be calm.
- Know your truth. Even if the whole world stands against you, don't stand against yourself.
- Don't post anything on an online public space or social media to defend yourself. A narcissist will use it against you.
- Set a limit to how much they can intrude into your space.
- Speak with only a trusted circle of friends and tell them your side of the story.

The best way to gain an advantage over a narcissist is to think the way they think and set up strategies to counter their moves whenever possible.

Your Quick Workbook

1. Identify triggers: Write down what specifically triggers you when interacting with the narcissistic person. How can you anticipate these triggers and prepare yourself emotionally?

_____

_____

_____

2. Practice self-awareness: Write down ways you can increase self-awareness and recognize when you are becoming emotionally involved in the narcissistic person's drama. What techniques can you use to shift your focus back to yourself? (This could be a breathing exercise, or body scanning where you focus your attention on each part of your body, often from your head to your toes.)

_____

_____

_____

3. Limit exposure: Write down specific steps you can take to limit your exposure to the narcissistic person. How will you maintain your emotional detachment in their presence?

_____

_____

_____

4. Focus on self-care: Write down specific self-care practices you can implement to support your wellbeing. How will you prioritize self-care in your daily routine?

_____

_____

_____

5. Seek support: Write down specific individuals (friends or family members) you can reach out to for support. How will you maintain your support network and ensure they are aware of your situation?

_____

_____

_____

6. Challenge negative beliefs: Write down the negative beliefs and thought patterns that may make it difficult to emotionally detach from the narcissistic person. How will you replace these negative beliefs with positive, empowering ones?

_____

_____

_____

7. Visualize a positive outcome: Write down how you want the situation with the narcissistic person to be resolved. What would be your ideal outcome and how will you visualize this outcome to maintain emotional detachment?

_____

_____

_____

Chapter Three Takeaway

A wise man once said, "Know thy enemy." And make no mistake, narcissists are your enemy. They have several tactics that they use, consciously or unconsciously, to manipulate you and get you exactly where they want you. And as you can guess, that's not where you want to be.

Understanding these tactics is key to remaining a step ahead in your dealings with them.

CHAPTER FOUR

Detoxification From Toxic Relationships

"Above all else, guard your heart, for everything you do flows from it."

—Prov. 4:23 (NIV)

"I can be changed by what happens to me, but I refuse to be reduced by it."

—Maya Angelou

Understanding the Six Relationship Types and Their Impact on Your Life

Have you ever had a great relationship with someone without knowing that person's place in your life?

It's important you pay attention to this. If you intend to set boundaries for certain forms of relationships, it's crucial you understand the relationships in your life and know the purpose and function of each. It's true that every relationship serves a purpose. But not all relationships are the same. For instance, your relationship with your partner can't be compared with your relationship with the lady who works at the grocery store down the street. They're different, but all are important.

Each relationship is meant to serve a unique purpose in your life, but no relationship can give you everything you need in life. The moment you understand this, you'll save yourself a lot of trouble in assuming every relationship is supposed to give you the same result. Through this, you can also identify which relationships to hold dear and which to let go.

Before I show you different types of relationships, try to understand that when you comprehend and correctly identify every relationship in your life, communication becomes effective, and problem-solving and decision-making in your relationships becomes easy. You'll be able to interact with everyone around you in meaningful ways.

So, here we go:

1. Family Relationships

For most people, the first type of relationship they experience is relationship with the people they're related to by blood. It's only in certain circumstances that people grow up outside a family system. However, from birth, a child begins to get acquainted with a certain culture, customs, and beliefs within the family setting. This implies that the family is the first foundational institution that shapes our minds and the way we see the world.

Although not all family relationships are positive, the cord that binds you to your family makes it hard to sever relationships with them. If a person experiences narcissism or codependency in the family, the relational bond remains intact, but their mind has been shaped to accept toxicity in relationships as a norm. This makes family relationships unique and different from every other relationship.

2. Friendships

Think of living on earth without friends. What do you think that'd look like? Probably not too good. Friends make the world go round, right? I consider friendship to be the next foundational type of relationship after family.

Most people begin having friends in childhood, either from their neighborhood, at school, or at their place of worship. According to an article from the Exchange Family Center (2019), the friends most people start keeping from childhood create in them a sense of belonging and security. This also contributes to the quality of life a person goes on to live.

There are different types of friends. Some are just acquaintances, others are social friends, and most people have a few intimate ones. Each of these friends has a place in our lives. The way a person is treated within a circle of friends influences their perception of themselves, their self-esteem, and ultimately their effectiveness in society.

When you understand the level of friendship you have with someone, you'll be able to determine how much they can influence you.

3. Social Relationships

Social relationships cover the relationships you have with your coworkers, distant relatives, and neighbors. We all have people we work with professionally in some capacity, either remotely or onsite. Our relationships with coworkers are usually at a different level from the ones we have with our family or friends; however, professional relationships determine our productivity.

An article from Mind Tools observes that the more comfortable colleagues are with each other, the more confident they'll feel to voice their opinions, share a workspace, and jump on innovative ideas. This fosters group morale and productivity.

Good work relationships allow you to focus on opportunities for personal development and to win new business and enhance your career. A negative work environment due to poor relationships, conversely, will demoralize you and affect productivity.

4. Romantic Relationships

Primarily, this type of relationship grows out of friendship. A romance starts when the level of communication with someone grows from casual to intimate. It's at this point you begin to admit that you're in love.

The person you claim to be in love with has more access to you than just a casual friend or even someone you call your best friend. Therefore, your romantic partner has a lot of influence over your emotional and psychological wellbeing. This romantic partner can also influence your perception of yourself because you'll easily believe anything they say about you.

A romantic relationship is a strong form of relationship. If you're in a romantic relationship with someone toxic, you're in for some bad moments. A toxic romantic partner will take advantage of your vulnerability and use it against you.

5. Marital Relationships

Usually, a romantic relationship, if sustained, leads to a marital commitment between two lovers. They reproduce and raise a family. Some just choose to remain as partners, but this can still be categorized as a marital relationship.

A marital relationship requires another level of commitment and responsibility that makes you not only responsible for yourself, but for your partner as well. You can no longer just think about yourself alone; you have to think about your partner. You're not only in it for the special benefits of a marital relationship, but you're committed to living a purposeful life of meaning together.

A marital relationship means making a deliberate decision to go on a lifelong journey with your romantic partner. You'll have to be flexible enough to cope and live with your partner. Once this relationship goes wrong at the level of friendship, it'll be wrong at every other level. So, before you allow your relationship to grow past the phase of friendship, be sure you want to go further in that relationship with the person you're beginning to develop funny feelings for. If you aren't sure about their character, draw a line immediately!

6. Spiritual Relationships

Walton (1996) notes that a spiritual relationship involves the connection you have with yourself, other people, nature, and God at the soul level. He further states that all relationships can be spiritual. The depth of this kind of relationship is directly related to one's personal acceptance of the existence of the inner self.

The moment you begin to accept that there's more to you than your physique, your perception of yourself and the world around you will begin to change. Spending daily time with God will strengthen the true foundation of your life—because if there's a spiritual side to you, then there's a spiritual side to the world around you as well. That's the only way you can connect at that level with the world around you.

This kind of relationship will open you up to the possibility of exploring the fullness of your being and reality. If well cultivated, it'll take you beyond the realm of anxiety and lead you to a place of rest and peace.

Signs You're in a Toxic Relationship

Relationships are a neutral institution. They are neither good nor bad. It's the individuals involved that determine the type of relationship it will be.

How can you tell whether your relationship is unhealthy? When you begin to see the signs listed below, it's an indication that you're in a toxic relationship.

- You don't seem to do anything right anymore
- You're not feeling happy anymore
- You're feeling disrespected
- Every argument and disagreement is an opportunity to dig up the past
- Your needs are not met
- Communication is strained
- You're stuck in the euphoria of the past

- The excitement of the relationship is being replaced with blame and complaints
- There's no productive discussion about the future
- You're feeling choked in the relationship
- You're beginning to resent your partner
- You're beginning to lose friends
- There's no balanced commitment in the relationship
- You're giving more and getting little
- You're feeling undervalued
- It feels like you go from one criticism to another
- You can no longer raise your head with high self-esteem
- You're usually scared to air your views
- You're feeling unsupported
- You're losing faith in your partner's credibility
- You're losing peace over trivial issues
- You're feeling depressed
- You're seeing only each other's bad qualities
- You're feeling your worth comes from what your partner thinks of you
- You're feeling your opinion comes second to your partner's
- You're not feeling free around your partner
- You're feeling manipulated
- You're feeling used
- You're feeling inferior to your partner
- You're feeling unworthy
- You don't feel emotionally or mentally sound around your partner
- You're feeling lonely when you're together with your partner
- You find it hard to trust your partner
- You feel you're responsible for their happiness

- You're being abused physically or verbally or both
- You're being mocked regularly
- You're not being appreciated for your effort
- You don't spend time together anymore
- Your suggestions are usually turned down
- You've lost your privacy
- You're being stalked
- You've lost your sense of self-worth

All these and many others that are not listed here are signs of a toxic relationship. Assess your relationship to check if any of these symptoms are present.

Six Main Types of Toxic People

Just as we have good and loving people in our society, there are also toxic people. Toxic people are numerous, and you can find them anywhere, even in the most religious corners of society. Here, I'll focus on six toxic people groups.

Be careful of these groups of people:

Manipulators

A manipulator will always make plans to control you for their own benefit. They do this without any regard for how you feel or what happens to you. They're only interested in getting their needs met.

Narcissists are in this category. They take advantage of you and leave you psychologically and emotionally wounded.

Pessimists

These sets of people always have their heads down. Their natural outlook on life is negative. They don't see anything good about anything around them. The best they can see is the worst in every situation.

The terrible thing about this group of people is that they are influencers. They're usually quick to register their negative opinions about a project or any step forward. So, they instill fear in their friends or partner about whatever that step forward may be.

If you hang around these types of people, you'll quickly give up on your dreams and never become the best version of yourself.

Talebearers

A talebearer doesn't have a closed mouth. They're only interested in sharing juicy news. They're not interested in the good news; primarily, they're interested in the faults, failures, setbacks, and downfalls of other people. They're quick to spread such news.

Spreading this kind of information could cause discord between friends and, sometimes, irreparable damage in relationships.

People Pleasers

People pleasers are only interested in being in your good book. Even if you're going down the wrong path, they won't tell you the truth you need to hear because they don't want to hurt you.

People pleasers have low self-esteem, and they derive their worth from what you think of them.

If you're trying to get your self-esteem up, associating with a people pleaser won't help you achieve that. They'll only encourage you that it's okay to feel low and inferior to others.

Judgers

Judgmental people are quick to put on their critic's lens to nail you to the cross. When what you're doing doesn't seem good to them, they don't think about how they can learn from it. They just criticize it immediately.

Things are only good as far as their lens sees it as good. They have a way of squashing your passion if they don't like it, thus stifling your desire to be passionate and expressive. They make you feel terrible about yourself and what you intend to do. They rarely appreciate or commend people for the effort they put into something.

If you associate with these types of people, you'll dampen your self-worth and never see anything good about yourself.

What Being in a Toxic Relationship Does to You

A toxic relationship is poisonous to your emotional and psychological wellbeing. I have identified a few effects a toxic relationship could have on you:

1. Loss of self

The first significant effect a toxic relationship has is that you lose a sense of who you are. This is the most crucial part of anyone. Once you begin to lose sight of who you are, it becomes difficult to do anything meaningful with your life because a sense of identity is what gives your life direction and meaning. Your vision and ambition ought to align with your identity. If identity is lost, purposeful living is also gone.

A toxic relationship gradually kills that sense of identity. If such a relationship persists for a long time, you might lose it altogether.

2. Low self-esteem and self-worth

The way other people treat us tells us a lot about ourselves. If you're in a toxic relationship where the other person doesn't care about you, you're denied love and support, you're constantly abused—verbally and emotionally—and you're always ignored, it'll take a lot of self-talk not to feel bad about yourself. Your first natural response emotionally and psychologically would be to think less of yourself.

While in a toxic relationship, chances are you'll lose the confidence to ever speak up and try something innovative, and you'll stop believing in yourself.

3. Stunted personal growth

Being trapped in a toxic relationship doesn't allow room for personal growth and development. When you're not even in control of your life anymore, how could you think about pursuing any form of advancement? It's your partner that decides how far you'll go or what you can do.

When they do things to convince you that you're not good enough, and they constantly remind you of your past mistakes and downfalls, you'll not bother to attempt anything progressive.

Other effects could include:

- Decline in your physical, emotional, and psychological wellbeing
- Distorted perception of a healthy relationship
- Anxiety and perpetual fear

These and many more are the effects a toxic relationship could have on you.

Your Quick Workbook

1. Identify the toxic behaviors: Write down the specific behaviors or actions that are causing harm in the relationship.

_____

_____

_____

2. Evaluate the impact: How are these toxic behaviors affecting your mental and emotional wellbeing?

_____

_____

_____

3. Consider your options: Brainstorm different options for addressing the situation, such as seeking therapy or setting boundaries. Which option are you going for?

_____

_____

_____

4. Prioritize self-care: Make a list of activities that bring you joy and peace and make time for them in your schedule. (Being in a toxic relationship is so depleting, you need to rejuvenate.)

_____

_____

_____

Chapter Four Takeaway

Once you've identified that you're in a toxic relationship, understand that you're in a sinking ship and the best way to survive it is to address the situation.

Overcoming Narcissism and Codependency in Origin Families

"Do you see a man hasty in his words? There is more hope for a fool than for him."

—Proverbs 29:20 (NKJV)

"It's not your job to manage the emotions of others. It's an exhausting role that may offer temporary bursts of self-worth, but ultimately will drain the life out of you."

—Jackson MacKenzie

The Enmeshed Family System and How it Works
One big happy family?
Meh. A sham.
Think again.

One of the reasons why Mel had a hard time admitting that her relationship with her mom was weird was because of the word "enmeshed." She said it sounded like she was a fly or maybe a fish trapped in a net, and that didn't sound pleasant at all.

As vivid an image as that conjures, I'd say that it's a pretty good definition of the concept. An enmeshed family is one where the members are so close-knit and reliant on each other that the natural boundaries and roles are blurred.

It wouldn't be hard to find the parents being overly reliant on their children for emotional support in such a setting, and the children not being allowed independence from their parents emotionally. People from enmeshed families tend to think that they're just super connected, but on close examination, a lack of boundaries gives the whole jig away.

This family system is dysfunctional and has damaging effects on both the children and the parents. It's easy to mistake a close family unit for an enmeshed one, but the difference lies in the fact that boundaries are in place in a healthy family. Once family members start to view non-family members as outsiders, it's a pretty good sign that it may be an enmeshed family.

A child from an enmeshed family doesn't have an identity separate from that of their parents or other family members. They don't think about their needs or place any importance on said needs, instead aligning their goals with what their parents want or what's best for the family.

They typically feel guilty for wanting some space from their family, and they are often bad at resolving conflict. You may find someone like that saying yes to things they don't really want just to avoid disappointing someone else. Another strong characteristic is the fact that they feel obliged to solve any problems that their family members may have, even when it's not directly theirs to solve.

Parents in an enmeshed family typically center their lives on their children and believe they can provide all the support and love their children need forever. This leads them to monitor their children's relationships with outsiders and dissuade them from getting too close to others. They expect their children to be like them, even down to having the same dreams, so naturally they prevent their child from trying to achieve their dreams, especially when it's not in line with what they want.

Children from an enmeshed family tend to have low self-esteem and fall into codependent relationships just because they're used to it.

Let's look at the individual interactions you'd see in this kind of setting.

Dealing with Narcissistic Siblings

We all know that growing up with siblings may be more of an obstacle course than a walk in the park, but have you considered the possibility that your difficult brother or sister may just be a narcissist?

Now, it's entirely possible that this sibling is not a narcissist but may have a few narcissistic traits that make getting along with them a herculean task. Either way, identifying these traits for what they are will teach you how to manage this relationship.

You probably haven't realized it yet, but growing up with a narcissistic sibling could be responsible for some of your character traits (usually negative ones) and has a profound effect on your mental health too. You may be used to avoiding that particular sibling or just resigning yourself to their manipulative behavior, and while you think you've survived just fine all this time, the impact of this relationship on you may very well extend to your other relationships and even other aspects of your life.

Having a toxic sibling makes you naturally distrustful of people. This is most likely because you've been deceived and manipulated by your toxic sibling. One minute you're best friends, the next they may do something to indicate that they never cared for you in the first place, and eventually you'll become hardened and distrusting.

You may also find out that you're willing to tolerate abusive relationships with others simply because you're used to enduring your toxic sibling's manipulation. If you're the type that's quick to make excuses for other people's behavior towards you, it's possible that you have accepted the fact that abuse is an inevitable part of every relationship thanks to the toxic narc in your life.

The incredible thing about narc siblings is that they're able to seem like innocent angels to your parents. In fact, they may enjoy painting you as the scapegoat of the family. They often position themselves as the model child who always does the right thing, which means confiding in your parents may be out of the picture. Naturally, you'll also find that you're almost deathly afraid of confrontations and any other kind of conflict, so you'll go the extra mile to avoid it.

Narcissists, as we know, hate criticism and often react dramatically to it. Being subjected to this dramatic performance over and over again will make you eager to avoid it as much as possible. That's probably why you roll over and give in to your narc sibling's desires, even when you'd rather not.

This behavior will be echoed in your other relationships—friendships, work relationships, and with romantic partners. It may even be so bad that you end up with a narc partner simply because that's what you're used to.

If you're used to being the one that other people run to for help or advice, there's a great possibility that you're not getting the same comfort from your friends. This is because you find yourself drawn to being the helper or confidant in most relationships. This may be because you're able to empathize with others better than the average person. It may even be because you're seeking to have the relationship you'd want with your siblings elsewhere, but you're not capable of trusting anyone else that much.

I think we can both agree that the effects of putting up with a toxic sibling spread farther than you may have originally imagined. If you have a sibling that's:

- Really cruel to you and seems to enjoy hurting you, whether physically, mentally, or emotionally;
- So toxic that you feel relief whenever you're not with them or in contact with them;
- Self-centered and makes everything about them;
- Excessively entitled even though they never reciprocate your efforts;
- Always portraying themselves as the good child while you're the black sheep; or
- Always striving to be in the limelight, even when it has nothing to do with them,

You most likely have a narcissistic sibling. So, how can you handle them? Here are a few steps to take:

Take back your self-confidence and self esteem

We can both agree that your self esteem will have taken a hit after putting up with a toxic person for so long. It can be hard to see yourself as someone other than whoever they've led you to believe you are. Taking the time out to destroy those negative notions about yourself is a crucial first step to breaking free of that toxic bondage. Spending more time with people who love and appreciate you goes a long way as well as affirming yourself as much as possible.

Set boundaries

This can look like choosing to walk away when they say hurtful things, refusing to engage when they're trying to bait you, informing them firmly that you'd prefer that they stop doing something you don't like, or even limiting your contact with them if need be. The hard work lies in cataloging their harmful behaviors and agreeing on what you don't want. Then you need to inform them of your new preferences and attach a condition to when they step out of bounds.

Enforcing these conditions may initially be challenging, but it's entirely possible.

Ultimately, focusing on self-care and being kind to yourself are important aspects of coping with a narcissistic sibling.

Codependent Siblings

Codependent siblings, like other codependent people, struggle with self-esteem and inferiority problems. Their selflessness usually hides a need to be in control and get validation or attention as a result.

Unfortunately, this affects both you and the codependent sibling because it puts the responsibility of making them happy solely on you. It also compels you to act a certain way to please them, even when you don't want to. It may also be enabling bad behavior and teaching you that you don't need to take care of yourself. As a result, you may turn out to be resentful and irresponsible.

It's important to set the right boundaries and stand by them. Prepare yourself for the fallout when you set these boundaries and steel yourself against the inevitable manipulation that's sure to follow.

You also need to work on your self-care practices. It's essential that you take care of yourself, and this includes taking responsibility for your feelings and actions. Taking the bold step to end your sibling's codependency can be tough, and you may even require help from others, but it's worth it in the end.

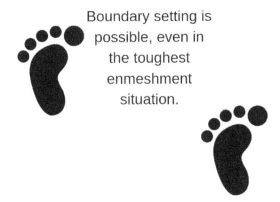

Boundary setting is possible, even in the toughest enmeshment situation.

Your Quick Workbook

1. Identify your boundaries:

a. Write down your personal values, beliefs, and boundaries.

_____

_____

_____

b. Reflect on how they have been affected by the enmeshment in your family.

_____

_____

_____

c. Identify what changes you need to make to assert your boundaries.

_____

_____

_____

2. Assess the impact:

a. Reflect on how your family's enmeshment has affected your life and relationships.

_____

_____

_____

b. Write down the specific behaviors and patterns you need to change to break free.

_____

_____

_____

3. Set healthy boundaries:

a. Write down the specific steps you need to take to establish healthy boundaries with your family, including the narcissistic family member.

_____

_____

_____

b. Identify what you are willing and not willing to tolerate in your relationships.

_____

_____

_____

4. Communicate your boundaries:

a. Plan a conversation with your family about your new boundaries and what you need from them.

_____

_____

_____

b. Practice the conversation in your mind or with a trusted friend.

c. Be clear, direct, and assertive when speaking with your family, including the narcissistic member.

5. Break the cycle of codependency:

a. Identify your codependent tendencies and work on breaking the cycle.

_____

_____

_____

b. Practice self-care and self-love to reduce codependent behaviors.

6. Keep reassessing:

a. Regularly check in with yourself to see if your boundaries are being respected.

b. Make any necessary adjustments to ensure that your boundaries remain intact.

c. Celebrate your progress and growth.

Managing an enmeshed family system is a challenging but rewarding journey. With clear boundaries, self-care, and support, you can create a healthier and happier life.

Chapter Five Takeaway

Blood is thicker than water, the popular saying goes. But is it thicker than toxicity? I don't think so. Dealing with narcissists is one thing, but dealing with narcissists who are also family members is something different. It can often make you feel closed in with nowhere to go, and because they are family, you may often feel like it's your responsibility to fix them.

Big mistake.

You can't change anyone who doesn't want to change. It's that simple. With codependent and/or narcissistic family members, it's best to learn how to use boundaries to manage your interactions with them.

CHAPTER SIX

Tips for Setting Healthy Boundaries

Confession :

i honor my boundaries

"Wounds from a friend can be trusted, but an enemy multiplies kisses."

—Proverbs 27:6

"Lack of boundaries invites lack of respect."

—Anonymous

Have you ever lived on a ranch before? Or perhaps you've visited one? If you have, one thing you'll realize is that, while the ranch hands have a variety of duties to attend to every day, there's always someone whose job is to go inspect the fence line for any damages and repair it at once.

That can be very tasking, especially if the ranch is a large one. It may require that the ranch hand ride for long distances simply to maintain the border, yet it's so important to the wellbeing of the ranch that someone's always assigned to this duty, come rain, come snow, or come shine. Keeping the border intact keeps the precious cattle in and prevents outsiders from sneaking into the ranch and causing havoc.

This is a great example of what setting boundaries looks like. Everyone talks about the great step you need to take to set your boundaries, but less emphasis is placed on its maintenance. This is a common mistake, and I tell anyone who cares to listen that maintaining and updating your boundaries is at least as important as setting them up.

Why You Need to Set Boundaries

Take it from me when I say that boundaries make a whole world of difference. The difference between having balanced relationships with the people in your life and being a people pleaser or always muddled up in obligations you don't want (eventually hating your life as a result) lies in your boundaries.

Yep. You heard me right. If you hate your life, you may need to examine your boundaries to see what you're letting in that's stealing your peace. Setting boundaries helps you to:

Be more confident about your needs

Realizing what you need and asserting these needs to others is a very crucial benefit of setting boundaries. This means that you have no choice but to evaluate what you need and how you feel. The very act of standing for what you want will permeate other aspects of your life, teach you how to be more assertive, and improve all areas of your life.

Meet your needs

How many times have your needs gone unmet in a relationship? Have you quietly accepted the fact that your needs aren't really important? If so, you need to start setting boundaries yesterday! This will help you recognize that your needs are valid and also get them met, be it by you or by others.

Get more time and energy

The fact that the opportunity cost of doing stuff for other people means you have less time and energy to do what makes you really happy should be a huge motivating factor for you to set those boundaries. You'll also be less angry and resentful because you won't be doing things that either waste your time or go against your values. I mean, would you choose to do stuff that weighs you down or stuff that fills you up and makes you happy? It's a no-brainer, right?

Be more compassionate

Being firm about your boundaries doesn't mean that you're wicked or selfish. Feeling guilty about setting boundaries doesn't mean that it's wrong to do so, either; it just means you've taught yourself not to ask for what you need because you think you don't matter. Putting up those boundary lines is a great way of respectfully communicating your needs to others. In respecting your boundaries, they also learn to respect and value themselves.

Stay protected

What if you didn't have to deal with the drama of your narc partner or codependent siblings? Think how much clearer your mind would be and how much your anxiety would lessen. Boundaries act as a shield against messy situations, physical violence, unwanted feelings, and even self-criticism.

Myths Holding You Back From Setting Healthy Boundaries

What are your worst fears about setting boundaries? A lot of people I've spoken to say that they don't want to set boundaries for a number of reasons, usually based on misconceptions they have about boundaries.

We've seen what boundaries are and why it's important to set them; now let's look at what they're **not**.

They don't mean that you're selfish

Having those boundary lines around you helps you take better care of yourself so that you're able to care for others. Remember, if your cup is empty, what will you share with others?

They don't have to be set in stone

Changing your boundaries from time to time won't make you look wishy-washy. On the contrary, it just means that you're open to change and growth. You're allowed to modify your boundaries if what you currently have doesn't work for you.

They won't hurt others or make them leave you

Make no mistake, a boundary is simply the way you tell someone that you deserve respect and the manner in which you'd like to be treated. Sure, it may be uncomfortable for some people, but that's not harmful. Also, people who see your boundaries as hurtful are indirectly indicating that they think you don't deserve the respect of being treated the way you'd prefer. Chew on that for a bit.

They won't make you become angry

Some people say that they've tried setting boundaries with some particular people in their lives and it just led to them getting angry a lot because those boundaries kept getting violated. Guess what? Even when you didn't have those clear-cut demarcations in place, you still got angry or resentful whenever your natural boundary was violated. Laid-down boundaries just makes it more obvious. As you keep asserting your boundaries over time, you'll find that you're getting less angry.

They don't have to look like anyone else's boundaries

It's tempting to want to emulate someone else's boundaries, especially if we greatly admire that person. However, boundaries don't look the same for everyone. It's more effective to set boundaries that apply specifically to your life and work best for you.

What other misconceptions do you have around setting boundaries? I would be delighted to hear about them via email. Now, let's break down these objections one by one, shall we?

How to Set Boundaries with Your Family

Setting boundaries with family members can be tricky, especially if your relationship with them is toxic in one way or another. However it's important for you to understand that your needs are valid. While you may not want to hurt the other person's feelings, you need to understand that they won't think twice about hurting yours. Yep. Repeatedly violating your boundaries really means that they can't be bothered about your feelings and they don't mind walking all over you for their own benefit.

Be clear and direct

This isn't the time to quibble. Tell your family what your needs are, and attach consequences if they violate your boundaries.

Be realistic

Just because you've summoned the courage to set out your boundaries, doesn't mean that your toxic family members will suddenly play nice. Understanding that maintaining your boundaries is where the work lies is the key to setting great boundaries.

Show them that your time is precious

Wasting time is an unfortunate result of poor boundary setting, and preventing this is crucial, as it's a great way to halt meaningless activities. Simply state that you need to attend to something else that's important or that your time is running out. You can point out that they're eating into your precious time as you make your excuses to leave.

Spend more time with people who appreciate you

There's a stark difference between people who don't respect you and people who actually value you. In the company of the latter, you're more likely to be relaxed, content, and happy. You may learn to see yourself in a different way than you're used to. When you spend more time with people that love and respect you, you're reminded that your feelings do count and you're not likely to accept anything less.

Tactics for Setting Boundaries and Maintaining Friendships

After proper evaluation, especially in light of the new information you now possess, you may find that you need to modify your relationships with your friends. Setting boundaries in this case can be hard; finding the balance such that your friendship isn't adversely affected can be a difficult balancing act. The fact remains, however, that our friends are such a huge part of our lives that the effect of a properly constructed boundary to protect that relationship with them is immediately felt.

You may need to check the boundaries of the relationship if you feel like you're the one doing all the work, you don't trust their integrity, you don't find their teasing funny, they don't respect your time, or maybe you're simply not as available as you used to be. Once you're dissatisfied with any area of the friendship, it's time to speak up.

A few things to keep in mind when setting boundaries for a friendship are:

Emphasize how valuable the friendship is to you

Explain that you're doing this to protect this important relationship. Truthfully, setting boundaries can be hurtful in this kind of scenario, but it's for the best. Explain that you're having this difficult conversation precisely because you care.

Be kind, firm, and direct

Let me say this now: setting a weak boundary is worse than not setting one in the first place because you'll spend valuable time and effort trying to reinforce it. It's better to steel yourself to set a strong boundary once and for all. This will reduce the likelihood of being frustrated or disappointed later on.

Start as soon as possible

If you've noticed a particular behavior that you don't like, set a boundary to deal with it as soon as possible so that it doesn't become a habit. It's also better to handle it quickly before it becomes a huge issue.

Don't focus on them

Using statements that start with "I" is a much more effective way to have the conversation. This way, your friend won't feel like you're blaming them, and you're centering the discussion on how you feel. It helps them to better understand where you're coming from and meet you halfway.

How to Create Boundaries in the Workplace for a More Positive Working Environment

Setting boundaries at work is more than just putting that nosy coworker in their place. It encompasses more than standing up to your toxic boss once and for all. Yeah, it's a whole lot more than that. It's realizing that you need to take care of yourself in the best way possible so that you can be as productive as possible in your career.

Setting boundaries at work utilizes the same basic idea as setting them anywhere else, but most people seem to discard thoughts of their wellbeing at work when they get caught up in the corporate hustle and bustle. If that's you, this is your sign to stop today.

So ask yourself: "What are the factors I need to have in place to be my most productive self?" Proper consideration will reveal that this question is the basis of every effective boundary you'll need to set because it encompasses your micromanaging, toxic manager as well as your nosy coworker.

Here are a few other tips to help you along the way:

Ask for help

If you have a supportive manager or a coworker who seems to be more productive, it won't hurt to ask them for some assistance. Apart from making you more effective, it also improves your relationship with them and may even blossom into a mentorship.

Decide your own limits

Now that you have an idea of your most productive environment, it's time to create it. If that means taking paid time off every quarter or insisting that you shouldn't be contacted after hours, then by all means make those decisions.

Communicate clearly to your team members and superiors

Once you have decided your limits, the next step is to communicate them to your team members. It's important to be as clear and direct as possible. Don't waffle about your boundaries, either; if you don't want to be reachable while on vacation, insist on it.

Get ready for the blowback

Did you think it was going to be that easy? I hope you didn't. You need to prepare for the consequences of your boundaries. This is where the toxic people at work start creeping out of the woodwork to make these boundaries difficult to maintain. But you won't be bothered because you already know that maintaining your boundaries takes a larger chunk of effort than setting them and you're appropriately prepared to stand by them, right? Great.

Setting Boundaries with Your Partner

This may be the aspect of setting boundaries that makes you the most uncomfortable. If you have a codependent partner with narcissistic traits, this may not be a walk in the park for you.

I'll say this right off the bat: putting up boundaries in that kind of relationship won't be pleasant, and your toxic partner won't take it lightly either. I think it's best that you're aware of this because, like they say, to be forewarned is to be forearmed.

Now, I know setting boundaries with a romantic partner feels like you're putting up walls between each other when you should be letting down your hair and being as vulnerable as possible. Yeah, it seems weird and counterintuitive, but trust me, that's not the case at all.

Even in a romantic relationship, you need to protect yourself and your values so that you can bring forth the best version of yourself. It's as simple as that. Yeah, you may be tempted to just keep holding on in the face of abuse and disrespect, but that's only harming you mentally and emotionally. You don't deserve that.

Your boundaries should reflect your important values and needs. This can look like:

- Asking for space to process emotionally weighty issues or to just breathe.

- Maintaining your identity outside your relationship by preserving your passions, interests, and hobbies.

- Separating your feelings from your partner's feelings. Don't let them assume your feelings or reactions.

- Saying no. If you truly feel uncomfortable with something, it's best to say no with the knowledge that you're preserving your relationship.

- Resisting emotional manipulation. Instead of taking the easy way out by accepting the blame even when you're not at fault, stick up for yourself.

- Asking to be respected. You deserve to have your opinions, emotions, and words respected, so don't hesitate to ask for it.

- Defending yourself when your partner tries to belittle you. Quickly speak up for yourself, state what you don't like, and ask for an apology.

- Deciding whether or not to be vulnerable with your partner. You should only open up when you feel safe, not because of pressure.

The bottom line is that realizing that intimate relationships need boundaries even more than non-intimate relationships will guide you when it comes to finding the willpower needed to reinforce your boundaries.

Imagine a situation where you're barely communicating with your partner because you're too full of resentment and frustration. Imagine constantly being unhappy but unable to communicate it for fear of hurting their feelings. If you're truly in a loving and healthy relationship, your partner will feel awful once they realize that you've been unhappy and didn't tell them.

The most important person in this relationship is *you.* This means that you have to put your wellbeing first so that you can love and receive love the right way.

* Ready to set empowering boundaries and soar with personal growth? Explore Worksheet #6 by grabbing your __BONUS #1__ or checking this QR code.

How to Express Your Boundaries and Avoid Arguments

I once worked with a young man who was so anxious about being confronted that he tolerated a lot of bad behavior from his friends, who were quite mean. We decided that he needed to work on his boundaries and assert his feelings. He was so terrified, but he came to see the necessity of that action. To make the process easier for him, before he confronted anyone, he'd walk away first and close his eyes while rehearsing how he'd set or reinforce his boundaries. It was a bit embarrassing for him, but he learned to get used to it, and in no time, he was standing up for himself without flinching.

—Stephen

We've talked a lot about setting boundaries, but you and I both know that it's not easy, especially if you hate confrontation. Well, you're in luck because I have a few strategies that'll help you set your boundaries without the fear of ruffling too many feathers:

1. Find out why you're so afraid of confrontation in the first place

The fact that you'd rather count the grains of sand in the Sahara than face conflict is a sign that you've internalized the notion that conflict isn't compatible with healthy or peaceful relationships. It most likely indicates some trauma that remains unresolved for you.

But if you take the time to understand that conflict can be healthy and even make the relationship better, then you have a stronger chance of setting and maintaining your boundaries without fear. This means exposing yourself to conflicting situations and allowing yourself to experience the emotions while evaluating them. Keeping a journal and/or meditating will come in handy here.

2. Do it early

Here's the naked truth: holding off on correcting someone or setting your boundary immediately only exposes you to similar incidents. You'll be increasingly irritated by their actions, and eventually you'll explode because you just can't take it anymore. Trust me, that day will be messy and complicated and may end up damaging a precious friendship or relationship. Why wait till then? If you speak out now, you're likely to be calm and rational with a higher chance of avoiding more conflict further down the road.

3. Mind your language

Yep, something as simple as the way you present your thoughts can be pivotal in avoiding confrontation. Ensure that you place a lot of emphasis on the fact that you're not opposing the other person and that you appreciate and value their needs too.

Help them understand that you want the relationship to last a long time, in a healthy environment, and that's why you're speaking out. Focus more on how you feel rather than accusing them.

I don't know about you, but these tactics have helped me salvage a lot of relationships, and I'm happier for it. I'm grateful to have these techniques in my toolbelt. I'm sure you will be too!

How to Handle People Who Violate Your Boundaries

Okay, we both know that your boundaries are going to be tested by people around you, just to see how serious you are. If you stand your ground, some people will adjust and respect them. Unfortunately, others (read: the toxic narcs and codependents in your life) will violently oppose them. I don't mean to sound negative, but they will.

These people will ignore you and your demands and even get defensive when you challenge them. That's not all, folks—these people are horrible at reaching a compromise and may even try to persuade you to relax your boundaries. Oh, did I say "persuade"? My bad, I meant *manipulate*.

Here are a few helpful ways to handle those situations when they arise:

Recheck your boundaries

Before you storm off to accuse someone of violating your boundary, do a thorough evaluation. Did you set clear, consistent boundaries? Or did you keep changing the terms at every interaction with the person? Has the person seen you enforcing that boundary with others? You also need to be crystal clear about the boundary in your own mind and stick to it; that way you won't be tempted to adjust it. If you do an assessment and you're certain that your boundaries are clear and consistent, then you can move on to the next step. If not, you need to redefine them and make sure you're enforcing them consistently.

Reassert your boundaries

Yeah, I know. It's most likely an exercise in futility to reiterate a boundary when it's already been violated, but it's necessary to stay consistent even when you can't control the outcome. This is the perfect time to state the consequences that come with violating the boundary and enact them. For example:

"If you don't stop yelling at me, I'm going to hang up."

Or,

"If you keep talking over me, I'm going to end this conversation and leave the room."

Then, you should hang up or leave the room or do whatever consequence is attached to that boundary violation.

Face the facts

Look, as much as you don't want to hear it, it's necessary to realize that some people will never accept your boundaries. Narcissists are very competitive and will not give in easily. In such cases, it may be easier to limit contact or reframe the context of the relationship.

I need to say that this isn't the same thing as giving up because the average narc will never let you win fair and square. In fact, I'd say that it's simply about you seeing the writing on the wall and protecting yourself. This way you're not available for them to manipulate and control. Sounds like a win to me.

Your Quick Workbook: Healthy Boundaries Worksheet

1. Identify the toxic behavior: Write down specific examples of the toxic behavior that you want to address.

_____

_____

_____

.2 Assess the impact: How does the person's toxic behavior affect you emotionally, physically, mentally, and spiritually?

_____

_____

_____

3. Define your boundaries: What are the specific behaviors and actions that you will not tolerate from the toxic person?

_____

_____

_____

4. Communicate your boundaries: Clearly communicate your boundaries to the toxic person in a calm, assertive manner. Be specific and avoid making accusations or attacking the person. Write down how you're going to express your boundaries to this person.

_____

_____

_____

5. Enforce your boundaries: If the toxic person continues with the same behavior, it is important to enforce your boundaries by taking concrete steps. Write down what step you're going to take for this particular person.

_____

---

6. Review and reassess: Regularly evaluate the situation and reassess your boundaries to ensure they are still aligned with your needs and values. It's your first time setting boundaries with this person; as time goes on, things might change that cause you to review your boundaries. Also, how often do you think this assessment should be done?

Remember, setting healthy boundaries with toxic people is an ongoing process, and it's important to be kind and compassionate to yourself during this time.

Chapter Six Takeaway

Creating boundaries is crucial to your wellbeing, but it must be done with the right mindset. If you create boundaries with the mindset of keeping people away from you, then you'll quickly realize that those boundaries become walls that lock you in and prevent you from any meaningful interactions with others.

PART TWO

Emotional Abuse Recovery

One possible scenario in dealing with narcissists is being bound together with one in a legal union, like marriage. If you're in such a situation, you might be wondering, "What do I do?" That's one of the questions this final part of this book attempts to answer.

In the pages ahead, I will guide you through how to handle narcissistic relationships without losing your mind. However, in the event that you can no longer manage such a relationship, this part will also guide you on how to transition into a new life where you'll enjoy much tranquility.

You won't want to miss the climax of this book. The next two chapters comprise the point where you'll learn to untangle, detoxify, and heal completely. The secret to your best life yet is waiting to be discovered in this final part.

Turn to the next page, and the next after it, till your thirst is quenched.

So far, if you've discovered something meaningful in reading this book, please click HERE to leave a review on Amazon. That will help other people in their personal growth.

CHAPTER SEVEN

What to Do When You Can't Leave: Communicating with a Toxic Person

BY SETTING BOUNDARIES

"A word fitly spoken is like apples of gold in settings of silver."

—Proverbs 25:11

"I used to think the worst thing in life was to end up all alone. It's not. The worst thing in life is ending up with people who make you feel all alone."

—Robin Williams

There's a class of people that is difficult to love: toxic people. With this kind of person, there's no special season that has them emitting some inner beauty. They constantly exude an aura of toxicity. It's who they are. These people might be physically beautiful, but their attitudes are draining and exhausting. The aura they carry makes it difficult to deal with them or even have meaningful conversations without experiencing pain.

189

I hope and pray you meet someone ready to do life with you without seeing you as an antagonist. I hope you have relationships that add value to you.

The truth is that we don't recognize toxic folks at the beginning. They may have become part of our lives, and there's little we can do to keep them at bay. They could be an estranged spouse or a baby mama or baby daddy. If children are involved, you might be sentenced to a long time of having to communicate with them. It's even worse if that person is a narcissist. It's no news that narcissists are difficult people. Not just that, they're hard to reason with. With a child in the equation, you're stuck with the narcissist, especially if they're bent on being in the child(ren)'s life.

Why Narcissists Are Hard to Reason With

If you've ever stuttered or lashed out in frustration while conversing with someone, you'll relate to the fact that some folks are hard to reason with. Have you ever gotten to a point where you nodded your head in frustration, then paused in the middle of a conversation like a laborer taking a break from trying to cut down a huge tree? Have you ever felt parts of your body tremble after a conversation? Do you find yourself crying after interacting with a particular person? Do you experience a sporadic change in your mood after speaking with this person?

These are just some of the things you'll experience when you're trying to reason with a toxic person. It's even worse when the individual is a narcissist. The question now is, why are they so hard to deal with? Why are they bent on being contrary, even if what you're saying is reasonable? The answer isn't difficult to decipher. It's engraved in their personality, so much so that they don't think they have a problem. That makes it even worse. You can't ostracize them from who they are.

Without further ado, let's dive right into it. Here are some of the reasons you can't seem to agree with that narcissist in your life.

Entitlement

When it comes to narcissism, entitlement can be defined as feeling like you deserve to get certain benefits regardless of whether you earned them or not. People can feel entitled to your money, gifts, time, attention, or any other thing that could be perceived to be of value. When the word "entitlement" pops up in a conversation, it's often accompanied by signs of disgust—but I want you to know that entitlement can be both good and bad.

Entitlement simply means that you have a right to access certain privileges as a member of a particular space based on your membership or contributions. It can be good in the sense that you're aware of your rights as an individual within your sphere of influence, whether it's in the aspect of class, race, creed, socio-economic status, or a system. Entitlement can be specific to a particular relationship, situation, or place.

In a home, a child is entitled to proper care and nurturing from their parent irrespective of the child's behavior because he/she was brought into the world by the parent. As a citizen of a country, you believe that you're entitled to social amenities and other government benefits because you pay taxes. Even as humans, we are entitled to love, respect, and honor irrespective of age, class, or social standing. Don't all the religions of the world agree on this one view—loving our neighbor? Isn't that a command from God most of humanity believes in? The examples I have listed are healthy forms of entitlement.

However, narcissists represent a different type of entitlement. This is one central feature of narcissism that makes communication difficult. Entitlement manifests differently for grandiose and vulnerable narcissists. Since narcissists are self-absorbed people who are preoccupied with their own needs and feelings, they can't see the larger picture that involves others.

For grandiose narcissists, it's about getting the best of something without consideration for others. Usually, they want preferential treatment or consideration. For example, they might want to be attended to when they're paying for a public service even if it's not their turn. In the workplace, they might evade certain duties and responsibilities. At home, they might make emotional or financial demands without considering your needs. Everything is about them. It gets even more difficult when you're trying to communicate your needs.

For vulnerable narcissists, it's about wanting to be admired for their specialness and accomplishments. If they don't get this from people, they see it as a failure on their part or an implication that nobody likes them and that the world is against them.

Consequently, they begin to play the victim and use it to justify their entitled behavior.

When a person believes he or she is being victimized when that isn't the case, how do you get through to them?

When a person believes he or she deserves to be served first in a restaurant, how do you communicate with them?

When a grown adult feels they must have their bills paid by a family member or friend, how do you make them see that the world doesn't revolve around them?

This is why setting boundaries is important when it comes to narcissists. Very important.

Lack of Empathy

It's difficult to communicate easily with someone who doesn't feel what you feel. Is that not what empathy is all about? Isn't it about putting oneself in another's shoes? Isn't it about imagining what it's like to experience what another person is experiencing and seeing things from their point of view? Narcissists are incapable of feeling what you feel because they're so consumed with their own needs. A person that's devoid of empathy acts cold and insensitive even in the face of intense emotion. It's like bullets bouncing off a bulletproof vest. When you're trying to converse with a narcissist, they are most likely going to dismiss your feelings.

Due to inattention and self-focus, narcissists will not feel what you feel, they won't see what you see, and they most definitely won't think what you think. Hence, communication fails before it even begins.

Exploitation

The language of exploitation does not include reason, logic, or morals in its lexicon. Exploitation is about using others to gratify your own desires. In our narcissistically-blossoming world, you can see governments exploiting workers, corporations exploiting rural communities, partners exploiting one another in relationships, and bosses exploiting subordinates. The list is endless. In a relationship, exploitation can be financial, physical, or emotional, and it's about having an advantage over the other person.

Sometimes exploitation feeds on ignorance, and sometimes it's unintentional. If a person or group doesn't realize they are being exploited, it won't stop.

The goal is to have an advantage, to dominate and control. Trying to confront or communicate your needs to someone bent on being in control is like hitting a brick wall. You won't easily have conversations with a narcissist when they're all about forcing people into putting them on a pedestal and showing gratuitous displays of respect.

In some other subtle forms of exploitative abuse of power, narcissistic parents can shove unfulfilled dreams, goals, or fantasies down a child's throat just to feel good about themselves. It can also come in the form of forcing children to imbibe the parent's thoughts or behavior, rather than allowing them to develop their own ideas and interests.

It's hard to communicate with narcissists when they're so focused on controlling you. Oftentimes, they sincerely think they're doing you a lot of good. Other times, they're comfortable with you being under their control. It's an affront to their ego and grandiosity that you have a mind of your own. Think of how exhausting it could be to try to get someone like that to see things from your angle.

How to Communicate with a Toxic Person and Still Keep Your Sanity

My relationship with a covert narcissist taught me that communication is work. Actually, it's not just work—it's an art. It's something that has to be studied and understood amid a world that's saturated with so much information and yet devoid of wisdom. In a world where everyone has something to say, it takes a lot of guts to listen. It takes discipline.

In the words of Earl Wilson, "Listening, not imitation, may be the sincerest form of flattery." Winston Churchill's views align with Wilson's, as he once said, "Courage is what it takes to stand up and speak; courage is also what it takes to sit down and listen." As sincere and true as these words are, it's something that toxic people resent. They'd rather have you roll in the mud with them than stare at them as if they were an actor on stage. When it comes to communicating with toxic people, you must know what to say and what not to say.

Now, let me tell you something. You'll learn to say the right thing if you know how to listen. In today's narcissistic world, folks only listen to give a clapback. The goal is not usually to understand but to give a piece of their minds. This is why there's chaos, leading to a break in communication. Let your goals be to understand, and then be understood.

Learn to listen

This is not just about listening. It's about active listening. This is about having clarity about what the other person is trying to say. By the time you're clear about the other person's views, you're capable of dealing with them healthily and more effectively.

Active listening is different from just listening. With the former, you're listening to understand what the person is saying and where they're coming from with all their claims and outbursts. It's difficult to listen when the speaker's comments are getting under your skin, but when you come to an understanding that it's not about you but about what they might be battling within themselves, you'll listen more.

Make sure your body language and tone aren't aggravating the situation

Without knowing it, you might be displaying body language that is quite confrontational. Even if you're silent, is your body language screaming for a fight? Your body language might be trivializing or challenging what the other person is saying.

For example, are you saying "I'm sorry," but your tone sounds nonchalant? Is your nonchalance accompanied with arms folded across your chest defiantly?

Sometimes, an "I'm sorry" is exactly what a toxic person *doesn't* want to hear.

I don't mean that you should apologize because you're in the wrong, but at times, you'll need to be brave enough to lay aside your pride to allow for your peace of mind and to avoid dragging the issue out. Try saying something like, "I'm sorry you feel this way."

Don't get drawn in. Just remain calm.

Limit time spent together

Time spent with a toxic individual can be draining. If you find yourself feeling drained and stressed after spending time with someone, you might have to keep your distance. When every conversation leads to a fight and a repetitive violation of boundaries, it's high time you took a step backwards and reduced your communication with such folks.

Set boundaries

Being aware of yourself and understanding what ticks you off and prevents you from becoming a better person is one major step towards setting boundaries, especially with toxic individuals. Let folks know what you like and what you dislike. You can adjust the dynamics of your relationship with toxic people based on your boundaries.

Walk away

Did you know that some people have wound up in jail because they didn't walk away from a toxic confrontation? Because they got triggered, they moved from being the victim to being the villain. To avoid this, plan an exit strategy by saying something like, "I'm sorry, I have to leave now. I don't like where this conversation is headed," or, "I suggest we talk when you're calm." Then take a walk.

Don't look at this list as another set of rules. These are necessary steps for keeping a clear mind when communicating with toxic individuals. The toxicity of an individual is never about you. As someone once said, "The goodness in you irritates their demons." Don't lose your sanity, but rather guard it jealously.

Expressing Your Needs and Truth in Every Relationship

When it comes to those we love, we make excuses for them. We make compromises for them. We hardly hold them to the standards that we would other people.

Talk about the things we do for love! In our fear of losing them, we let go of our own needs. Sometimes we let go of ourselves. We let go of our Truth and relish in the lie we tell ourselves. If care is not taken, you might end up seeing your mistreatment as a sign of love.

It's high time you started having difficult conversations. If you don't address the issues in your relationships, you will end up harboring resentment, overthinking, and experiencing irritation and anxiety. Issues that are always swept under the carpet will lead to a mountain of conflicts in the long run if communication is absent.

For any relationship to thrive, openness is important. How do you begin?

Know what you want

You must be aware of your needs. Do you know that at times you get moody and sad without being able to place a finger on the reason? Many times we can only get answers when we do a soul search into what might be missing. It's hidden somewhere in your subconscious. To help keep track of your thoughts, you can write them down. After a while, you'll find the answers. Take time out to figure out what's bothering you. It might be a need for connection, communication, emotional intimacy, physical intimacy, independence, or other needs that are not being met.

Arrange a rendezvous

Make preparations to meet at a time and place that's comfortable for you both. Make sure it's a quiet and serene place that will help you focus on your conversation. It's best to have this conversation when your partner is well-rested and energized, ready to listen to anything you have to say.

Don't be accusatory

Now that you're ready to bare your mind, don't begin your statements with comments like, "You never..." or "You're always..." Statements like this will put your partner on the defensive and can lead to an argument. Instead, say, "I feel like..."

You can begin by stating the good qualities of your relationship before moving to the problem. Make it all about you. Don't direct it towards your partner. It should be about you talking about your experiences and how you feel about them without making your partner look like the bad guy in the picture.

Avoid blaming or complaining. Don't say things like, "I need you to..." That's accusatory and can lead to another wave of arguments. When you make your conversations less accusatory, you make it a situation of "us against the problem."

Figuring Out When You Should and Shouldn't be Sorry

"I'm sorry" is one of the most abused and trivialized statements ever made. Nonetheless, it's still one of the most difficult to say. Many have made it such a habit that it has lost its soothing effect on the hurting. Many a time, it's an indication that a person hasn't learned their lesson.

Apologizing is a skill. You have to know how best to go about it. Sometimes "I'm sorry" doesn't suffice for the gravity of the offense. On the other hand, due to the manipulative nature of some people in our lives, we tend to get guilt-tripped for choosing what's best for us because it doesn't sit well with them, and we end up apologizing for things for which we shouldn't be sorry. For others, it might be the way we were raised, and apologizing has become instinctive.

These are times when you *should* be sorry:

1. When you use derogatory remarks towards your partner in a fit of anger

2. When you start an argument

3. When you're nonchalant about the relationship

4. When you're emotionally and physically unavailable when your partner needs you

5. When you forget special events or occasions that mean a lot to your partner

6. When you refuse to pay heed to the yearnings of your partner

7. When you're harsh, rude, or sarcastic about critical matters

8. When you cross a boundary that has already been clearly stated

Now, these are things that you *shouldn't* be sorry for:

1. Don't be sorry for calling out a person for their bad attitude and behavior.

2. Don't be sorry for setting boundaries.

3. Don't be sorry for stating your needs.

4. Don't be sorry for saying no.

5. Don't be sorry for being assertive.

6. Don't be sorry for standing up for yourself.

7. Don't be sorry for expressing your displeasure about a wrong done to you.

8. Don't be sorry for speaking the truth when the need arises.

We must be clear on the things we should be sorry for and those we shouldn't. When we're clear about this disparity, we are less susceptible to manipulation from toxic individuals.

Saying No Without Feeling Guilty

People-pleasing is common amongst those who have frequently been made to feel guilty for saying no. This class of people easily fall prey to toxic manipulators who are ready to manipulate your vulnerabilities and insecurities.

Remember:

- You can say no without feeling bad about it.
- You can say no without feeling like a villain or standoffish person.
- Sometimes you have to say no for your convenience.
- Sometimes you have to say no to protect yourself.
- Sometimes you have to say no to set boundaries.

Some people don't say no effectively. Instead, they make excuses. This leaves room for more requests from the person making a request. There are several ways that you can say no effectively.

1. Say, "No." Yup! Just say it. There's no point beating around the bush and making excuses. If you have to explain, do so briefly. But never feel compelled or coerced into doing something that you aren't keen on doing.

2. Be assertive about your decision. You don't have to be rude about it. You gain control over the situation when you say things like, "I'm sorry, I won't be able to do that right now, but if I can, I'll let you know." While saying no, let your body language also say no. Don't give an air of not being sure about your decision.

3. Boundaries must be set. If you're in a relationship with someone, you might have issues saying no to them. Saying no allows people to understand your stance on certain issues. Knowing yourself and the dynamics of your relationship will make it easier to say no.

Your Quick Workbook

1. Here is a simple worksheet to help you communicate with toxic people in your life:

Identify the toxic behavior: What specifically is the toxic behavior you are trying to address?

_____

_____

_____

2. Reflect on your feelings: Take some time to think about how the toxic behavior makes you feel and how it affects your relationship with the person.

_____

_____

_____

3. Set clear boundaries: What are the boundaries you need to set in order to protect yourself?

_____

_____

_____

4. Choose a calm time and place: When and where will you have the conversation? Choose a time and place where you both can be calm and won't be interrupted.

_____

_____

_____

5. Stay focused on the behavior, not the person: Remember to focus on the behavior you want to change, not attacking the person themselves. It's easy to get angry in this situation, which is why you should remind yourself of the behavior here:

_____

_____

_____

6. Use "I" statements: Express your feelings and needs using "I" statements, such as "I feel hurt when you do/say x." Let's practice—write down what you'll say:

_____

_____

_____

7. Listen to their perspective: Try to understand the other person's point of view and let them know you are open to hearing their thoughts.

8. Find common ground: What areas do you think you both agree on? Where can you work together to resolve the issue?

9. Agree on a solution: Work together to find a solution that works for both of you.

10. Follow up: Check in to make sure the solution is working and to hold both parties accountable.

Remember, effective communication with toxic people requires patience, empathy, and a strong sense of self. The goal is to find a solution that works for both of you and to maintain healthy boundaries for yourself.

Chapter Seven Takeaway

Having to stay in contact with a narcissist can be hard. But it is in times like this I want you to remember something: you're in control of yourself, not the other person. The narcissist can behave how he or she wants to behave, but you're the one with the final say on your response.

CHAPTER EIGHT

Loving and Prioritizing Yourself When Dealing with Narcissists

"For no one ever hated his own flesh, but nourishes and cherishes it, just as Christ does the church."

—Ephesians 5:29, ESV

"The challenge is not to be perfect—it is to be whole."

—Jane Fonda

Overcoming Narcissistic Victim Syndrome for Good

People react to narcissists in different ways. Your reception to a narcissist can be attributed to your exposure to narcissistic behavior, especially in your formative years.

If you were nurtured by narcissistic parents, constantly teased or scorned by your siblings, or were a timid child that got abused or exploited, your trust has been violated repeatedly. This will make you more paranoid and sensitive than others who don't share your experiences.

From our knowledge of social history, we know that we have expectations of other people and we feel about the people around us. This explains why the most important step in dealing with narcissists is studying the patterns that make up our experiences and how our reactions bring pain to us. For example, your tendency to people-please has likely exposed you to the whim and caprices of the narcissist. Maybe your lack of boundaries has made narcissists trample on your self-esteem.

The moment you begin to see the role that you've played in your own pain, you'll begin to be able to impede the cycle of pain that we allow narcissists to inflict on us.

I know it's easier said than done. You're probably screaming, "It's not that simple!"

Yes, I know.

Narcissists aren't always negative. We see them as this larger-than-life entity and then put them on a pedestal. We can't imagine our lives without them. We surrender to an illusion and end up losing ourselves, getting bruised and feeling empty.

Here's how you can rid yourself of narcissistic victim syndrome for good:

1. Pay attention to how you're feeling. I remember someone telling me, "Energy doesn't lie." I've held on to that. If you're constantly feeling uneasiness, anger, shame, and fear while in the company of a particular person, this can be a telltale sign that you're in the presence of a narcissist. The moment you sense this, it's best to take a step back and seek ways to defend yourself.

2. Once you identify these feelings, pay attention to what buttons are being pushed to trigger you. This is why self-awareness is important. This way, you know when a narcissist is trying to hit a nerve. You know you've felt this same way in the past. Do a soul search and own your narcissistic vulnerabilities. Are you easily shamed by condescending comments? Do you feel so low that you're bent on pleasing people even to your detriment? These are questions that you need to ask yourself.

3. Now that you've identified your weaknesses, which the narcissist recognizes, move to your feelings. How have your feelings enabled narcissists in their devices?

4. Separate yourself from any form of self-loathing that the narcissist might evoke in you. Recognize that their projections do not define you. It's a form of control to keep them dominating. It'll help you to see them in a less-grandiose light when you realize that they put you down to feel superior. The more you give them admiration, the more you feed their narcissistic supply.

5. After detaching yourself from this self-loathing, resist the urge to retaliate. Don't stoop to their level. Keep in mind that it's baseless to challenge them or preach to them about the error of their ways. Save yourself the effort and walk away. Narcissists are comfortable in their delusions, so much so that the truth about themselves lies dormant in their subconscious. And you know what? They want to keep it that way.

What am I saying? Don't waste your breath trying to resurrect a truth that they choose to leave in the subconscious. It can only worsen matters. Don't even think about it.

Detoxifying After Years of Emotional Abuse

You must have heard a lot about detoxification in the world of physical wellness. Your mind, which determines the course of your life, also needs detoxifying. This isn't about detoxing your mind from negative emotions. This isn't about ending suffering. It's more about being in touch with your feelings, understanding the roots of those feelings, coming to terms with your pain, and not allowing it to distract you from truly living.

It's about clearing out the residue of wrong mindsets and emotions that remain engraved in your subconscious. Did you know that your trauma still lurks around in your mind? Could that be the reason you're experiencing constant mood swings? Could that be the reason you still have PTSD from an experience that changed your life?

Do you know why the mind has to come first when it comes to healing from emotional abuse?

Psychiatrist Bessel Van Der Kolk, MD (author of *The Body Keeps the Score: Brain, Mind, and Body in the Healing of Trauma*) states, "Research revealed that trauma produces actual physiological changes, including recalibration of the brain's alarm system, an increase in stress hormone activity, and alterations in the system that filters relevant information from irrelevant" (2014). So, the state of your emotions is connected to how your body functions effectively.

Let's look at these emotional toxins and their roots.

- Hurt is rooted in victimization, helplessness and blame.
- Sadness is rooted in self-pity and regret.
- Shame is rooted in humiliation and embarrassment.
- Hopelessness is rooted in loneliness, despair, and desperation.
- Fear is rooted in anxiety, panic, and immobilization.
- Anger is rooted in resentment and bitterness.
- Hate is rooted in meanness and vengefulness.
- Jealousy is rooted in insecurities, envy, and possessiveness.
- Pride is rooted in self-righteousness and self-exaltation.
- Greed is rooted in insatiability and emotional hunger.
- Guilt is rooted in unhealthy responsibility and self-blame.
- Criticism is rooted in judgment and false projections.

How can you detox yourself emotionally? How do you go about a soul purge? Let's dive into some useful techniques.

1. Identify your triggers and their roots. Once you're aware of these things, you can seek self-soothing ways to take charge of your emotions. You can try relaxation rituals to help you relax, like meditation, prayer, laughter, or listening to classical music (or some other genre of music that keeps you calm).

2. Now that you're aware of what triggers you, plan out how you can keep yourself in check when the need arises. If you've got anger issues, plan to go on a walk in the moment. Don't say a word. Don't pick up anything. Just take that walk. If someone is trying to put you down, separate yourself from what's been said. Understand that what's been said is an expression of the other person's insecurities. It has nothing to do with you. You're good.

3. Take up a charitable course. It's high time you started living. To do this, you'll need to step outside yourself. The more absorbed you are with your emotional instability, the more you'll miss out on how much good you can do for the world around you. Have you considered mentoring young people, volunteering, checking up on a sick friend, or even simply listening to another's problem? You'll see how much healing will come from just breathing life into the things and people around you.

4. Take a break from complaining. There's surely something to be grateful for. This isn't trivializing your emotional challenges or ignoring that something is wrong; rather, it's accepting that some things can be overwhelming, but that you can quit complaining and be grateful for the seemingly inconsequential things that you rarely pay attention to. The moment you cease complaining, positive thoughts will begin to flood your mind.

5. Know your vices. Are you fond of binge eating or reaching for the bottle when you're in distress? Tell yourself the truth about what's making you over-indulge. These emotional vices that are causing you anxiety might just be rooted in something you're afraid to confront. When you identify them, it will be much easier to limit and control your addictions to these vices.

6. Get help. When I say help, I don't mean your friend, family, or next-door neighbor. I'm not saying they aren't helpful in soothing your pain—you need them—but you need a professional too. With therapy, you'll exhume all that trauma, the buried emotions and anxieties that are holding you back from being your best self. You don't have to be going through a meltdown to go to therapy. Look at this as a luxurious treat that you choose to give your mind.

7. Take on a 7-Day Challenge with God. Sit down in a silent place and spend 30 minutes meditating on His Word for 7 days.

Think of the furnishing of your mind when it comes to emotional detox. Your body and organs will thank you for it.

Don't Blame Yourself

The older you get, the more you'll realize that there are some things that you shouldn't blame yourself for. After exiting a relationship, it's not uncommon for people to blame themselves for the pain they went through. Before I get ahead of myself, let's dive into some of the things you shouldn't blame yourself for.

1. Don't blame yourself for being rejected. Oftentimes, we internalize rejection and make it all about ourselves when truly it's never about us. Find your tribe. You aren't for everyone, and that's okay.

2. Don't blame yourself for expressing your emotions. This is what makes you real. There's no such thing as "doing too much" when it comes to emotions. The sooner you accept this, the more you'll embrace your authentic self. (This applies as long as you're not inflicting physical harm or being emotionally abusive.)

3. Don't blame yourself for making mistakes. It's part of being human. Focus on being a better person today than you were yesterday. It's time to move forward.

4. Don't blame yourself for having needs. Others might treat your needs as if they don't matter. It doesn't mean that they don't.

5. Don't blame yourself for another's insecurities. Sometimes people try to treat you badly and project their insecurities onto you. It's not your fault.

6. Don't blame yourself for looking out for yourself. There's nothing wrong with taking care of yourself. Sometimes you need to, for you to be healthy for others.

7. Don't blame yourself for being too trusting. Humans are flawed. If we don't take risks when it comes to love, we're not truly living. Treat failed relationships as a lesson and an opportunity to grow and evolve.

8. Don't blame yourself for the pains of the past. The past is the past. The only direction you need to be looking is forward. Decide to live in the now and work towards a brighter future.

How to Prioritize Yourself Every Day

Have you been a people-pleaser in the past, where you gave so much of yourself? Have you gotten hurt in the process of trying to win a certain someone's heart, only for it to get broken? How can you be a blessing to your world when you put yourself in positions that leave you hurt?

Here are simple ways that you can look out for yourself daily without feeling guilty about it.

1. Set apart a time for deep reflection. Revamp your thoughts, set your goals, do a review of your life, practice gratitude, and breathe. I had to add "breathe" there because many times we hold our breath out of anxiety and fear. Breathe.

2. Eat healthily. Fruits, vegetables, and other whole foods are readily available in markets and stalls. It gets even better when you complement a good diet with the right supplements. Doing an overall health checkup will let you know which vitamins and minerals you're deficient in.

3. Take breaks. Hustle culture has taught you that if you sleep a certain number of hours per day, you must be lazy. You don't have to work by these rules. Know your limits when it comes to your health. If your body is telling you that it's time to lie down, listen to it. Don't hesitate to take a break if you have to. And remember, screen time isn't taking a break. If you're taking a break, it has to be rest for all your senses.

4. Manage your time well. Set deadlines for yourself. Work effectively and manage your work well.

5. Drink water. Yep! Good old H2O. You can't deny the many benefits of water. Your organs will be cleansed, your skin will be moisturized, your joints will be well lubricated. And yes, you'll exude confidence when you're glowing differently. Water ain't old school. Treat yourself to a lot of it.

Support Systems and Support Groups

One of the greatest gifts that we'll ever have is the gift of people. A support system is a network of people, be it family, friends, or peers, that are available to walk us through tough times. Imagine not having any friends to call on while in a relationship with a narcissist. That's dangerous, if you ask me.

One of the ploys of toxic people is to isolate you from loved ones. Don't fall for that ploy. However, in situations where it seems that the people close to you might not believe you when you explain the abuse, it's best to reach out to a formal support group. A support group is made up of people who are going through the same things you are. They are willing to listen without judging you or blaming you for your wrong choices.

Here are the benefits of having a support system, whether in the form of family and friends or a formal support group:

1. They help you stay strong in the face of loss, stress, or setbacks. They will even help you find the humor in those moments.

2. They will help you see the things you don't see in yourself and your relationships. They will change your perception of things and challenge you to grow.

3. They can help distract you from your worries, keep you feeling secure, and bring out the best in you.

4. They will provide you with guidance, support, and advice when you're at a crossroads about certain issues.

If you have friends, family, and loved ones that do this, keep them close. Never sacrifice your friendships or family relationships on the altar of your romantic ones.

If you're wondering how to get a support system in place, here are some suggestions.

1. Start volunteering. Commit to it and you will feel a sense of belonging through being around people that are working towards the same goals.

2. Engage with neighbors and colleagues at work. The conversation doesn't have to be all about work. You can talk with your coworkers about various ideas, ideologies, or issues that affect the world.

3. Start a book club. You'll not only widen your mental horizon, you'll also have the opportunity to see things in different ways through the perspectives of others.

4. Be active in your local community. Being involved in the community and making contributions to its development will provide protection for you as well.

Emotional Detoxification Worksheet

Honestly answer the following questions:

1. What are your triggers? Is there an event in your past that causes you to become angry when something similar occurs?

2. What's toxic about your reactions to those triggers? Do you inflict emotional or physical harm on others when angry?

3. What do you hope to do instead of reacting in an unhealthy manner? List your ideas.

4. How can you regulate those emotions?

5. List the bad habits that you hope to remove from your life.

6. What are some of your toxic behaviors that led you to these bad habits?

7. What are your insecurities? List them.

8. What do you hope to do to address those insecurities?

9. List out the qualities you want your future self to possess.

10. Affirm those qualities as if you already had them.

Note that you can write your wishes and affirmations on sticky notes and post them just above your desk or on your bathroom mirror as reminders. When you constantly see these affirmations, your resolve to be a better person will be strengthened.

Radical Self-Love Worksheet

1. Ignore the negative comments said about you. Write out a list of things that you love about yourself.

_____

_____

_____

2. Now that you've listed great things about yourself, write out how you intend to care for your entire being, whether it's physically or emotionally.

_____

_____

_____

3. List out the things or the people you're grateful for.

_____

_____

_____

These are some self-care techniques that I don't want you to forget:

1. Don't talk down to yourself.
2. Feel free to express your needs.
3. Be assertive when you feel that your boundaries are being violated.
4. Don't feel obligated to apologize for expressing your displeasure about a wrong.

5. Nurture yourself like you would a flower. List the things that bring you peace.

6. Let the past remain in the past. Make peace with it.

7. Make your health and happiness a priority.

8. Keep reminding yourself of your uniqueness every day.

9. Open your heart to loving again.

Self-Reflection and Self-Compassion for Healing Worksheet

1. Find a quiet, comfortable place where you won't be disturbed.

2. Take a few deep breaths and try to relax.

3. Reflect on your experiences as a victim of narcissistic abuse and try to understand how they have affected you. Acknowledge and validate your feelings.

4. Treat yourself as you would treat a friend who is going through a similar situation. Speak to yourself with kindness and understanding. Offer yourself words of comfort and encouragement.

5. Repeat positive affirmations to yourself, such as, "I am worthy of love and respect," "I am strong and resilient," and "I am deserving of a happy and fulfilling life."

6. Take some time to focus on your strengths, accomplishments, and things that bring you joy. Try to remember that your experiences do not define you, and that you have the power to create a new narrative for yourself.

7. When you are ready, slowly open your eyes and return to your day, carrying the feelings of self-compassion and self-worth with you.

Repeat this exercise as often as needed, meditate on God's Word, and try to incorporate self-reflection and self-compassion into your daily routine.

Chapter Eight Takeaway

Leaving a toxic relationship is a lot of work, and you should applaud yourself for this. However, it is equally important for you to remind yourself of what you left and the fact that you need to heal. It's easy to blame yourself for the abuse you suffered, but there is no use in that. Rather, revel in your newfound wisdom and rely on your support systems to carry you through.

You've got this!

A Much-Needed Biblical Roundup

In my experience, many Christians feel really guilty about setting boundaries. They think that it's unbecoming to say no when they're asked to make a sacrifice that they don't want to make. Well, the truth is that letting people erode your boundaries because you think that makes you look good is not a healthy way to approach life. I'll give you two important principles from the Bible to back up my views.

1. God loves a cheerful giver. Note the word: **cheerful**.

2. Even if you give up your body to be burned at the stake, without love, you're **nothing**.

Now, let's example these two principles.

2 Corinthians 9:7

"Each one must give as he has decided in his heart, not reluctantly or under compulsion, for God loves a cheerful giver."

God considers cheerfulness a really important ingredient whenever you're giving something—your money, time, energy, resources, support, or whatever. Without cheerfulness (and trust me, cheerfulness is always absent if you're feeling forced), your gift isn't acceptable to God. When you have boundaries that are clearly set, you'll have communicated without mincing words the extent to which you're willing to go for anything or anyone at any given point in time. That's you programming cheerfulness into your giving, thereby making it acceptable to God. Get it?

On point 2:

1 Corinthians 13:3

"If I give everything I own to the poor and even go to the stake to be burned as a martyr, but I don't love, I've gotten nowhere."

It's crazy, but it's possible to let people walk all over you, take your stuff without permission, show up to your house unannounced, and even gobble up your dinner, and yet you don't love them. But it's all empty—again, unacceptable to God. Doing "good things" without love is completely pointless and, if we're honest with ourselves, is just a waste of resources. Without setting boundaries, you'll inevitably find yourself having to do things that you really don't want to do even if they're supposed to be "good."

Boundary setting will keep you where you want to be. A lack of boundaries will always force you out of God's will because then you'll find yourself doing things you don't want to do for people you don't even like, and that, in God's sight, is hypocrisy.

Finding Peace with Godly Boundaries

In this world of turmoil and highly dysfunctional relationships, many people hesitate to enforce boundaries because of the initial conflict it brings. I want you to know that setting boundaries will bring you peace of mind, but I'm not going to sit here and tell you the big fat lie that you'll find that peace right away. At first, it'll most likely be full of struggles. The person you're settling boundaries against will revolt and might even resent you for a bit. Two things I want you to take note of here are:

1. Never, *never, ever* give up on your boundaries.
2. Give it time.

Even for the person setting boundaries, it can be a real tough one if you have mostly allowed people to get away with walking all over you in the past. Know for sure that this time, though it may not be easy at first, your boundaries will work as long as you stick with them.

Above all, pray for strength to go through with this and let the joy of the Lord energize you.

Here are a few Scriptures to help you find peace as you carry on with this journey:

"The Lord gives strength to his people, and the Lord blesses his people with peace." Psalm 29:11

"You will keep in perfect peace those whose minds are steadfast, because they trust in you." Isaiah 26:3

"Cast all your anxiety on him because he cares for you." 1 Peter 5:7

"I have said these things to you, that in me you may have peace. In the world you will have tribulation. But take heart; I have overcome the world." John 16:33

"Be careful for nothing; but in everything by prayer and supplication with thanksgiving let your requests be made known unto God. And the peace of God, which passeth all understanding, shall keep your hearts and minds through Christ Jesus." Philippians 4:6-7

"And let the peace of God rule in your hearts, to the which also ye are called in one body; and be ye thankful." Colossians 3:15

"Peace I leave with you, my peace I give unto you: not as the world giveth, give I unto you. Let not your heart be troubled, neither let it be afraid." John 14:27

"Depart from evil, and do good; seek peace, and pursue it." Psalms 34:14

"Now the God of hope fill you with all joy and peace in believing, that ye may abound in hope, through the power of the Holy Ghost." Romans 15:13

Conclusion

Be Gentle
With
Yourself

I'm glad that you've come this far. Toxicity comes with different faces and in different garbs. The moment you realize you're beginning to lose your sense of individuality, there's a problem. The moment you begin to seek wholeness and validation in another, you're likely to become toxic yourself. Why? You might end up manipulating another person into doing certain things just for you to feel good about yourself.

Toxicity is deeply rooted in our formative years or in past traumas—but we might not know what the other person is going through; we just feel this person is being a jerk. While we may make excuses for them depending on our relationship to them, we need to look out for ourselves. We should be careful not to form an identity out of a relationship. What if you're falling prey to someone's manipulation because you've failed to identify your own traumas? Note that traumas aren't only about what happened to you; they're also about what didn't. The first step to healing is identifying the fact that you might be an enabler of your abuse without even knowing it. Like the codependent, you're constantly pouring all of yourself into someone just to fill a void. The other person then begins to capitalize on your low self-worth to dominate you.

217

The world would be a better place if folks were committed to setting boundaries and sticking to them. If you have boundaries and are assertive about them, you won't easily become a doormat for others. Know when to say no—and when you do, mean it.

Self-awareness is a form of self-care, which will help you navigate a toxic relationship. This is how you achieve wholeness emotionally and psychologically. This is how you know when and how to set boundaries.

Practice the self-care techniques that have been mentioned in this book. If you need to, you can refer back to this book for reminders. Keep your head high.

Let the peace of the Lord keep and strengthen you, my dear reader.

I'm very glad, you've made it through Book 2!

Out of the vast sea of choices, you dove into my series and reached this point. That's truly incredible, and I am deeply grateful.

Since we're midway on this journey together, I have a small ask. **Would you take a moment to share your insights on Amazon?** Your review isn't just feedback— it's a spotlight, guiding others towards transformative lessons on setting boundaries.

Join me in spreading the word! Your insights will empower others. Can't wait to hear your thoughts as we venture into the next leg of our journey.

>> Leave a review on Amazon US <<

>> Leave a review on Amazon UK <<

BOOK #3

Independence over Codependency

A Survival Guide to End Toxic Relationships, Develop Radical Self-Love, Stop People Pleasing, and Learn How to Set Healthy Boundaries for Your Growth

Introduction

Codependency

J essica was a happy young woman who went into marriage with high hopes and expectations. She had dreams and she was ready to make them happen. Her husband seemed like a great catch—just the kind of guy she could build an amazing life with.

So, nothing prepared her for the rude awakening she experienced during her honeymoon: her husband was an alcoholic. Initially, she believed he would get better for her sake. He had to, because she loved him, and she believed he loved her—certainly more than a bottle of beer, right?

Over time, the signs became more difficult to ignore. There was more liquor than love in her house, but she continued to hold on to her dreams of a happy home and a wonderful marriage. At first, it was easy enough to take care of the house and do everything that needed to be done, including things her husband was responsible for.

The marriage wasn't getting sour just yet. She could still enjoy a good tangle in the sheets with her husband, even though the fact that he couldn't hold down a job bothered her. Kids were part of her dream marriage, so having them brought no hassle for her. She added caring for them to her list of to-dos.

Unfortunately, the weight of propping up her marriage, parenthood, and running their household soon began to show. She had an essentially irresponsible husband to cater for, she had all the house chores to attend to, and most importantly, she had her kids. She was responsible for everything and everyone, so there was no time left to attend to herself.

Eventually, love turned sour. Care was doled out with obsessive rage. Chores were done in anger. Dreams turned into toxic fantasies. But her husband was to blame for it all!

She hated herself for defending him when she'd first found out he was an alcoholic.

Hate. Bitterness. Rage. Cold responses. These behavioral patterns became her new normal. She got to the point that nothing looked beautiful and rosy to her anymore. The beautiful soul who'd had the strength to fight for her marriage initially had become completely overwhelmed by the tidal waves of negative behavior from her partner. The ugly anger that lay beneath her soul had started manifesting in every part of her life, and it had become so obvious that even her young children could discern, "Mom has gone crazy..."

Why should we care for people so much to the point of getting obsessed with them and unknowingly beginning to control them, manipulate them, get angry at them, and/or become overwhelmed and burned out by the need to take care of them while losing sight of self?

This is a manifestation of what psychologists have identified as codependence. That's not all there is to it, of course; that's why you've got this book in your possession. In this book, you'll learn the rudiments of codependency and how it operates. Have you ever looked at your current or past relationships and wondered why you behaved the way you did? No one sets out to become obsessive when they start to care for someone, but for some of us, it seems like we often find ourselves there, in a state of obsession. So, how did you get there? This book will provide you with that answer.

But just so you know, it's not all your fault. Behaviors don't just happen to people. We inherit a good number of those traits from our parents, and others we learn in childhood, from our peers or authority figures. That's why there's an entire chapter of this book dedicated to the effect your childhood has on your character as a codependent person.

If all this talk about codependence is new to you, and you're thinking that you might be codependent but you aren't sure and/or you don't know what that means—well, you're in the right place. This book will clear up your doubts. I'll share stories of people who were codependent to help you understand what people have been through and how they came out of it. We'll also cover the diverse stances of different psychologists on codependence, and what it actually means to be codependent in a relationship.

This book is also a practical workbook that will help you immensely as a part of your journey to recovery and wholeness. I'll walk you through every inch of the path to recovery; consider me your skillful self-help tour guide. Get your hiking stick ready—you're in for a great journey!

Welcome to your survival guide for ending codependency

PART ONE

UNDERSTANDING THE SITUATION

One of the greatest benefits of being a human being is the ability to form relationships with others. No matter how great you are as an individual, you'll always need social connection with others. You can see the beauty of these connections in everyday life.

A happy family at the park.

A couple whose love for each other radiates from them.

Kids playing with their beloved dog.

Unfortunately, these connections that make living worthwhile are also one of the easiest aspects of life to turn sour.

Why?

Because in some relationships, the benefits of the relationship aren't mutual. You can think of a relationship where a mother thinks of her children as an extension of herself, and consequently seeks to control every facet of their lives so they can arrive at an outcome she desires. Or think of a situation where a father is living off the kindness of his adult children while he galivants off and lives recklessly. These same negative dynamics can play out in romantic relationships as well, placing a strain on the person who has to sacrifice lots of things, including their happiness, fulfillment, dreams, and aspirations, for the sake of the other person in the relationship.

In this part of the book, we'll focus on two negative kinds of relationships—codependent relationships and narcissistic relationships—that could exist between parent and child or between romantic partners.

We'll also examine how the bond we formed with our parents as children influences our relationships as adults. There's more that we'll dive into as well, but you'll need to see for yourself. Let's jump in!

CHAPTER ONE

How Codependency Works

"Trust in the Lord with all your heart, And lean not on your own understanding."

—Proverbs 3:5 (NKJV)

"A codependent person is one who has let another person's behavior affect him or her, and who is obsessed with controlling that person's behavior."

—Melody Beattie

The Dynamics and Psychology of a Codependent Relationship

Psychologists were the first group of people to stick a label on the trait that Melody Beattie (1992) describes in the quote above, but there's no universal definition for codependency. Different psychologists, authors, and researchers have divergent perspectives on the concept. However, there are a few common traits of codependency that are shared across all definitions.

Jessica, in the story I shared in the introduction to this book, was a codependent person who was affected by the lifestyle of her alcoholic husband. But codependency doesn't always have alcohol in the mix. Let's read about another couple's story.

Ian and Alicia happened to meet and start chatting at the mall and instantly felt a spark. They found out that both of them had just gotten out of toxic relationships, so they could empathize with each other.

They decided to start off as friends, but eventually they inevitably slid into romance. After confessing their feelings for each other, they decided to start a fresh relationship together. Sounds good, right? You'd think that since they were experienced with toxic relationship dynamics, they'd be smart enough to avoid the pitfalls from their previous relationships. But sadly, it didn't work out that way.

They enjoyed the first year of their relationship; then the baggage from their past began to surface. Alicia had a spending issue. Despite her stable, well-paying job, she was often in debt. She tried to conceal the incessant calls from loan companies from Ian, and when they moved in together, she hid the fact that she still owed her old roommates on utility bills.

Let's not forget about Ian here, who in this case became the one going the extra mile to care for his partner while bearing the brunt of the stress alone. When he found out about Alicia's debts, he took it upon himself to pay them off and "fix" her life. Almost as soon as he embarked on that mission, he started feeling the repercussions on his own finances.

He had to delay paying his credit card bills. He couldn't meet his own financial needs because he was scared of declining Alicia's requests for money or assistance with her debts. Ian had a long list of things that bothered him about his girlfriend, but he never seemed to get the chance to sit down with her and talk about them.

Alicia became skillful at guilt tripping him, withholding her love and affection anytime he didn't do exactly what she wanted him to do. Ian was silently suffering; he wasn't comfortable enough with anyone else in his life to unburden himself to them. He secretly wished that Alicia would get a better paying job to sort out her debts, but that remained only a wish.

As though trouble in paradise wasn't enough, Ian was also having trouble at work. He couldn't say no to requests. He routinely worked overtime, and a lot of those hours were spent covering for the professional shortcomings of his colleagues. He worked during Christmas break because his boss demanded that he put in extra hours on an upcoming company project.

Despite knowing he needed time off to recharge, Ian kept going. The demands on his time increased, both by his job and by Alicia. He continually felt pulled in two directions, feeling increasingly angry and clueless about how to sort out his life.

As you can see, neither Alicia nor Ian's work colleagues were drug addicts or alcoholics, yet Ian is still demonstrating codependent behavior. His life ended up at the same climax of every codependent tale—bitterness and anger, where the rottenness beneath the once-beautiful soul begins to emerge, and the codependent becomes resentful and enraged by everything that happens to them. Their capacity to love and be good to others while neglecting themselves becomes overstretched, and their only response is an ugly outburst.

So, now that we've seen two examples, what does codependency mean?

Codependence isn't exactly a word you hear every day. Let's first try to understand where the word comes from.

A closer look at the word "codependence" reveals that it's formed from the combination of the prefix "co" and the word "dependence." *Dependence* is a common word; as you probably know, if you are dependent on someone or something, it means you can't do without them, right?

Co is a prefix that means "together" or "mutual."

In other words, codependents are *mutually dependent* on each other.

Is it bad to be mutually dependent? After all, most couples are mutually dependent, aren't they? Even colleagues at work can be mutually dependent on each other to get things done, right? It's true—none of us can really do anything all alone. As we mentioned in the introduction to this part of the book, we are social creatures and we rely on our relationships with others. However, there is a version of mutual dependence that can become very unhealthy, and that's what codependence is.

Now let's take a look at some signs of codependence.

Am I Codependent?

Before we look at the symptoms of codependence, let's dive into another story.

Gerald was a handsome man in his forties. He was a successful businessman, but couldn't transmit that skill into keeping his romantic relationships with women alive. His first marriage of 13 years ended in a messy divorce. He mourned his dead marriage for two months, then fell in love again. She was an alcoholic just like his first wife. He spent months trying to help her out of her addiction, but he ended up hurting himself. Instead of getting help for his partner, he became resentful because every attempt proved fruitless. She wouldn't stop drinking. Gerald was devastated and eventually ended the relationship.

A hopeless romantic, Gerald fell in love with another woman shortly after, and guess what? She was also an alcoholic. Gerald hadn't given himself time to recover from his past woes. He was in shambles himself, yet he kept throwing himself into new relationships and bearing the burdens of others.

Like Jessica, who we talked about in the introduction, Gerald remained willfully blind to his new girlfriend's problems. He defended her. He lied to himself that she wasn't the problem—he was. He tried to enjoy his relationship with her, but it only got uglier.

After a while, he felt he needed help and he went to see a counselor. After a few sessions, the therapist suggested that Gerald's problem was rooted in his family, because his father and older brother were alcoholics, and having to take care of them had affected him deeply.

The therapist brought up the idea that he might be codependent, but Gerald rejected the diagnosis and concluded that nothing was wrong with the women he had dated. Attributing the failures to simple bad luck, he hoped his luck would turn and threw himself fully into dating once more. This should not be surprising, as self-denial is a key trait of codependency (Elder, 2018).

Our focus in reading this story should not be on judging Gerald's situation. Rather, the point is to understand that you don't have to linger in a state of self-denial that leads you into the depths of pain and resentment before you come to the truth.

The following signs will help you figure out if you're codependent or not. Circle the appropriate answer after each statement.

- You're obsessed with taking care of other person's needs. **yes / no**
- You perceive yourself as completely unselfish and dedicated to the wellbeing of others. **yes / no**
- You judge what you think, say, or do as never good enough. **yes / no**
- You're embarrassed to receive recognition, praise, or gifts. **yes / no**
- You have a hard time with self-acceptance. **yes / no**

- You find it difficult to make decisions in a relationship. **yes / no**

- You keep redefining your personal boundaries to accommodate other people. **yes / no**

- You find it difficult to express your needs in a relationship. **yes / no**

- You're quick to say yes to your partner's every wish without considering the effect on you. **yes / no**

- You always make excuses for your partner's bad behavior. **yes / no**

- You've lost your sense of identity, interests, and desires. **yes / no**

- You give more to your partner than you're getting back. **yes / no**

- You become resentful when your partner declines your help or rejects your advice. **yes / no**

- You lack trust in yourself and have poor self-esteem. **yes / no**

- You're afraid of being abandoned. **yes / no**

- You depend on unhealthy people in relationships, to your own detriment. **yes / no**

- You magnify your sense of responsibility for the actions of others. **yes / no**

- Your relationships are built on conditional, controlling, and coercive behaviors. **yes / no**

- You use indirect or evasive language to avoid conflict. **yes / no**

- You believe that displaying emotion is a sign of weakness. **yes / no**

The list above isn't exhaustive; however, with that list, you should be able to establish which side of the codependent coin you're on. But there's still more you need to learn about this pattern.

Codependency in Families

A family unit is one of the relationship contexts in which codependence can be experienced. Most times this happens between parents and children. According to Lewis (2020), one of the ways to identify codependents in a family is when a parent has an unhealthy attachment to their child, going overboard to exercise excessive control over the child's life because of that attachment.

Lewis (2020) explains that, for example, a codependent parent may expect their child to keep them mentally stable and emotionally happy, essentially viewing the child as responsible for their wellbeing. Furthermore, if this behavior is perpetuated for a long enough time, it will lead to chaos and throw the family into a dark spiral of resentment and dissatisfaction.

From another perspective, when a family member struggles with addiction of any kind, it can prevent others within the family from living their own lives happily. It's not difficult to see why; our natural response is to help our family members however we can—and that's a great intention. But, as great as that is, it could also create a codependent relationship that will hurt other members of the family, and might eventually hamper the recovery of that loved one from the addictive situation.

Being emotionally connected to problems in the lives of other people can make us lose our identity, self-worth, beautiful soul, integrity, happiness, serenity, and individuality. We'll begin to compromise our boundaries and value system just to help the other person.

If you find that you constantly feel the need to save someone in your family who has a destructive behavioral pattern, or you feel drawn to someone who is struggling emotionally or physically and constantly put their needs before yours, you're tilting towards codependence.

But shouldn't you help people with such issues in your family? Quite frankly—no! Does that answer surprise you? This book isn't an advocate of selfishness or cruelty by any means. You have the liberty to help others, but your decisions shouldn't lead to severe behavioral patterns that cause you to unintentionally endorse the addictive or toxic behaviors of your family member, or lead you to go out of your way to meet their physical or emotional needs while you get lost in the midst of that genuine effort. Your beautiful soul might end up turning sour and resentful when everything that you loved about the other person begins to be darkened.

Either of your parents could be physically or emotionally attached to you in an unhealthy way, and this could make them develop obsessive behavioral patterns.

One final note: This could also be generational. Maybe you were the child of a codependent parent growing up, and now you're a parent and you're witnessing the same obsessive behavioral pattern towards your child in yourself. The things I'll share in this chapter will be helpful to you.

The Codependent Mother

Mothers are amazing caregivers, but sometimes they overdo it. And when they do, it strains their relationship with their children. Carter (2022) shares some real-life comments from mothers who unintentionally found themselves in the codependence conundrum. This could be you, too:

"My aha moment came when I paid 3 months of my 21-year-old son's rent (and skipped a mortgage payment of my own) because it's easier knowing his housing is secure than to properly and formally put boundaries in place that may require immediate investment and change from him." – @elle_acha

"One of my kids would get angry/frustrated when I asked him to do chores or follow through on things when he was little. I did a lot for him growing up. Summer before he left for college, he told me he was super worried because he didn't know how to do a lot of things for himself—like laundry, cook, make a doctor's appointment. And of course, this was my fault. I was protecting him and myself and took away the opportunity for him to feel self-sufficient and feel like he can take care of himself." – Anonymous

Dr. Ashurina Ream, a clinical psychologist, notes that codependency in mothers (or parents generally) "creates worry and internal pressure to be others-focused" (as cited by Carter, 2022).

Mothers should be part of their child's growth up to a certain stage of life. They are often so connected to their child that they know what the child is feeling or thinking. This is a great quality for a mom to have—and if you're reading this and you're a mother, you might notice this trait in yourself. But where the strain starts is when your child grows older and yet you still feel you have the same role as you did when your child was just a toddler. Once your child matures and becomes a teenager or young adult, you cannot continue to make certain decisions for them. You must realize at some point that you're not meant to tell them what to do all their lives. They'll rebel one day. Nobody likes to be controlled or to have decisions made for them.

As a mother, when you begin to overdo what you perceive to be your God-given responsibility to your children, you may also begin to lose your relationship with your partner. You'll be so focused on tending to the needs of your child (or children) that you cease to see your partner. Your romantic relationship begins to wane because you have a new priority. Additionally, out of fear of what might happen to your child if you don't do what you feel you need to do, you begin to take less care of yourself than you should. You become so attached that you no longer know the line that separates caregiving from codependency.

These are further signs that indicate you're a codependent mother. Remember to circle yes or no so you can easily track your answers.

- You find yourself fighting to control your child's behavior. **yes/no**
- You try to rescue your child from painful emotional experiences. **yes/no**
- You excessively feel the need to create a perfect world for your child. **yes/no**
- You sacrifice your romantic relationship with your partner to focus on your child. **yes/no**
- Your self-esteem is tied to your relationship with your child and their feelings, behavior, wellbeing, etc. **yes/no**
- You have a difficult time enforcing boundaries because you're afraid your child will become hostile towards you. **yes/no**
- You invest so much in your child that you gradually lose sight of yourself and abandon your own interests. **yes/no**
- You depend on your child for emotional support, which you might not always get. **yes/no**

If you've been exhibiting any of these behavioral patterns as a mother, don't panic. I know you didn't mean to go to the extreme. I understand that you want the best for your child, and that's what every good and caring mother should want. Being a codependent mother doesn't make you a bad mom; it's only an indication that you've overdone certain things, and you can rectify them.

Your child might have misinterpreted your acts of love as something else, but that's okay. You don't need to become more anxious, resentful, or hostile. Focus on channeling the same energy you've been using to release negative vibes around your home towards loving yourself and paying more attention to your own needs.

The Codependent Father

Fathers represent many things in their homes. In an ideal family setting, a father is the primary caretaker of the family. He is always around to provide support and to guide his children. He stays close behind them to catch them if they fall, both physically and metaphorically.

But you know that when we dote on people, we tend to overdo it sometimes. We may unintentionally hurt the people we dote on, or even ourselves. Just like mothers, fathers can also carry out their parental duties so excessively that they become overly attached to their child. Don't view executing your duties as a father as all there is to your life. If you feel that doing the things you do for your children is your only way to gain a sense of fulfillment, you're a codependent father.

Look, you're right to love your children. You're right to support them. You're right to stand by them. Those are amazing responsibilities that make you an amazing dad. But the moment you begin to feel you need to put more energy into carrying out your parental duties than into caring for yourself and your partner, you need to check yourself. When you start feeling you need to go out of your way to control the lives of your children and guard them from harm, then you're already beginning to slide towards codependency.

If you continue to adopt this kind of mindset, you'll no longer see yourself as a priority. You'll work and toil just to make your children happy while depriving yourself of rest and happiness. This mindset will also cause you to forget that you met your partner before you met your kids, and your romantic relationship will begin to decline. Pull yourself out of self-denial. Your identity is more than just a father.

Codependency in Romantic Relationships: What it Looks Like

I've already given you practical examples of codependency in romantic relationships. Jessica was the first example, and Gerald was another. The common thread between the two stories was the trait of self-denial. At some point in their relationships, they were under the illusion that their self-worth and actualization came from their responses to the needs of their partner. But their partners kept taking advantage of their vulnerability.

They felt guilty for not meeting their partner's needs, even if it meant neglecting their own needs. They sacrificed their aspirations on the altar of their partner's extravagance. They suffered loss of identity. They became resentful. They became hostile.

That's because what keeps relationships going for a long period of time isn't becoming the sacrificial lamb who gains nothing while losing their voice, self-worth, power, and identity. Relationships work well when partners understand the balance of meeting each other's needs without incessantly sacrificing for the other person. That balance is the ideal for any relationship.

According to Sanam Hafeez, a neuropsychologist and professor at Columbia University, (as cited by Santilli et.al, 2022), codependency in romantic relationships usually ensues from the parent-child relationship. Hafeez (2022) notes that codependent romantic relationships tend to form more often when people have had toxic relationships with a parent or other family member in the past.

But even if you are simply a naturally selfless and devoted giver in romantic relationships, with no history of codependency, you can still become codependent. To be a devoted giver isn't a bad thing, of course; it's one of the most beautiful characteristics of a beautiful soul. But if your need to give is wrapped in a need to be needed while you're excessively meeting the needs of your partner and neglecting your own, you've become codependent. And that relationship is unhealthy.

If you feel the need to apologize for everything, even for what your partner did wrong, that's another sign you could be codependent. This could be done because

234

you're scared to offend your partner or you want to keep the peace in the relationship. There's nothing healthy about a relationship where one partner begins to feed off the other. Trying to keep such a relationship alive makes you a codependent person who's deluded by self-deceit.

Why You Need to Stop Codependency

Codependency in any form of relationship is really toxic. While the codependent is trying to put everything into the relationship, the enabler (the other person, for whom the codependent is giving their all) gives nothing or very little of themselves. This type of relationship is harmful for both parties, but is especially dangerous for the codependent individual.

You have a life to live. You have dreams to pursue. You have a purpose on Planet Earth to fulfill. Being codependent will hamper all these things. If you don't want to remain under the self-deceptive illusion that Gerald was under in one of the stories I shared, you'll need to jolt yourself back to reality. It's not bad luck that put you in the codependent family or romantic relationship you're in. Don't become hostile to God. The choice to be all you've been created to be lies with you.

You can work on yourself if you've been exhibiting the signs of codependency as listed in this book. Later on, I'll show you some steps to help you stop being codependent—don't be complacent about following them. Let's get to work to get you living independently of anyone or anything.

Workbook One

Exercise One: Understanding Your Situation

This workbook will focus on helping to ascertain whether you're codependent or not. You have to recognize some of the signs that come with codependency.

Tick either yes or no.

NUMBER	QUESTION	YES	NO
1.	Are you obsessed with taking care of people's needs?		
2.	Do you neglect your own needs?		
3.	Do you ALWAYS (or 90% of the time) make excuses for people's actions?		
4.	Are you vulnerable to people's emotions?		
5.	Do you have a sense of fulfillment when you provide for people?		
6.	Is it challenging to say no to people's requests?		
7.	Is it difficult for you to talk about your needs or burden?		
8.	Do you like controlling people?		
9.	Do you trust yourself?		
10.	Are you always happy when working for people?		
11.	Do you doubt your decisions oftentimes?		

12.	Do you feel guilty when doing something for yourself?		
13.	Do people's moods affect your personality?		
14.	Do you always apologize for everything?		

If you answered YES to all or most of the above questions, then you are codependent.

Exercise Two: How Do You See Yourself?

At the core of codependency is someone who has lost so much faith in himself or herself that they view other people as more important than they are. This exercise is focused on helping you track your inner beliefs to see what damaging thoughts you might be harboring about yourself that may be fueling your codependency habits.

Examining My Self-beliefs

True or False Statements

Read each statement and write if it is true or false about your inner thoughts

1. I don't see myself as important. _____

2. People should make sacrifices for me _____

3. It's not easy to love someone like me _____

4. I'm happy even if others aren't _____

5. I'm beautiful and valued _____

6. I'll only be happy when my family is happy _____

7. I'm ready to sacrifice everything, even myself _____

8. I need to focus all my attention on protecting my loved ones

_____

9. I deserve all the happiness that this world can give

_____

10. Sometimes, I'm just a waste of space

_____

11. God must hate me

_____

12. My life is worth nothing if my loved ones aren't happy and satisfied

_____

13. I'm valuable

_____

14. I shouldn't be unhappy because I want to make
.   others happy

_____

From your answers, you'll be able to see for yourself the extent of the self-damaging thoughts that you've been harboring.

Chapter One Takeaway

Codependency is a serious problem that eats up many relationships that otherwise would have been great. The first step to thrashing out this issue is checking for sure signs that you're codependent. When you realize that you need help, half of the problem is solved.

CHAPTER TWO

The Impact of Childhood Experiences and Attachment Styles

"Fathers, do not provoke your children, lest they become discouraged."

—Colossians 3:21 (NKJV)

"All hurt is founded on attachment to anything regardless of its nature. When we detach we vibrationally send ourselves back into the flow of life."

—Dr. Jacinta Mpalyenkana, Ph.D., MBA

Does Childhood Impact Codependency?

Just like many other psychological traits, positive or negative, codependence may be rooted in childhood experiences. Most children form the basis for future relationships through their relationship with their parents. Does that apply to you?

I invite you to test this briefly. Reflect on how your relationship with your parents and other members of your family has shaped your present relationships with people.

What did you discover?

One of the things I've learned about codependency is that any child who was raised by over- or under-protective parents has a higher chance of developing codependency issues.

If you were raised by an overprotective parent, you'll remember that they shielded you from anything or anyone they perceived as a threat. That sounds good, right? But what does that loving act do to one's mental state? It takes from you the confidence to face your own threats when your parents aren't there to protect you anymore. Instead of growing a lion heart, as an adult you end up running away when confronted by situations that your parents used to protect you from.

You'll grow scared of ever stepping out to try new things because you were shielded from facing challenges or tough things as a child.

For example, your parents may have prevented you, out of pure love, from learning to ride a bicycle because they feared you would break a bone. Doesn't that sound logical? But it can only be logical up to a point in your period of development as a child. If such overprotectiveness continues as the child grows older, it creates negative psychological consequences that will influence the child's future relationships, leading to codependence on other people and making fear the basis of critical decisions.

Consider another scenario. If, in your childhood, your parents pampered you so much you couldn't acquire the basic life skills you need to survive as an independent adult, you'll always be looking for someone to fulfill those needs for you.

The reason there is an astounding number of freshman college students who have no basic household cleaning skills is due to this unhealthy type of parenting. Whatever motivated the parents to not let their child learn these skills, it isn't good for the mental formation of the child. When they become adults, they'll always feel entitled to be served and expect other people to do things for them while they enjoy a luxurious life without caring how those things get done.

This style of parenting is one of the things Amy Mitchell, in the 2016 American comedy *Bad Moms*, fights against. She takes on the responsibility of doing virtually everything around the house, including driving her two kids to school. Her husband does next to nothing at home, and her kids think they're entitled to having everything done for them, including their school assignments. Amy becomes stressed and starts to revolt against the school system that makes moms do virtually everything for their children.

She succeeds. The result? Her son starts taking responsibility for his homework. He doesn't wait for her to serve him breakfast before going to school.

Unfortunately, one of the reasons there are lots of codependents in our society today is because they were raised with this entitled mentality.

Okay, so we know lots of parents are overprotective. How do parents under-protect their children? This is the flip side of the overprotective coin. While overprotective parents give their children everything they need and more, under-protective parents do the exact opposite. They don't provide enough support for their child during their different developmental stages. This leaves the child vulnerable; the child will grow up feeling insecure and lonely and become an adult who feels less deserving of any form of love. It breeds low self-worth, low self-esteem, and low self-love.

From my own study and observation, I've seen lots of children who were raised by parents who had substance use issues as well. These children have a greater tendency towards codependency too. In this context, the child becomes the caregiver while their parent becomes the receiver. That's an unhealthy kind of relationship, and it's against the natural order. When children find themselves in such a situation, they learn to neglect their own needs to meet the needs of the parent or family member. They'll grow up feeling responsible for everyone around them, but not themselves.

People who experience this will, most times, derive happiness from other people's satisfaction—that is, they will only have a sense of satisfaction after they've met the needs of people around them.

Which side of the coin do you belong to? Have you been raised by overprotective parents or under-protective parents?

The Different Attachment Theories

Attachment theory was first propounded by two psychologists, John Bowlby and, later, Mary Ainsworth, in the 1960s and 1970s respectively. According to them (as cited by Gonsalves, 2022), people's attachment styles are shaped and developed in their early childhood. And this happens in response to their relationships with their earliest caregivers.

According to Mancao (as cited by Gonsalves, 2022), the spectrum of our attachment style ranges from how we respond emotionally to others to how we interact with our partner in relationships to how we behave generally in relationships.

The chart below is a depiction of how the four attachment styles are measured on the basis of an individual's degree of avoidance and anxiety in relationship:

Avoidant	Fearful-Avoidant
Secure	Anxious

Parents (especially moms) are often the first caregivers that children meet upon their arrival on Earth. Although parents' roles are numerous, they have one important one in the midst of the many: just being there.

The influence parents have on children through their presence cannot be overemphasized. A parent's presence makes a child feel loved and secure. Just being there is what also produces attachment.

As portrayed in the chart above, there are four basic types of attachment:

- Secure attachment
- Anxious-insecure attachment
- Avoidant-insecure attachment

- Fearful-avoidant attachment (also known as disorganized-insecure attachment)

Let's examine each of these attachment styles in greater detail.

Secure Attachment

This is the best identified form of attachment. It's an attachment that forms a secure and loving relationship with other people. This kind of attachment is formed when parents or caregivers are available, sensitive, accepting, and responsive.

Parents who form a secure attachment with their children allow them the freedom to spend time with their friends and with other kids in the community. But they also wait for their children to come back to hear about how they spent their day and to comfort them during hard times if the need arises.

One of the processes that also leads to the formation of this attachment style is when parents learn to have fun with their children. Through play and fun activities, the child learns to express positive and negative emotions and receives the right responses from the parent. Children who develop a secure attachment style don't have issues trusting people. They have a good sense of self-worth and self-esteem. They don't doubt what they're capable of doing. These are the kinds of children who grow up into well-rounded adults and go on to have healthy relationships.

That's what we're aiming for!

Trust, love, and acceptance are common traits for securely attached people. They feel sufficient in themselves and they don't feel their happiness in life is dependent on their partner.

Anxious-Insecure Attachment

What do you think an anxious attachment will produce? That's right—fear. There's no way an anxious attachment can be secure. It's an insecure attachment style that is laced with fear of abandonment.

This attachment style is formed when parents are not always available to attend to the needs of their child. Since the parents are distant, either physically or emotionally, the child cannot trust the parents to be around when needed. Therefore, the child has no guarantee of security coming from the attachment figure. The result is that the child will be afraid to explore since there's no guarantee of safety from the parent.

The child will sometimes activate a distress mode, hoping this will compel their parent to respond. The child will also become needy and resentful. When these people grow into adults, they're unlikely to feel secure in their relationships. They'll be afraid that their partner might abandon them in the same way their parents usually did. Thus, they'll desperately seek reassurance and validation from their partner.

Avoidant-Insecure Attachment

This attachment style is a bit different from the anxious attachment style. Even children are aware when their parents are trying to avoid them, and it creates an insecure attachment. For whatever reason, some parents might find it difficult to accept or respond sensitively to the needs of their child.

For example, when the parent refuses to comfort the child when needed, but instead chooses to reject and reduce the child's feelings, it can produce an avoidant-insecure attachment. The parent may also refuse to assist with difficult tasks. The child will then begin to consider the parent nonexistent since the parent refuses to respond when needed.

The child is thus trained from that tender stage to lock up their feelings and not expect anything from anyone. They feel there's no point in expressing emotions since they have no one to share them with. Such children grow up to be adults who are not moved to tears by sad or touching events, and even when they feel pain, they refuse to show it.

They grow up believing that nothing good can come from relationships, and therefore, there's no need to trust anyone. These kinds of people prefer to be independent and consider romantic relationships stressful. If they are in a relationship, they try to maintain emotional distance from their partner.

Fearful-Avoidant (Disorganized-Insecure) Attachment

This is the worst form of attachment and the most hazardous for any relationship. In many cases, you won't want to share the same room with people who grew up with this form of attachment. It's almost certain the relationship will be toxic and not produce anything good—at least, not unless some serious steps are taken.

I say all that because children who have formed a fearful-avoidant attachment style with their parents were rejected, ridiculed, and frightened by their parents. Parents that display this kind of hostility towards their children are often those who have an ugly past themselves, such as some form of trauma. Unfortunately, the only thing such parents can give to their child is negativity, instilling fear and insecurity in the child.

This final attachment style is also known as disorganized-insecure because, unlike the first three attachment styles where the child is organized and consistent in their behavioral pattern, the child's strategy here is disorganized and inconsistent. This also influences the child's behavioral pattern. In order to feel safe apart from their parents, children who form this attachment style become aggressive in adult relationships, refuse to care for others, and are entirely self-reliant.

This attachment style is rare, but unfortunately, many people who form this type of attachment in childhood will grow into violent partners.

Identifying Your Attachment Style

Each of us was raised in different contexts by different parents. Our behavioral patterns in our relationships with others are partly due to the attachment style we formed with our parents in our childhood. That means that there's a link between your relationships as an adult and the type of relationship you had with your parents during your childhood.

John Bowlby, a British developmental psychologist and psychiatrist, wrote a lot about attachment theory. He showed how each attachment style begins to come together from as early as infanthood.

The following are signs of each type of attachment in adults so that you can assess your attachment style.

Secure Attachment

People with this attachment style:

- Have high self-esteem
- Can control their emotions
- Have no issues trusting other people
- Have great communication skills
- Can seek emotional support
- Feel comfortable being alone
- Have good conflict management skills
- Are comfortable in close relationships
- Are able to self-reflect in relationships
- Are easy to connect with
- Manage conflict well
- Are emotionally available
- Are not scared to share feelings with partners and friends

Anxious Attachment

People with this attachment style:

- Are sensitive to criticism
- Are often clingy and/or jealous
- Are afraid of being alone
- Suffer from low self-esteem
- Feel unworthy of love
- Have a fear of rejection
- Have a fear of abandonment
- Can't trust others easily

Avoidant Attachment

People with this attachment style:

- Have issues with intimacy
- Are almost emotionless in social and romantic relationships
- Are unwilling to share their thoughts or feelings with others
- Avoid emotional intimacy
- Avoid physical intimacy
- Have a sense of independence
- Have difficulty trusting people
- Feel threatened by anyone who tries to get close
- Enjoy being alone
- See no need to have others around them

Fearful-Avoidant Attachment

This attachment style creates:

- Contrasting behavioral patterns
- Fear of rejection
- Unstable emotions
- Anxiety
- Inability to trust people

You can test where you belong on the attachment style chart by paying attention to these signs in your own behavior. Whatever you find out, especially if you turn out to have an insecure attachment, it's just an indication of your current state. It doesn't imply you'll be tied to that style forever. In fact, that's why you have this book in your hands: you can form a new, healthy attachment style because you have the capacity to change and form new behavioral patterns.

How Your Attachment Style Is Formed

How did your attachment style develop? Most attachments develop at a very tender age. Mental health counselor Grace Suh (as cited by Gonsalves, 2022) says that the relationship parents develop with their children in the first 11 months of existence is paramount in the formation of the child's attachment style.

If you've been paying attention to the last few sections, you should have realized by now that it's not entirely your fault that you behave the way you do. Because, really, what could you possibly have done to change something for yourself when you were just 11 months old? Your behavioral formation is first dependent on your parents or primary caregivers.

Generally, even though babies can't speak, they still have a mode of communication with their parents. Attachment is formed based on the parents' response to that communication. If you're a parent, keep in mind that your responses to your baby in the first few months of life will shape what becomes the bedrock of their future relationships.

What kind of responses lead to the development of each attachment style?

Secure Attachment

Responses:

Consistent availability and being sensitive to needs.

You felt safe and secure in childhood because your parents were always there for you. You got reassurance from your parents for certain actions, comfort when you were hurt, and loving discipline when you erred.

This response builds up to make you feel valued, loved, safe, and understood in your early interactions with your parents.

The responses you got from your parents at that stage of your life indicate that your parents were emotionally stable themselves.

Anxious Attachment

Responses:

Inconsistent availability, unpredictable affection, and occasional withdrawal.

249

This response instills fear, especially fear of being abandoned, in children. If in your childhood your parents were not always available to attend to your needs or comfort you when needed, you'll likely grow up into an adult who's scared of trusting people you're in a relationship with.

You'll look for constant reassurance from your partner that you're still needed in the relationship.

Avoidant Attachment

Responses:

Dismissive and distant. Disconnected from the needs of the child.

This kind of response leads the child to believe that nothing valuable could come to them from relationships; thus, they grow up with the mentality of being self-reliant, and they avoid any form of emotional expression.

They view relationships as burdensome and, if they are in a relationship, try to avoid meaningful conversations or maintain emotional distance from their partner.

Fearful-Avoidant (Disorganized) Attachment

Responses:

Outright neglect and/or abuse. Frightening and traumatizing.

This attachment style is the most extreme of all four styles. Here, the child has no sense of what a healthy relationship looks like. It's difficult for people in this category to trust people in relationships. Their behavioral pattern is usually disorganized because their parents were a source of both comfort and fear.

Changing an Unhealthy Attachment Style

In a personal blog, Seth Blais (2020) shares his personal story of traumatic experiences during childhood. Those experiences shaped his adulthood, especially his relationships with people. The attachment he formed with his parents was the extreme one: fearful-avoidant or disorganized attachment. As a boy, he became acquainted with violence as a rite of passage, a critical event in his childhood experience. He grew up in a dysfunctional family under the rule of an abusive and emotionally unavailable father who had his own problems to deal with. Seth's emotional needs were unintentionally neglected, and therefore he grew up with feelings of abandonment and fears that his future romantic relationships would have the same outcome.

His story is a rare case of fearful-avoidant attachment. Can such people be helped? Yes! It's possible to change an unhealthy attachment style as an adult—unless you want to remain as you are, that is, doling out negativity to the people around you.

Here comes the golden question: "How can I change my unhealthy attachment style?"

1. Recognize and Admit

The first step to changing an unhealthy attachment is to be sincere with *yourself* to recognize that the attachment you formed with your parents as a child could be responsible for your current relationship woes. Essentially, you must admit that the relationship you had with your parents or primary caregiver as a child has shaped (or is still shaping) your present-day relationships.

To do this is to take the first and most critical step toward liberation—liberation from the influence of unhealthy childhood experiences on your adult life.

2. Be Willing to Change

Bowlby, the first psychologist to promulgate attachment theory, didn't believe we could change our attachment style. However, advanced studies in neuroscience have proven that people can indeed change the way their brain works.

But you know how these things are; change doesn't come served to you on a golden platter. Rewiring the brain to work differently from how it's been used to working over many years is extremely difficult—almost impossible. However, it can be done. The key factor that will help you stay in the process of transformation is your willingness to make the change.

Sure, you might want a change in your behavioral pattern… but are you willing to put in the work to make that change happen?

3. Raise Your Self-Esteem

Each form of insecure and unhealthy attachment dampens your self-esteem. At the extreme of the attachment spectrum is a battered self-esteem. However, irrespective of the level of damage, your self-esteem can be recovered.

Although you may have been raised in an atmosphere that took your self-esteem from you, you can create an atmosphere that lets you see how valuable and lovable you are. Be assured that you're not a bad person. You only grew up in a toxic relationship, which taught you that you're less deserving of love and attention. But that's a lie. You deserve all the love in the world. And you deserve to be listened to. Your needs are valid.

Raise your self-esteem with the truth about *you* that I just shared. It'll take you further in changing your unhealthy attachment style.

4. Confront the Real Need

Insecure attachment styles develop due to how our parents responded to our needs. As adults, when we allow that style to linger in our relationships with people, the real underlying issue is that we still have needs, but we feel that if we share those needs with our partner, we'll get the same response we got from our parents in childhood. Thus, we sometimes choose not to express our needs for fear of re-experiencing what happened in the past.

Securely attached people have healthy relationships because they know how to express their needs. Thus, if you want to enjoy good relationships with people, learn to express your needs sincerely.

Childhood experiences are life-shapers, both positive and negative. But the good news is that as adults, we can fix whatever was broken during our childhood. If having a great life of self-actualization and purposeful accomplishment is your goal, committing *yourself* to change is a worthy effort.

Workbook Two

Exercise One

Circle and write your answers.

- Do you think your parents were overprotective? YES / NO
- Write down four things you wish you had done during childhood that your parents didn't permit.

1.

_____

2.

_____

3.

_____

4.

_____

- How did not doing those things affect you?

_____

_____

_____

- Do you think your parents were under-protective? YES / NO
- Write down four things your parents were supposed to do for you that you had to do by yourself.

1.

_____

2.

_____

3.

_____

4.

_____

Exercise Two

In light of the discussion about attachment styles, which of the four styles do you belong to, and why do you think this is the style that best describes you?

_____

_____

_____

_____

_____

Do you like the attachment style that you have?

_____

_____

How has this style affected you (whether positively or negatively) in times past?

_____

_____

_____

Chapter Two Takeaway

Your attachment style is intricately linked to the issues you are having now with codependency. It's important to identify your attachment style in order to arm yourself with more useful information as you proceed on this healing journey. Feel free to go back into the exercises to be sure that you've identified your attachment style correctly. Now it's time to take a look at something else that's closely linked to codependency: narcissism.

CHAPTER THREE

Codependency and Narcissism

"Before destruction the heart of a man is haughty, and before honor is humility."

—Proverbs 18:12 (NKJV)

"To a narcissist they always take the lead, they want to dominate the conversation and make things about themselves. Their sense of importance makes them think that as their partner, you are there to serve them…"

—Courtney Evans

The Relationship between Codependency and Narcissism

Naina didn't know what narcissism was until she had a firsthand experience in the space of 12 months.

She was introduced to the "love of her life," Jeff, through a family friend. They got off to a great start; the young man seemed like a great, kind, and respectable person.

Early in their dating relationship, he showered her with gifts and affection, like she was all that mattered to him. They went on extravagant and romantic dates. Their relationship blossomed, or so it seemed. She thought that if she could marry such an amazing man, it would be happily ever after.

They got engaged in a matter of weeks. That was when it dawned on Naina what kind of man she had tied the knot with and things began to sour. However, she tried to shut her eyes to the slight changes she noticed in him. The changes in his character had begun to unfold in the weeks leading up to their marriage, but she had always defended him. They'd fought and disagreed over issues before marriage, but she'd decided to let them slide each time.

To keep the marriage alive, Naina allowed Jeff to control her in every way he wanted. She sheepishly did whatever he told her to do. Despite this, her husband cheated on her, and her in-laws were as cruel and aggressive towards her as the lord of hell himself. They rejected her, and they made it clear. Naina was gaslighted, restricted from visiting her family or friends, verbally abused, and ridiculed until she mustered the strength to walk away from the marriage.

Naina's husband is just one of many narcissists walking the streets of our communities. You might have met one yourself. And if you have, you might have seen a glimpse of what it means to live with one. When you live with one, you're basically living in a state of confusion.

The word "narcissism" is used in different contexts today, but it has a specific connotation in psychology. Narcissism is not an appreciation of self in the genuine sense. People with narcissistic personality have an idealized image of themselves. They're in love with this magnified self-image. They only feel uneasy whenever their narcissistic confidence is threatened. This tendency makes people with narcissistic personality take others for granted or exploit them. People with this personality are not just hostile to the people around them, but they also don't feel or understand the effect of their behavior on other people.

Narcissism is a personality trait, but it is also a personality disorder. Not everyone who has a narcissistic tendency has narcissistic personality disorder (NPD); people at the lower end of the narcissist spectrum only exhibit some of its traits. It's those at the highest point of the spectrum that fall into the NPD category.

Just like Naina's husband, narcissists are often charming and confident. At the outset of their relationships, they don't usually show any negative tendency right away. At that stage it's difficult to know their true nature.

Narcissism vs. Codependence

Narcissism and codependency are similar in that they are connected to a distorted view of self. Both categories of people place a lot of importance on what people think about them. To get a sense of their self-worth, they need people. The only difference is that their method of getting validation from people differs.

Narcissists have an excessive focus on themselves. Everything in the room must be about them, and if that doesn't happen, they explode. And when they do explode, they don't care what effect it has on other people.

Narcissists always need people's affection and admiration to feel good about themselves.

On the other hand, codependents are often excessively focused on others. In their distorted perspective of themselves, their essence, relevance, and esteem come from meeting the needs of other people. In their zeal to serve others, they may assume control and dominance over the person they're trying to help because they perceive that what they're doing for the person is what's best for them.

Unlike narcissists, they don't need people to magnify their image; they just want to feel needed.

One other similarity between the two personality traits is that both are excessive in their expressions.

Signs That You're Being Abused by a Narcissist

The signs that point to the fact that you're in a toxic relationship with a narcissist are usually accompanied by some excessive negativity. Merciless violation of boundaries, manipulation, and demeaning treatment that make you lose your sense of self-worth are all signs that you're in a relationship with a narcissist.

Also, when you feel like you no longer know yourself, and you've been so devalued that you feel worthless, know that you're almost certainly being abused by a narcissist.

Other signs include:

1. Broken hedge

Narcissists enjoy breaking through the "hedge" of their victims. Thus, their victims are handicapped—their power to make independent choices is taken away from them. Some victims have reported that they no longer have me-time or security because their arrogant abuser takes the liberty of going through their personal stuff, including their personal journal or private emails.

It can get so bad that the victim can't make independent decisions about their own body. Their body is cruelly violated, and its care is at the beck and call of their abuser. If this is you, your partner is a narcissist.

2. Aggressive threats of physical violence

Narcissistic abusers are obnoxious con artists who focus on emotional manipulation. They can achieve this through different vicious acts, including violent outbursts, self-harm, and other scary episodes. They crave attention and will do whatever they deem necessary in their distorted mind to achieve it.

3. Verbal abuse

Does your partner derive joy and self-satisfaction from insulting you till you don't trust your personal judgment? Your partner is probably a narcissist. Verbal abuse is one of the tools at the disposal of narcissists, used to belittle their partner. They may even make a joke of the verbal abuse or say things subtly, but it's always done to degrade the victim.

4. Public destruction of image

Narcissists are also good at manipulating their partners by lying about them to trusted loved ones. With that, their victims are at their mercy. They distort valuable information about their partners and share it with those whom their victims esteem highly. This ruins the public image or social standing of the victimized.

5. Overwhelming self-doubt

When you're in a relationship with a narcissist, one of the telling signs is that you'll begin to doubt yourself. The battering, blaming, and accusations from your partner will make you feel uncertain about things, including yourself. At this point, the victim will have no other choice than to seek validation from the narcissist about anything they want to do.

6. Isolation from other people

Narcissists take their cruelty further, doing anything they can to push their victim's friends and kin away. Victims of this form of abuse will also intentionally isolate themselves because they feel ashamed of their situation, or because they're afraid no one will understand them, and thus they feel it's best to withdraw and be alone.

Understanding the Tactics of a Narcissist

Neuharth (2017) suggests a number of tactics narcissists employ to victimize the people in their circle. Let's have a look at his list:

1. **Emotional appeals:** This happens when a narcissist plays on the victim's emotions using logic and reasoning in order to conceal their own false claims and, eventually, control their victim.

2. **Peer groups:** Narcissists join groups where their self-image and ideas are propagated. Within such groups, they feel important and gain a sense of satisfaction because they're with people who support what they do. In turn, they use this to victimize their partner or people around them by mounting pressure on them to join the bandwagon, or make them feel guilty that they're missing out on something good if they don't.

3. **For or against:** Narcissists usually narrow all options to just two: "You're either with me or against me."

4. **Always right:** Narcissists hate to be wrong. If someone tries to prove them wrong, they constantly try to thwart that effort. Even when you spot their errors and successfully point them out, they either dismiss it or change the subject entirely.

5. **False flattery:** Narcissists are as devious and subtle with their compliments as with their critiques. They give insincere compliments because they want something in return.

6. **Labeling:** Narcissists feel most powerful when they're able to attach humiliating labels to their victims.

7. **Empty promises:** Narcissists can easily throw around grandiose promises, but they never have any intention of fulfilling them.

8. **Gaslighting:** Narcissists get at their victims by quoting a part of whatever their victims have said, twisting it, and using it against them. When they do this, they make their victim launch into defensive mode to defend themselves. And when the victim fails at self-defense, which the abuser will ensure happens, they'll begin to doubt themselves. They may even arrive at the point of thinking they've got a dysfunctional mind that can't be trusted to retain information.

9. **Ridicule:** Narcissists don't take other people seriously. They dole out sarcastic comments to ridicule the acts or speech of their victim.

10. **Dehumanization:** Narcissists have a superiority complex. They treat every other person as inferior and they make it obvious, such that people around them feel small and not good enough.

A few other tactics narcissists use are:

- Lying
- Oscillating between cruelty and charm
- Discouragement
- Diminishing others' accomplishments
- Criticism
- Dismissing people
- Stalking
- Intruding
- Emotional blackmail

- Guilt tripping
- Objectifying
- Threats
- Blaming
- Shaming
- Feigning innocence
- Brainwashing

Recovery and Healing from Narcissism

I've met with victims of narcissism who have been so damaged psychologically that they've accepted and adapted to the maltreatment they receive from their narcissistic partner. Sometimes they even feel they deserve what they're getting.

In fact, some become so delusional that they find a way to numb their pain and suffering because they think it's a normal way of life. Others feel their partner truly does love them, and that's why he/she treats them the way they do.

People with such perspectives are difficult to help. Until they're ready to step out of their delusional state, they'll not be free.

It's only those who desire help that'll get it. If you desire to be free and healed and to recover from the psychological abuse you're suffering at the hands of your abuser, here are things I'd suggest you do:

Stage 1: Admit the Truth

- **Admit you're in an abusive relationship:** Some victims of narcissistic relationships don't believe their partner is treating them badly. They believe they deserve what they're getting because their abuser makes it seem so. But until you admit you're being abused, you'll never believe you need help.

David Tzall, a licensed psychologist in New York, notes (as cited by Cox, 2022) that the first step to healing from a narcissistic relationship is to acknowledge that abuse has occurred and has had a serious impact on your life. Tzall states that admitting this will help you to make sense of your experiences and emotions.

To get to this point, you'll need to know the signs and symptoms of a narcissistic relationship (I've already written about this in previous sections of this book). This will help you to diagnose your situation and better assess what you're going through.

Educating yourself about this issue is vital to getting to the point of admitting the truth.

- **Admit you're not the problem:** One of the strategies of narcissists is to manipulate the mind of their victim to believe that they're problematic. A narcissist will always point out your errors and weaknesses and make you believe that you deserve to be treated the way you're being treated.

That's far from the truth. If they're truly helping you to be better, why is it that you've lost your sense of self-worth? How is it that you no longer believe in yourself? Why do you think less of yourself if they've been helping you to be better all this time?

You're not the problem—they are! It's true you're not perfect, but no one is! Not even your abuser. Therefore, anyone who's using your weakness against you so that they can manipulate you emotionally, and then turn it all on you as if you're the problem, is narcissistic.

- **Admit you need help:** Being in an abusive relationship drains you of a lot of the strength you could have used to ward off your abuser or even get out of the relationship. This is why you need help, and you need to admit it.

You'll get so little from this book if you don't admit you need help. This book was put together to help you out of that abusive relationship. Your acknowledgment of this will prepare you and open your mind to accept my counsel.

Stage 2: Act Now

- Go for the life preserver

When someone is sinking, a life preserver helps them to stay afloat. Being in a narcissistic relationship is like falling off a ship into a sea of stormy waters. The inability to swim (or navigate the abusive relationship) will naturally put you in danger of drowning. There's no school or institution that prepares you for what to expect in such a relationship. But when it happens, a life preserver will come in handy.

Your life preserver in this context could be your body. According to the National Alliance on Mental Illness (NAMI), you can heal your mind through your body. Tzall (as cited by Cox, 2022) explains that trauma is stored in the body and mind, but you can release it by engaging in a form of exercise that helps you release the grief, rage, and hurt. Running, kickboxing, and dance cardio are examples of exercises NAMI recommends.

NAMI also suggests that listening to empowering music or positive affirmations can reinforce the effect of the exercise and help you control your emotions when the negativity you're trying to release starts to get hold of your mind.

A life preserver could also come in the form of engaging in a creative exercise. In 2018, the National Center for Biotechnology Information (NCBI) carried out a study where they asked a group of participants to create artwork based on the theme of nature, religion, and colors. This exercise was carried out in about eight 75-minute sessions. As the participants continued this exercise, they expressed their trauma through their art, but over time the rate at which they did so began to decline; instead, they began to create something more positive.

You can release trauma and its negative effects on you through artistic hobbies like writing, painting, drawing, and playing and/or writing music. You can also share this with the world as proof that healing and recovery from abusive relationships is possible.

Another life preserver could be joining a support group. The good thing about a support group is that you don't have to be ashamed of your experiences because you know you're with people who've had similar journeys. In such a group, you can get the right encouragement and the inner strength you need to confront your psychological issues.

Rebuild the hedge

Did you remember that one of the things narcissists do is to defy your boundaries and break past your "hedge" into your personal space? They ensure your boundaries are so porous that they can freely intrude any time they want to.

Continuing on this track of recovery, you can begin to rebuild those boundaries. You could start with securing your personal time so that your abuser cannot intrude or question what you're doing. It could also be something as simple as putting a lock password on your phone.

You shouldn't be emotional about doing this. Don't worry about what your abuser will think. Just focus your energy on rebuilding the hedge. With that, you can decide who or what goes in or out of your space. Even when your narcissistic partner returns and tries to wriggle back into your space, the boundary will hedge them out, putting *you* in charge of your life once again.

An important boundary to set is on the definition of who you are. Up till now, you've probably been taking in just about everything your abuser says about you. You must draw a line on that. Take away that right from them. Their comments about who you are shouldn't sway you anymore.

This implies that during this recovery process, you must begin to rediscover your true image. Whatever you discover about yourself is the truth, not what someone who has been taking advantage of you says.

You'll also have to draw the line on the extent to which your abuser can influence your choices. One form of proof that you're no longer under their control is that you can make decisions independent of your abuser. These choices include how you spend your money, where and whom you visit, what and when you eat, and what you wear on your body.

Note: The easiest way to give a narcissist control over your life is to tell them personal things about yourself. They'll gladly take the information and use it to manipulate and hurt you. It's vital that you draw a line on how much of your information you divulge to them, if you need to at all.

Plan to set sail again

While you're building the hedge, you should also make plans to set sail again. That is, make plans to get your life back on track. While you're in that toxic relationship, you were denied a lot of good things. You sacrificed dreams, purpose, aspirations, wishes, and goals on the altar of narcissism. But the good news is you can set sail again.

Your experience as a victim of a narcissistic relationship might not be so extreme that you lost your job, but a narcissist can still deprive you of some activities that give you pleasure. Think, for example, of the places you wanted to travel but your abuser refused to let you. It's time to make plans for that journey now.

Your life shouldn't be stuck because of someone else. Get your life on track again and do those things you've always loved to do. If you lost a job during the relationship, apply for another, or start your own venture if you'd like. Be enthusiastic to set sail again. You're now the captain of the ship of your life; you can steer the course to whichever direction you desire. Having quieted that external voice that usually dictates the coordinates of your life and got you stuck in the first place, you are now free to set your life in motion again.

Take that professional class. Oh, is it a music lesson or a cooking class you're interested in? Go for it!

You must go for the things you've always imagined doing. There's no better time than now to do them. Stop settling for pseudo-happiness hemmed with tons of regret and self-pity. Your happiness is now your responsibility.

Stage 3: Build Appreciation

Forgive yourself

In this third stage, the first thing you'll need to do is to forgive yourself. Don't think of it as a one-time thing, either, where you can just say, "Okay, I forgive myself for defending my abuser." That's not enough! Or you might be inclined to say, "I forgive myself. Now what...?"

Forgiveness doesn't work that way. It's not something you just say casually without being sincere about it.

This is how forgiveness works on you psychologically: you'll know you've forgiven yourself if you can remember an event that used to make you feel angry and bitter towards yourself, but it no longer does. Generally, the effect of unforgiveness is anger, but when you stop feeling negatively about yourself every time you remember your past mistakes, you're beginning to forgive yourself.

To forgive yourself is to let go of past hurts.

Stop holding things against yourself. It can halt this recovery process. You're not stupid to have gone into that relationship in the first place. You went into it because you were in love. And it's not wrong to love. You just didn't see the signs because they were subtly concealed.

However, forgive yourself for choosing to love. Forgive yourself for not seeing the signs. Forgive yourself for defending the abuser. Don't ever blame yourself for those things. You didn't choose a narcissist. It's love you chose, and you can't blame yourself for choosing to love.

If you think you should have known better because you're smart and intelligent, then I need to remind you that you're not a superhuman, and you have emotions too. Anyone, regardless of intelligence, status, or background, could be a victim.

Stop blaming yourself for how the relationship turned out. Accept that you're human and you're prone to mistakes. Admit and embrace your vulnerability, and never feel bad for whatever happens to your abuser.

Repeat this over and over again till your mind is able to let go of the past completely.*

Discover how to challenge negative thought patterns through Worksheet #7 from BONUS #1 or check this QR code.

Anticipate grief

If you think that now that you're beginning to get a hold on your life again, you won't have moments of grieving, you're mistaken. Coming out of a traumatic experience causes grief occasionally. You might find yourself longing for your abuser. You might feel sorry for them or consider giving them another chance. There are times you might even feel you miss them because of the days they lavished you with love. You might feel like you shouldn't have left them in the first place. You might blame yourself for not giving them enough chances to get better.

Don't worry, all of these are normal psychological reactions to the grief you're going through. Your mind is taking time to adjust and heal, so you shouldn't expect that all those experiences will be wiped away in a single moment.

Another form of grief you could feel is shame. During your recovery process, there'll be times you reflect on your past experiences and how you got into that situation and feel ashamed of yourself. You could be ashamed that you stooped so low as to accept such maltreatment despite your intellectual, financial, or family status. It could arouse anger and bitterness against yourself.

You could also feel ashamed for ending a romantic relationship you've broadcasted to others in your life so much.

Those feelings are legitimate as well. It's all part of the recovery process. It's just like how medicine that can heal an illness may leave a bitter taste in your mouth. It doesn't negate the fact that you're recovering. Therefore, don't let any of those feelings get to you. They're transient. They'll dissipate with time.

You can distract your thoughts when you catch yourself in that puddle of negative feelings. Try going over those exercises I recommended in the first stage of recovery again, especially the one that has to do with expressing your emotions through exercise and creative arts. Do this for as long as you need to in order to distract your mind from thoughts of the past.

Get your gaze back on your recovery process!

Find *you*

One of the dangers of being in a narcissistic relationship is that you lose your sense of identity. Your passion, values, and beliefs usually get lost in such a relationship. It's only through the recovery process that you can rediscover yourself. Therefore, during this recovery process, focus your attention on self-rediscovery. You won't be able to find happiness and fulfillment if you're unable to find *you*.

Rediscover your passion.

Rediscover your values.

Rediscover your beliefs.

Rediscover YOU!

There's something unique about you. Find it again.

Your voice was silenced in that toxic relationship. You can find it again. Your voice deserves to be expressed. It's been muffled for so long.

This is possible if you begin to practice what I'll recommend next.

Cultivate self-love

Happiness and peace with yourself thrive in the environment of love. In place of the rage and bitterness you used to feel during the traumatic experience, cultivate love. Love emits positive energy against the toxicity of rage and bitterness.

Love yourself without restriction. You have permission to do so. There are many ways you can do this:

- Accept your personality.
- Acknowledge your imperfections and allow yourself to grow during the recovery process.
- Be kind to yourself when you err.
- Learn to choose yourself over and over again as the first person who deserves your attention.
- Prioritize your wellbeing.
- Treat your body with respect by eating good food, resting enough, and exercising properly.
- Always be thankful you survived the traumatic experience.
- Affirm to yourself how unique you are.
- Be patient with yourself during the recovery process.

- Allow yourself to grow at your own pace without comparison to others.
- Be committed to your recovery.
- Don't indulge in self-pity.
- Invest in your growth and mental development.
- Be determined and disciplined to become better daily.

Also, engage in activities that promote your self-esteem, self-worth, and happiness, and that give you a sense of purpose. Be intentional about this.

It's important to note that this process will take time to crystalize into tangible results. You must be persistent and insist on seeing the process through. You deserve to be loved and cared for.

Forgive your abuser

Holding on to the grief of the past is like tying a rock to your neck. Once you dive into the river, you'll drown. No one wants that for themselves. Unforgiveness gives your abuser the power to control your emotions. Whenever you remember all you went through at their hands, you'll certainly feel embittered, but this will only arouse negative energy in you, even though they're no longer with you. Don't give them that much power again.

Forgive them. Let go. It's not possible to forget the experience totally, but you can choose how you respond to it whenever you remember it. Instead of feeling bitterness and rage towards your abuser, be compassionate towards them. They're suffering, but they don't know it. Speak to yourself as if you were talking to them: "Though I feel awful about everything you did to me, I won't allow you to hurt me any further. I choose to let go. I forgive you. I want peace. I want happiness. If I don't forgive you, I'll still have the gall of bitterness in my heart. So for my sake, I forgive you."

You might not choose to say those exact words—feel free to use your own—but repeat it over and over again every time you remember your abuser.

Craft your experience into a tool

Having experienced what it means to be a victim of a narcissistic relationship and, now, an independent soul, take time to reflect on the lessons you learned from those experiences. You can use those lessons to help so many other people out of that situation. For example, Melody Beattie, author of *Codependent No More: How to Stop Controlling Others and Start Caring for Yourself*, decided to write the book after having been codependent herself. Now, her books are helping lots of people in similar situations beyond what she could ever have imagined.

You might not become a writer. But even if it's a small community you're going to raise around you, go ahead and do just that. The most important thing is that you're helping other people get out of darkness and into light.

Become the lifesaver that throws life preservers to drowning souls when they cry out for help.

Don't rush into another relationship

Dear reader, enjoy your independence! Don't be in a rush to get into another relationship when you're yet to fully recover from the hurts of the previous one.

Allow yourself to heal. Then allow yourself to find yourself and live to the fullest. Don't be under any pressure to jump into a new relationship. Just enjoy your independence. Take time to develop your relationships with people. You don't have any obligation to go beyond the surface level in your relationships with anyone just yet, and that includes your close relatives, colleagues, or neighbors. Don't doubt your ability to love someone again, but give it time.

Workbook Three

Exercise One

Write down three instances when someone you care about made you feel devalued or worthless.

_____

_____

_____

Would you call this person from the answer above a narcissist?

_____

_____

_____

Which of the narcissistic tactics do you feel you've suffered from the most? (Examples: gaslighting, victim playing, projection, etc.)

_____

_____

_____

How long have you been dealing with this narcissist?

_____

_____

_____

Do you feel like you're too weak to break free from them?

_____

_____

_____

_____

If yes, why do you think you're weak?

_____

_____

_____

If not, what attributes or advantages do you have right now that put you a step ahead of this narcissist? Write down five of these.

_____

_____

_____

_____

_____

What will you do if the narcissist fights back?

_____

_____

_____

Based on the information in this chapter, what do you think is the next best thing for you to do now?

_____

_____

_____

Do you have support systems to help you as you break away from the narcissistic relationship? Write down these people's names and why you've chosen them.

(E.g., "Aunt Mary because she's kind and has been there for me in the past.")

_____

_____

Chapter Three Takeaway

Codependency and narcissism are two negative behavioral patterns that ruin relationships. They're direct opposites that attract like magnets. If you're codependent, chances are that a narcissist is in your life. However, regardless of the impact of the damage, there's hope for redemption. Healing and recovery are possible, as this chapter has proven.

PART TWO

SOLUTIONS THAT WORK

My goal as an author is to encourage all my readers to become the best version of themselves, they can. This is in spite of anything they might have been through at any phase of their life. And speaking of things people go through, toxic relationships are one of the most common situations people get into, unplanned, that almost always reduce their chances of becoming the best they could be in life.

So, I've decided to tell you everything you need to know about toxic relationships in this part of the book. I'll also talk about a specific behavioral pattern I believe to be toxic and that could inhibit your chances of living your best life. And, as with the previous part, I'll guide you through the nitty-gritty details of eradicating toxic relationships and behavior from your life.

This is where you get to see the power you have to take charge of your life and destiny through assertiveness. Don't skip any chapter in this part. Each chapter connects to the rest, and they could help to illuminate your life. Now, let's dive in!

CHAPTER FOUR

Understanding Toxicity in Relationships

"The fear of man brings a snare, But whoever trusts in the Lord shall be safe."

—Proverbs 29:25 (NKJV)

"Sometimes trying to fix them, breaks YOU."

—Steve Maraboli

"Hey, you can't have that!"

"But I'm craving it."

"Well, you still can't have it. The doctor said it's not good for you!"

That was my mom trying to stop my younger self from eating a tasty slice of pizza covered in ketchup, just the way I liked it. I tried to protest, but she insisted, and she won. The dermatologist had told her to take away some things from my regular intake if she really wanted my face to be free from acne. Pizza was one of those foods. She didn't hate me, but I felt like she did because she made me eat more veggies. I didn't know any better then, but now I see it all. I know why she had to ignore my incessant whining to ensure acne didn't take away my self-esteem. I sneaked a few pieces behind her back sometimes; she caught me most times. She showed no sympathy; rather, she ensured I got used to the new eating routine. I share this now because it all paid off, not just for acne, but for my overall health.

You'll need to have my mom's attitude if you want to get rid of toxic relationships in your life. You need to just… lose them. Delete them. Remove them from your life. Rip them off your skin. Need I say more? What else is there to do anyway? Toxic relationships involving things like codependency and narcissism, in most cases, stick on you for a long time, like acne, till you lose your beautiful self. But the good thing is that you can get rid of them if you just have the right attitude and persistence.

A Background Thought

Does anyone set out to have a toxic relationship? I doubt anyone would. Any sane human being desires to have a healthy relationship. But what many people don't know is that even a healthy relationship requires lots of effort to be healthy. And it's not just a one-sided effort. Both parties must be committed to the health of the relationship.

Here's why:

None of us grew up as perfect people. We all have flaws in our behavior, mannerisms, upbringing, and other things that have contributed to our character and personality. Many of us are warped in some ways. But within each of us is also a wealth of goodness. So, we're neither totally perfect nor totally warped.

From day to day, we meet people–from our home to the street, and at school or our place of worship or workplace. We meet people everywhere. Things go sour if our imperfection rules the day. But we'll be the happiest people if we keep our imperfections at bay.

What makes a relationship healthy in spite of our imperfections? It's the commitment of the parties involved to learning how to accommodate and adapt to the other's imperfections. Not only that, but we also must learn to accommodate the other person's personality, ideals, and perspectives, and adapt to their moods. This effort must be mutual to make the relationship healthy.

The difficulty experienced in relationships (which could mutate into toxicity) is dependent on the people in the relationship. A relationship itself is neutral; it's the parties in the relationship that determine what kind of relationship it will be. Difficult partners will have a difficult relationship. Difficult children will have a difficult relationship with their parents, and vice versa. If you apply that to any context of relationships, the same will hold true.

The more difficult the relationship, or the people in the relationship, the more work will be required. Anyone who values their relationship will put in that work.

Toxicity in relationships sets in when the parties involved don't want to accept their imperfections, and they're not ready to put in any effort to make the relationship work. Such nonchalance has the potential to harm one or both people.

But how do you know if your relationship is toxic? That's what I'm about to show you.

What Are Toxic Relationships? How Do They Encourage Codependency?

When a professional in the medical field says something is "toxic," it means that thing is not good for you. It's usually associated with things we eat or take into our body. Generally, when we think of "toxic," something poisonous comes to mind. Regardless of the way you define it, "toxic" doesn't sound great. It never comes off like a word that connotes something delicious. So, let's just hit it straight on the head: anything labeled toxic is poisonous! It's bad.

A relationship can be toxic, too. What does that mean? Yeah, you guessed right: it's a bad relationship! It's a relationship that's poisonous. It's not good for the wellbeing of anyone, and that includes you.

Let's take that a little further. A toxic relationship creates a sense of discomfort, like any poisonous substance will do. Scott (2022) describes a toxic relationship as any relationship where someone feels unsupported, misunderstood, humiliated, or assaulted. She adds that some toxic relationships involve threats to one or both people's emotional, psychological, or even physical wellbeing.

Cory (2022) similarly describes a toxic relationship as a relationship made up of behavioral patterns that damage the other partner emotionally and, more often than not, physically too.

Basically, a relationship that makes you feel worse instead of adding real value to you will evolve into a toxic relationship (Scott, 2022). You'll be amazed to discover that this kind of thing happens in different contexts as well—on the playground, in an elitist boardroom, and even in the bedroom.

A relationship can also be toxic when one of the parties in the relationship takes all the responsibility for keeping the peace while the other person keeps doing things to tear it apart. Unfair, right? It's a lot of hassle to be the only one putting in all the effort. Sacrificing your time, resources, personal space, vision, goals, and more for a one-sided relationship is beyond tedious.

Such effort is commendable, but it's not the healthiest thing to do. It could lead to codependency, especially when you're not being appreciated for your efforts. Let's look at a case study.

Marlyss was a typical example of a person who put so much into her relationship, but it didn't turn out well. She was an attractive woman and a good wife, and she spent most of her time living up to that title. She was always busy taking care of her five children and her husband, who was a recovering alcoholic. She made it her priority to prove that she was a good wife and mother, devoting her life to making her family happy. Unfortunately, she didn't succeed. She grew frustrated over how difficult it was to carry out her role. Coupled with that, she felt unappreciated for her efforts. Instead of appreciating her, her family complained to her. She got even angrier.

But she didn't stop trying. She kept putting a lot of effort into keeping her relationship with her husband healthy, but this drained her and made her lose the good years of her life. She resented this so much, but she felt guilty whenever she wasn't making any effort to live up to that standard of being a good wife and mother.

Marlyss' relationship turned toxic. That wasn't her intention. She planned to make her family happy, but she was doing it alone and she ended up becoming codependent, bearing the full weight of keeping her family afloat while slowly being crushed under that weight.

Another interesting example is Randell. He grew up with an alcoholic father and three alcoholic brothers. He wasn't enjoying his relationship with them, so, as a smart and sensitive young man, he spent a large chunk of his free time obsessing over helping his alcoholic relatives. He tried to clean up the messes they created with the aim of fostering a serene environment where they all could enjoy a healthy relationship. But it didn't work as expected.

Nonetheless, he felt obligated to them. Sometimes he got upset because the people around him behaved in such absurd ways, and he wondered why. He felt sorry for them, and felt he needed to get involved in their problems. To him, that was kindness, love, and genuine concern. But at what expense? He rarely had fun; instead, he spent all his time bearing the burden of other people's issues.

Randell was also codependent; he was committed to "fixing" his relatives or making them better in order to have a healthy relationship with them—but that, too, is toxic. He alone was laden with a yoke meant for two people, each pulling their own weight in the relationship.

When only one person is doing the work—that's a toxic relationship.

Signs You're in a Toxic Relationship

Some poisonous substances don't look dangerous. They could be packaged in a shiny cover, and you only discover they're unhealthy after you've consumed them. Similarly, the toxicity of a relationship is not always obvious from the outset. Even though the signs of a toxic relationship are not the same in every context, there are some common ones, and we'll go over those. But ultimately, there's only one person who can tell how bad or good your relationship is: you.

In a general sense, any relationship that constantly threatens your wellbeing through words, actions, or inaction is likely a toxic relationship. It's also important to note that any relationship that involves physical or verbal abuse is absolutely toxic.

These are other signs that indicate a relationship is toxic. These include:

1. Breached communication

Communication is the foundation of any relationship. Relationships grow when the lines of communication, verbal or nonverbal, are intact. The moment that line is broken, bad things are bound to ensue.

Lack of communication causes friction in the relationship. When you stop talking, you'll start stepping on each other's toes. You'll misunderstand each other's actions and inaction. You'll fight over every little thing because you don't have sufficient information to understand the other person; you only act on assumptions. Assumptions can be dangerous in any relationship, and they're also a sign that the relationship is turning sour.

2. Defensiveness

Some psychologists believe that arguing in a relationship isn't all that bad if handled correctly. It's believed that a healthy argument will take the relationship to a deeper level of understanding and intimacy. According to Jane Greer (as cited by Del Russo, 2017), arguments are healthy when you have a specific reason for the fight and a specific problem you're trying to solve. During this kind of argument, there's no devaluing of each other or calling of names. Both parties are able to listen to each other.

But an argument becomes toxic when you become defensive and critical of each other, or you blame one another. Instead of finding compromise, you argue unendingly till you no longer have the strength to continue, and the matter remains unresolved. Later, when something as trivial as who should empty the trash comes up, the bigger, unresolved issue will rear its ugly head to fuel your reaction in this smaller issue.

3. Competition instead of complementing

Have you seen partners who are always competing against each other? I've seen a few. The end result usually isn't good. Each person in the relationship ought to complement the efforts of the others to get better results. The moment we start competing against our partner, we'll be pulling each other down rather than building each other up in order to ensure we're the only one sitting at the pinnacle of success. Competitiveness in any relationship is a sign that the relationship is toxic.

4. Resentment

It's dangerous when partners hold grudges against each other. It's a sure route to distrust and distance. If you tend to nurse grievances quietly for whatever reason, and you can't trust your partner to listen to your concerns, you're quietly breeding a toxic relationship.

5. Glossing over issues

If you never talk about important matters like finances, division of chores, interests, future goals, and values, your relationship could end up being toxic. These topics are important to people and are part of our everyday lives. When the person you're in a relationship with doesn't seem to show interest in or care about your opinions on these things, it could lead to strain in the relationship, and eventually unending fights.

The Dynamics of a Toxic Romantic Relationship

A romantic relationship occurs, typically, between two people who have an intimate connection based on attachment, mutual understanding, interdependence, and a sense of fulfillment. A simpler way of putting this is that when two people are in love with each other and committed to each other, their relationship includes making each other happy.

Love is a beautiful thing. There is no bitterness, envy, hatred, or fear in love. When any of those negative behavioral traits begin to manifest in a romantic relationship, the relationship will become toxic.

A toxic romantic relationship is characterized by the following behavioral patterns:

- Jealousy
- Isolation
- Lack of respect
- Possessiveness
- Emotional and/or physical abuse
- Dominance
- Gaslighting
- Strain in communication
- Manipulation
- Desperation
- Selfishness
- Rejection

This list is not exhaustive, but it'll guide you to identify the negative patterns in your own relationship.

Workbook Four

Exercise One: For Partners

Understanding your relationship is key. Can you confidently say your relationship is healthy and not toxic? The questions below will help you decipher the nature of your relationship. Be honest with yourself when answering the questions.

1. How often do you talk to your partner?

_____

2. Have you ever felt disrespected during an argument with your partner?

_____

3. If yes, give one example.

_____

_____

_____

_____

_____

4. Is your partner a rival to you?

_____

5. Does your partner still love you like before?

_____

6. Can you independently make decisions for your partner?

_____

7. Does your partner degrade your emotions?

_____

8. When did you last engage in an activity with your partner?

_____

9. Do you engage in name-calling in your relationship?

_____

10. How often do you discuss critical issues with your partner?

_____

11. Based on your above answers, would you say your relationship is toxic?

_____

_____

Exercise Two: Toxic Family Cycles

Is your family of origin toxic?

_____

_____

If your answer to the previous question was yes, why?

_____

_____

_____

_____

Do you think you'll ever be able to draw boundaries with them?

_____

_____

How do you propose to do that?

_____

_____

_____

_____

Which family member(s) is/are particularly toxic, in your opinion? Add one reason why you mentioned this person/these people.

(E.g., "James, because he's the golden child and always wants everything to go his way.")

_____

_____

_____

Do you still want to have a relationship with your family of origin?

_____

_____

How do you hope to set boundaries from this point on for these particularly annoying folks?

(E.g., "Inform James he's no longer allowed to come to my house unannounced.")

_____

_____

_____

_____

_____

Chapter Four Takeaway

Personally, I don't believe that there are certain people for whom you *can't* set boundaries. There's always a way, and that's what I communicated in this chapter. If you're dealing with a toxic relationship and you're ready to break free, the ball is in your court. You'll no longer be responsible for anyone else's mess. You're becoming responsible for yourself, and as a person who is recovering from codependency in leaps and bounds, this chapter is your cue to say no with love.

CHAPTER FIVE

Putting an End to People Pleasing

"For do I now persuade men, or God? Or do I seek to please men? For if I still pleased men, I would not be a bondservant of Christ."

—Galatians 1:10 (NKJV)

"I finally know the difference between pleasing and loving, obeying and respecting. It has taken me so many years to be okay with being different, and with being this alive, this intense."

— Eve Ensler

Maybe you have a general idea of what people pleasing is, but let's go a little deeper into exactly what that means. Professor Alena Papayanis shares her personal story of people pleasing in a Huffington Post article; while she was in college, she dated a "sweet" guy who never matched the effort she put into their relationship. The guy's dad cautioned her not to do everything for him or try to be *too* nice to him, but she didn't understand this advice.

She tried to balance the deficit in their relationship by being overly nice. She tried hard for both of them. By giving herself to the relationship fully, she thought she'd become indispensable and it would be impossible for the guy to reject her. She felt her niceness would shield her from ever being abandoned. Turns out, that was wrong.

Nevertheless, Papayanis carried this perception long into adulthood until she realized that she was not just being nice—she was being a people pleaser, and this was dangerous because it kept her boxed in, unseen, and unfulfilled for decades.

Before you start thinking you'll stop being nice to people, you should read this out loud to yourself: It's not just being nice that makes you a people pleaser; it's being *overly* nice, to the point that **you** get lost in the niceness. That's a pretty accurate description of people pleasing.

People Pleasing Is Not Selflessness

To illustrate this point, let's take a look at an example from the Bible. Martha, the sister of Lazarus and Mary of Bethany, thought she was doing the best thing possible by running around, trying to take care of every guest that came into their house uninvited. While everyone else, including her sister, was sitting down, listening to the edifying words of a certain Jewish Rabbi (Jesus) that could transform their lives, Martha was completely wrapped up in trying to please this honored guest.

At the point when the weight of the cooking was crushing her, she complained. She wanted Jesus to take her side and ask Mary to assist her in the kitchen. Martha's sense of hospitality wasn't getting the kind of notice she'd hoped, and she wasn't getting noticed either. So she decided to take it out on her sister, insinuating that Mary was lazy and not as hospitable as she ought to be. If the Rabbi didn't see through this, no one would have thought that her sense of hospitality was turning to hostility. But the Rabbi named it as it was. He told her that her effort at trying to impress Him wasn't necessary. In His judgment, it would have been better if she was seated with everyone else to listen.

Martha might have felt disappointed, but it was the truth. You know how some of us sometimes try to do certain things for someone we honor, love, or have a crush on even when it's not convenient (or it feels like it's killing us)? We might try to convince ourselves that it's an act of selflessness, but at the core of that sentiment, you know it's not. There are other things that make you do what you do.

Let's shine some more light on that behavioral pattern.

People pleasing has a very similar description to concepts such as selflessness, generosity, and kindness. On the surface they look alike; however, a deeper look shows that they're not the same. People pleasing doesn't look good on its practitioners. They go all the way for other people while concealing their pain, smiling like nothing's wrong. So, people get accustomed to seeing them happy all the time and never complaining about anything whatsoever—until the people pleaser can't take it anymore.

In sharing her experience as a recovering people pleaser, Alena Papayanis made it clear that it's misconstruing to associate people-pleasing with being genuinely selfless just because people pleasers show extreme kindness and are sincerely compassionate. Yes they do. That's not all there is to those superficial acts. True kindness doesn't make you betray yourself, and the weight of your kind act shouldn't crush you to the point that you explode in anger, bitterness, and resentment.

During Papayanis's years as a people pleaser, while she was selflessly doing things for other people, her own needs became insignificant. How she felt didn't matter. She was the last person to care about how she felt about anything and was more interested in how everyone else felt. This meant that she wasn't even paying attention to herself. Her needs weren't a priority.

She later found out that her selflessness wasn't true kindness; it was the result of her personal fears and insecurities. She had thought (wrongly) that if she pleased everyone, they'd love her in return. People pleasers tend to believe that nobody loves anyone just for the sake of loving them—that people have to do things and make sacrifices to get anyone to like or accept them.

Such a perspective is wrong, and it has grievous side effects in our relationships. I'll show you how unhealthy it is before I close this chapter.

Many people hold the same mistaken perspective on people pleasing as Martha and Alena Papayanis. And I don't blame them for it. If you're one of them, don't be hard on yourself. Remember that most of us cultivate certain behavioral patterns from our childhood, and others we pick up from our environment or based on our experiences as adults. You're not at fault. This is your moment of truth. Everyone who has gone through some form of toxicity in their relationship and is healing and recovering has had the same moment. This is yours. Don't miss it!

Think of these individuals as examples of true selflessness: William Pitsenbarger, Scott Davidson, Neerja Bhanot, and Martin Luther King Jr. Something fascinating about these folks is that they sacrificed their lives to save many others. Doesn't that sound like people pleasing? No! Here's why:

- They sacrificed for a just cause.

- They weren't seeking attention for themselves. Other people did that for them.

- They didn't feel crushed under the weight of their actions. They carried on till death. Martin Luther King Jr. thought it a glorious thing to lay down his life.

- They found fulfillment in their actions.

- They didn't need people's validation to keep doing what they did.

- Most of the people they saved weren't people they intended to curry favor from. They just did it to preserve life and posterity.

Unfortunately, the same things cannot be said of people pleasing. Here's what happens in people pleasing:

- You're focused on what people think about you.

- You fear criticism, so you try everything you can to get in people's good book, even if it means doing something foolish.

- You're a yes-person. You don't have the courage to say no because you don't want to offend anyone.

- Sometimes you remain passive in making decisions because you don't want to take sides. You don't want to offend anyone on either side.

- You don't have your own defined emotions. You feel how other people feel.

- You're indecisive until the person you're trying to please makes a decision.

- You do everything you can to fit into the pack. You just want to feel accepted.

- Unlike with selflessness, you don't feel fulfillment from what you do. You feel used and drained.

- Anyone can invade your personal space. No boundaries.

- You accept just about everything. You go to any length necessary to please others, not because it feels right, but because you feel satisfied when someone says, "Oh, you're so sweet."

- Your sense of self-worth and self-esteem come from what people think about you.

- Your identity is with the mob. The mob defines what and who you are. And that's what you believe about yourself.

- You regret many of the things you do, and when you're alone you may end up crying over them. Sometimes you resent yourself and think you're not good enough.

This list isn't exhaustive, and it's not possible for one person to manifest all these traits all the time. You could recognize yourself in just parts of what is on that list. But the bottom line is that people pleasing isn't good for you. It's toxic, and it makes you depend on other people to do anything worthwhile with your life. Your relevance and essence will always revolve around people as a people pleaser. But here's the thing: people cannot always be trusted to be nice and never take advantage of you.

Effects of Unhealthy People Pleasing

People pleasing has side effects, and they're not pleasant. You might already know that, but maybe you weren't sure if it was people pleasing causing those effects. Here, we'll highlight the negative aspects of people pleasing.

The most devastating damage people pleasing does is not on your body, but your inner being. Here's what gets affected when you take the path of people pleasing:

Loss of Self

While you struggle to fit into everyone's idea of who they think you are, you lose the real you. You lose your identity while trying to please everyone. All that's visible is what the mob has created. This means that you'll have multiple self-images that appear at different times and in different places. If that sounds weird, it's because it is. Losing your sense of self can be very damaging to your mental health.

Neglected Self

As a people pleaser, your spirit, soul, and body will get little or no care. Your physical health could begin to fail in the process. YI might also begin to quietly lose your mind from trying to fit into everyone's idea of you. You're good at taking care of others—you check up on people to ensure they're fine—yet you can barely end a day without feeling aches all over your body from the stress. Perhaps you've not yet realized that you can't truly take care of people if you're unhealthy yourself.

Loss of Ideals

No one can try to please everyone without losing their core principles. To please everyone, you must be ready to compromise, bending your principles to fit theirs. This is a short route to becoming a puppet that can be controlled at will.

Try to do a personal assessment about your core values right now. Ask yourself:

- What do I stand for?
- What do I believe in?
- What am I without my personal values?

If you don't have answers to those questions, it could be because you've allowed people to define your life the way they deem fit. Humans can be bad puppeteers. They love to take advantage of others when given the chance. And in a real sense, you won't do much in life if you spend all your time trying to please people. At best, they'll use you to get to their destination. And you? You'll be left regretful and angry, feeling you've been used and dumped.

Resentment. Anger. Bitterness.

You'll end up resenting the fact that you never have time for yourself. You use up the time you ought to spend caring for yourself on other people, and now you're worn out. There are things you innately care about, things you wish to get done, but you're just too busy prioritizing other people that don't really care about you. This could lead to resentment, and make you bitterly angry with yourself.

But that changes nothing. It only drains you emotionally.

Your anger will skyrocket if the reason you've been trying to please someone ends up being pointless. But you won't be able to channel your anger to other people — you'll still be the victim of your own outburst. Sometimes you might subtly demonstrate hostility (like Martha did) towards your loved ones, like making little jabs, using sarcastic jokes, or throwing shade. When you try to suppress your resentment, it'll work, but only for a short time. If not nipped in the bud, more negative feelings will show.

Another side effect is that people pleasing can increase your stress level to the point where you no longer find pleasure in anything. The enjoyment you used to derive from certain events or activities is likely to decrease. In a real sense, you don't have time to enjoy anything because you have so many commitments to other people. Even when you're not doing anything, you're constantly thinking of the things you have to do next.

Do you know that this can make you lose good friends? If you no longer show up to an activity that you used to enjoy with your friend or partner, you might lose that relationship in the long run. And that can create even more anxiety for you.

Purposelessness

To be purposeful means that you have a definite destination, vision, or goal. But how can you have a definite place you're going to when other people can intercept you and divert you from your path? And because you want to make people happy, you painfully feign a smile and accept.

What if your vision doesn't align with the vision of your boss or the group you belong to? It dies a natural death even before it starts becoming tangible. And your goals? You'll forget them altogether because you're pursuing something else for someone else.

If this continues, you'll never dare to make plans for anything again because it won't matter in the end. Your ability to aspire to lofty and great things will be maimed because even if you do aspire, it'll only remain a figment of your imagination that can never come to fruition. You'll doubt your ability to ever become anything more than what people want you to be.

This is a dangerous place to be. All your potential and talents will lie dormant and untapped in this state.

Loss of Confidence in Self

When people tell you that you're not good enough or you're not suitable for their group, what happens? You probably feel like your whole world is crumbling. If this is the group of people you've been trying to please, then because you respect their comments more than anyone else's, you believe their words to be true. That could begin to impact how you see yourself and what you think about yourself. That's the moment you begin to think you're a massive failure and you can never excel at anything. You doubt yourself.

When people you're trying to please also constantly trash your opinions, you'll lose confidence in your ability to ever say anything meaningful.

Think of the times you tried to voice your opinion. What happened? Were you heard? How did you react? Your courage dies a natural death every time you are ignored. If you do not do something about this, the idea that your opinions are not worth hearing will grow into your subconscious and sentence you to a life of silence and timidity. You'll tell yourself to always accept what everyone else says and never say anything to the contrary.

Stress

People pleasers are naturally everyone's go-to person. They never say no. Everyone loves to have those kinds of people as team members or as their colleagues.

Even if they have their own piles of work to finish up, a people pleaser will still accept requests for help from others. Just the thought of all that work is exhausting. It's a direct invitation to stress, which will eventually lead to a breakdown. When you take on more than you can handle, you'll always be a victim of health issues. That's not difficult to diagnose.

Unfortunately, you're not a superhuman. No one can constantly shoulder their own burdens plus the burdens of other people* and remain mentally and physically healthy. Thus, you've been endangering yourself.

* *Are you set to nurture self-love and break free from people-pleasing? Dive deep into personal growth with Worksheet #5 from __BONUS #1__ or check this QR code.*

How to Create a Balance – Selflessness Can be Balanced

I'm an advocate of selflessness. I hope I've made that obvious to you. But I'm also a realist. I've had enough experience with people to know what they're capable of.

Not everyone sees things the way you see them, so don't assume that while you're transforming from people pleasing to genuine selflessness, things will go smoothly right away. There are people out there who will want to take advantage of your genuineness.

Before you think it's not possible to live harmoniously with people, let me drive this sentiment home to you: selflessness is a virtue that can build nations.

But there's a balance to selflessness, too—one that won't make you be at the beck and call of everyone else, all in the name of trying to be selfless. Now, we don't want you to crawl back into people pleasing. But while I try to create a balance here, your knowledge of the distinction between people pleasing and selflessness will come in really handy. (You might need to go over that distinction again before continuing.)

So, how do you live selflessly without being a people pleaser? Here's how:

Eliminate Feelings of Guilt

You must learn to eliminate any guilt that pops up. Selflessness does not mean you'll say yes to every request. Thus, you shouldn't feel guilty for turning someone down. If it's a task that would not fit well with your schedule or simply something you don't want to do, don't do it. Kindly decline and move on. A people pleaser will feel guilty for declining a request. But that's no longer you! You're coming out of that already.

Don't Judge Yourself Based on One Action

Don't label yourself as cruel or selfish for declining a request. Being selfless or otherwise is largely about your behavioral response in certain circumstances. That doesn't mean that's who you are. You could learn to be a genuinely selfless person, but there are situations that would warrant acting selfishly. That doesn't make you a selfish person; you just made the best decision for yourself as the occasion demanded.

Therefore, you shouldn't tag yourself as being selfish just because of one circumstance. People are free to call you anything they want, but you should resolve in your heart that you're not other people's labels.

Be Prepared to Own Your Decisions

Be bold enough to own your decision to act selflessly (or not) in any given situation. If you choose a behavior, stand by it. That means you'll also have to face the outcome of the decision head on. Even if it doesn't turn out great, you can take solace in the fact that you made an independent choice without being intimidated by how people might think or what they might say about you.

Mix Selflessness with a Bit of Selfishness

MMA fighter and motivational speaker Charlie Brenneman has a good description of this on his blog. Brenneman explains how he had to make an important decision for himself and his marriage, and since he was in a relationship, his decision wasn't about him alone; he had to be considerate of his partner. That sounds like a **selfless** thing to do. But he also had a clear vision for his UFC career, and he made it his priority. This sounds **selfish**. But the motive for his pursuit was to be able to inspire other people to attain their greatest self. Now that sounds **selfless**. But to achieve any of that, he had to be in a good state of mind. That's **selfish**.

Oscillating between selflessness and selfishness like this could seem daunting, but it's not so hard to do. Here are some tips:

Admit You Need the Self-Care

Hagar (2023) notes that it's important to learn to fill our own cup first (that is, take care of our needs first), not only for our personal wellbeing but also for the wellbeing of others. Self-care might seem selfish, but we can only give as much goodness to people as we have in ourselves. It's only right to ensure we are mentally and physically healthy in order to have healthy relationships with other people.

Take care of yourself. When you practice self-care, you're responding to your personal needs while at the same time considering the impact of your own good health on the people around you.

Dig Deep Enough to Give More

Naturopathic doctor Sherwood (2021) reiterates the golden rule to love others as much as you love yourself. In his view, we are stewards of our lives, and our key responsibility is to cater to our own needs.

He uses the analogy of digging a well to explain the balance between selfishness and selflessness. To get a sufficient amount of good water from a well, you have to dig deep. In the same way, putting enough work into your spiritual, emotional, and physical wellbeing is not really all that selfish. According to Sherwood, it's actually an extreme act of selfishness to fail to take care of yourself, as you'll become a liability to the people around you. Therefore, you must make the right choices regarding your lifestyle.

Create a Serene Environment

Pablo (2021) adds his thoughts to this discourse as well, stating that the beautiful balance to be found in living life to the fullest is in learning to look out for yourself and your interests—but also the understanding that the greatest form of fulfillment comes from helping others. You give love, you get love in return. But how can you give what you don't have?

Pablo warns against overdoing self-care to the point of hurting people. He also suggests weighing the need and the circumstance before acting selflessly. For example, it's not right to go bankrupt for a drug addict who's not willing to change. You don't need to defend or support someone who's acting badly and doesn't intend to improve their behavior. You'll only be subjecting yourself to constant ridicule and unfair treatment in your supposed act of selflessness.

It's not smart to give away what you need yourself. Don't become a beggar to feed a beggar. Nothing will change that way.

Both Matter

This is what I consider to be the peak of the middle ground between selfishness and selflessness. Don't prioritize one over the other. Don't make the mistake of focusing on self-care while you lack in generosity to others. You can do both. As you create time for yourself, also schedule time to be with your friends or to do things for people in need. It's not a matter of you versus them. Both matter. This mindset will help you form healthy relationships with others.

You can have healthy relationships without crawling to people as if they hold the key to your self-worth. You can independently care for yourself and still be selflessly generous towards others, but not at your own detriment.

Workbook Five

Exercise One: Are You a People Pleaser?

People pleasers are prone to certain behaviors. This exercise will help to pinpoint some of these characteristics in yourself. Having more yeses than no's in this exercise means you're definitely a people pleaser.

Tick either yes or no.

NUMBER	QUESTIONS	YES	NO
1.	Do you have principles?		
2.	Do you easily change your plans for people?		
3.	Do you seek people's approval?		
4.	Do you complain or nag when you're working?		
5.	Have you ever gotten to a point where you lack enjoyment in everything you do?		
6.	Are you selfish?		
7.	Do you easily judge yourself?		
8.	Do you say "yes" to everyone's requests?		
9.	Do you feel guilty for not giving a positive response to people's requests?		
10.	Do people take you for granted at your workplace?		
11.	Do you feel purposeless?		
12.	Do you get angry when no one notices your effort on a project?		

Exercise Two: Debunking Myths

What myths did you use to believe about people pleasing? Write four.

_____

_____

_____

_____

Based on what you know now, would you say people pleasing is cool? Give reasons for your answer.

_____

_____

_____

_____

Do you still want to remain a people pleaser? Why or why not?

_____

_____

_____

_____

What's your game plan to stop people pleasing?

_____

_____

_____

_____

Chapter Five Takeaway

Selflessness and people pleasing are not the same. You can be selfless without losing your mind. You can be selfless without being a doormat. Yes, I said it. At this point, you really need to come to terms with the fact that you've only got one life, and you can't spend all of it pleasing people. In a healthy relationship, the needs of both parties will be equally prioritized, rather than one person's needs being more important.

We're more than halfway through this book, and by now I really hope you've started to think about your life. People pleasing will hurt you badly. You've got to move on from it.

So far, if you have learned something from the book, please click HERE to leave a review on Amazon. That will help other people in their personal development.

CHAPTER SIX

The Assertiveness and Boundary Setting Guide

"A soft answer turns away wrath, But a harsh word stirs up anger."

—Proverbs 15:1 (NKJV)

"Assertiveness is asking for what you want, turning others down, and making decisions that are right for you without anger, threats, manipulation, or fear of repercussions."

—Patrick King

Earlier in this book, I mentioned the crucial role of communication in a relationship. Communication involves more than just talking. For you to be taken seriously and as someone who is capable of making independent choices, you must learn to communicate your thoughts assertively. That's how to let people know that you know what you're doing.

Are you just recovering from a toxic relationship? This is an important lesson for you.

Learning to Be Assertive

Speed et al. (as cited by Sutton, 2021) describe assertiveness as "standing up for oneself without significant anxiety, expressing one's feelings comfortably, or exercising one's own rights without denying the rights of others." When you lack assertiveness, you won't be able to do any of those things. This can tilt towards people pleasing and hostility, as well.

Here's a practical example of assertiveness. My uncle asked his daughter to send a message to their realtor about getting an electrician to come and fix something at the house. Here's what my cousin typed:

"I'd like the electrician to come this morning."

My uncle told her not to send that message. He said this would be better:

"Tell the electrician to come this morning."

Which of the two sounds more assertive?

My uncle's wording sounds authoritative and stern. His approach is a mild form of aggression in a conversation. But being aggressive doesn't make you assertive. At best, it'll send the wrong message to the recipient. On the other hand, my cousin's wording makes it sound like she's pleading, but her message is nevertheless assertive. The request was serious, but she didn't make it sound that way (which could put the other person under unnecessary pressure). She knew what she wanted, she was clear about it, and she stated it concisely.

Assertiveness is an essential communication skill (Mayo Clinic Staff, n.d.). Being assertive during communication allows you to express your thoughts more effectively and makes you sound like you know what you're talking about.

Since assertiveness is a communication skill, it can be learned. Even though you may have lost the confidence to speak up for yourself during a toxic relationship, now that you're going through a period of recovery, you can learn to find your voice again.

Perhaps knowing the benefits of being assertive will motivate you to learn. Being assertive will:

- Boost your self-esteem
- Help you to earn other people's respect
- Help you manage stress by declining requests to take on responsibilities that may wear you out
- Make you more likely to get what you want
- Improve your communication with others

- Let you create honest relationships with people around you
- Help you create healthy boundaries

Now, are you convinced you need to learn this communication skill?

This is how to be assertive during any communication:

Start with "I," Not "You"

During a conversation, when you start sentences with "you," you're unintentionally putting the other person on the spot. Oftentimes the other person will naturally jump into defensive mode. But when you start with "I," the other person will see things from your perspective and listen to what you have to say.

For instance, instead of saying, "You're wrong," start with, "I disagree."

When you want to make a request, you can say, "I would like you to help with…" instead of, "You need to…"

An article from Coursera illustrates this concept well and provides a formula for this kind of conversation. Follow this pattern:

"I feel ____ when ____ because ____. What I need/ want is ____." (Coursera, 2023)

For example, "I feel disrespected when you talk back to me in public. Could you correct me when we're alone together, instead?"

Here's another example: "I was already loaded up with different tasks when you asked me to help you with yours."

Using this formula will help you to express how other people's behavior makes you feel in a respectful way, instead of pointing an accusing finger and putting them on the defensive.

Softly Decline with a Smile

Having been a yes-person for a while, you need to set your boundaries and prioritize your wellbeing. I suggest you learn to say no. Of course, you won't just start saying it with all the audacity with which you've been wanting to say it for so long;

internally, you might feel a bit unsure about saying it, but do not let that be reflected in your voice.

The next time a request comes asking you to take on more responsibilities, softly say, "No" with a smile. It could turn out to be the best thing you've done for yourself in a long while.

According to recent research, the stress that comes with overwork could lead to serious health problems such as sleeplessness, depression, diabetes, heart disease, damaged memory, and decreased productivity (Carmichael, 2015). This is to say that accepting every task that comes your way can have serious long-term effects.

Hold Firm to Your Decision

Not everyone easily takes no for an answer. They'll love to push further to get you to change your mind, testing your resolve and looking for a hole in your armor—a weak spot they can use to get through to you.

In that moment, weigh the impact of their request on you. If complying will not do you much good, or will be harmful for you, insist on your initial response. Don't argue with them. Just persist in saying no with a smile on your face. You can add "sorry" when you're declining the second time if you'd like to. You could even give them an alternative option or refer them to someone else. But hold firm to your response.

Body Language Matters

Nonverbal communication has always been important, but it's even more relevant in our post-Covid-19 world (Michail, 2020). It's become a part of our daily existence. The pandemic forced us to learn how to communicate more with gestures, eye contact, and other nonverbal means. According to body language research, 7% of all communication is verbal, whereas the tone of our voice and our body language represent 38% and 55% respectively.

This means that learning to communicate with body language comes with great rewards for assertiveness. You can act confidently, even if you don't feel confident. Here's how:

Sit upright, leaning forward a bit. Make regular eye contact. Keep a neutral or positive facial expression. Don't cross your arms or legs. You can rehearse this in front of a mirror or with a friend before having a conversation you're nervous about to help you master the art.

Learning assertiveness could take a while, but if you persist, it'll pay off in the long term.

Balancing Assertiveness with Compassion

Public speaking coach Sims Wyeth (2015) notes that leadership "is a constant tug between assertiveness and empathy."

While empathy nudges you to show understanding towards what others are thinking and feeling, assertiveness involves expressing yourself confidently (without being aggressive).

Have you met people who couldn't cope with your standard of assertiveness? It's true that you're trying to create a system for yourself that will ensure no one takes advantage of your selflessness and generosity, but you still need to balance that assertiveness with empathy.

Research shows that empathy, compassion, and understanding for others are three things that give us the peace and happiness we desire. As much as we want and need to create boundaries to protect ourselves, we must also balance those boundaries with the skill of empathy. This will help us to express ourselves confidently while maintaining a consideration for the feelings of the other person.

Here's how to do it:

Analyze the Situation

You can choose which behavioral pattern to display depending on the situation. Analyze the situation first, then choose to either be assertive first, then show empathy, or vice versa. Remember that you're dealing with different people in different contexts; you can't expect the circumstances or the personalities involved to always be the same. Analyze first, then decide on how to respond.

Learn to Listen and Pay Attention to Details

To effectively analyze the situation, you must learn to be a good listener with a good eye for detail. Listening is a great empathy skill. You're able to show empathy when you see things from another person's perspective, not by watching their emotional displays (these could be deceptive), but by paying close attention to their speech and intuiting how they might be feeling.

Go Head-First, Then Follow with the Heart

Empathy is a skill that allows us to build great relationships in different contexts. You need a good heart to show empathy. With a compassionate heart, you can be considerate in your decision to be assertive. But before you go all-in with your heart, ensure your head is involved in the interaction. You can see through toxic people's schemes and antics when your head is involved in the exchange. Don't get overly emotional.

Usefulness of Boundaries in Relationships

One of the objectives of this book is to guide individuals on how to end unhealthy relationships and begin to live the life they were designed to live. One of the things that I've suggested to you as an important means to recovering from unhealthy relationships is boundary setting.

This can't be overemphasized. Boundary setting comes with a lot of benefits for someone who wants to live independently of people's selfish interests. Before learning the benefits, let me remind you again what boundary setting looks like.

According to Martin (2016), boundaries are guidelines that inform people how you want to be treated. This includes letting them know what behaviors you will accept and what you won't. This could range from simply letting someone know that they can't keep yelling at you to excusing yourself from a conversation or a group, or blocking someone on your phone.

Now, the benefits of setting boundaries:

- **Helps you set clear expectations:** Having boundaries doesn't make you a mean person. It just helps you to set clear expectations and limits to what you can take and what you can't.

- **Gives a sense of peace and security:** Boundaries protect us from physical and emotional harm. This includes physical violence, unwanted touch, verbal abuse, and manipulation. Boundaries also provide emotional freedom from self-criticism and second-guessing. Personally, when I don't set boundaries, I get stuck in shame and self-doubt. I criticize myself for not asking for respect and allowing others to mistreat me. In contrast, when I set boundaries, I feel empowered and safe.

- **Tones down resentment:** When you don't have boundaries, you're likely to overcommit to things and spend more time on other people's problems than you planned. You'll go overboard to please other people to your own detriment and waste time doing things that don't add any value to you, or even things that go against your values. You might lose your self-worth and identity in the process, as well. You'll do these things with a fake smile on your face while you groan inwardly. When you're alone, you'll probably hate yourself for taking on so much more than you can handle.

When you set boundaries, you're less likely to feel this resentment towards yourself or anyone else because you'll be able to speak up for yourself, and decline whatever will hurt you.

- **Helps you build a better self-image and self-esteem:** Without boundaries, you fit into everything that everyone calls you or says about you. You don't have a defined image of yourself. With boundaries, you can have time to focus on yourself and redefine yourself from your perspective. This will boost your self-confidence and give you a sense of self-worth.

- **Boosts your mental and emotional wellbeing:** With the boundaries you set, you can be free from the mental stress and emotional breakdown that arise from doing everything everyone else wants you to do.

- **Reduces burnout:** When you build boundaries around yourself, you won't take on too many commitments anymore. This way, you'll have ample time to rest and refresh yourself, thus avoiding burnout.

How to Set Boundaries

The need to set boundaries can be different in different contexts and with different people. Some people need to set boundaries with family, others in the workplace, and others in their romantic relationship. Regardless of the context where you need to set boundaries, you have to remember that you're the same person in all contexts. The boundaries you set for one context could be applicable in other situations. Essentially, there are *generic boundaries* and *specific boundaries*.

For instance, if you're the go-to person at work and in your family, people will always want to dump tasks on your lap regardless of the context. When you decide to be assertive in declining people's requests, it'll be reflected in all your relationships. This is a *generic boundary*.

Generally, boundary setting begins with **self-awareness**. You don't like the way you behave in your relationships or you don't like the way people treat you? You can change it. It starts with *you*. It's a form of self-awareness to recognize that you can no longer accept the way things are going in your relationships.

What If My Boundaries Are Disrespected?

The boundaries you set for yourself are meant to improve your wellbeing, but they aren't for you alone; you need the cooperation of other people for the boundaries to be effective.

But what if the other person isn't cooperative? Sounds like another thing to worry about, doesn't it? Don't worry—there's a way around this.

Martin (2016) suggests that you assess your situation first using the following questions.

- Who is disrespecting your boundaries? The type of relationship you have (family member, romantic partner, coworker, etc.) will determine your response.

- Can this person change? Talk with the person to find out whether they're intentionally crossing your boundaries and whether or not they're willing to make a change.

- How long have you been dealing with these boundary violations? If they've been doing this for years, for example, it might be harder for this person to change (though not impossible).

- Is the person being physically violent? At this point, your safety comes first seek a way to get away from them because they're not likely to change anytime soon. Don't hesitate to ask for help from a support group or relative. If you're a minor, you could also reach out to a trusted adult at school, church, or your parent's friends, or a hotline. It's dangerous to assume you can do it alone.

- Are you enforcing your boundaries? Don't assume other people know what they are. Ensure the boundaries you've set are clear to those around you, and more importantly, ensure your response to a violation is always consistent. Don't compromise, regardless of the situation or persons involved. Be consistent in defending your boundaries.

After this analysis, you may decide on any of the following actions to ensure your boundaries are respected (Martin, 2016):

1. **Reiterate them:** In the previous analysis, you identified the person who is violating your boundaries. Perhaps they didn't take you seriously the first time. Restate your boundaries firmly and emphatically, but not aggressively, over and over again to drive the message home.

2. **Choose your reaction:** Some people intentionally violate your boundaries to get a reaction out of you. You can choose how you respond. Instead of allowing them to anger you, choose to laugh instead or just silently leave the situation. It'll make a huge difference.

3. **Accept what you can't change:** The only person you have control over is you. Don't expect to change people by setting boundaries. If the person who is disrespecting your boundaries refuses to change, you can either re-

strategize regarding how to communicate your boundaries to them, or find other ways to keep yourself protected from their negative influence.

Workbook Six

Exercise One: Violated Boundaries

What boundaries have you set in the past? Write down five.

_____

_____

_____

_____

Do you agree that setting boundaries has saved you a lot of trouble? Summarize your view on this.

_____

_____

_____

_____

_____

_____

_____

Who has violated your boundaries in the past? What did you do when those boundaries were violated?

_____

_____

_____

_____

_____

_____

_____

Exercise Two: Setting Boundaries

Write down five people in your life for whom you feel you need to set boundaries.

_____

_____

_____

_____

What barriers do you feel you're likely to face when setting boundaries for these people?

_____

_____

_____

_____

How do you hope to overcome these barriers in order to make your boundary setting a successful venture?

_____

_____

_____

_____

Chapter Six Takeaway

Abusers, narcissists, and other toxic people who are out to prey on the vulnerable will never take kindly to boundaries. They will try to convince you that boundaries are unnecessary. You now know that boundaries are extremely important. Of course, you can have boundaries and still be kind to people.

PART THREE

COMPLETE HEALING IS POSSIBLE

Back in high school, when I was a senior, it seemed like everyone was in a relationship. It was important to be liked and to like someone. Everybody knew this and strove to be accepted. Everyone. But not my best friend, Zoey.

Happily, for me, the girl I liked, liked me back, and we started dating—but unfortunately, I crossed a line before I realized what was happening. Maybe it was because my tender heart was still too immature to handle matters of love, but anyway, I grew really paranoid and jealous. I imagined my girlfriend cheating on me, and I accused her of doing so, too, until I finally pissed her off and she dumped me.

In the midst of my pain and regret, I sought comfort from Zoey.

Do you think I should call her?

Should I get her flowers?

Do you think buying her an expensive dress would fix this?

I tried to make him tell me what to do. Instead, Zoey only said, "You don't need a relationship right now, man."

The more he said that, the more annoyed I got. My turning point, however, came when he stood up on the park bench we'd been sitting on, spread his arms in the air, and said, "Unlike y'all, I'm free as a bird." Then he lunged forward to jump off the bench, flapping his arms like wings, and gave me a smile.

I saw that contented look of freedom in his eyes, and instantly I knew: *I wanted that.*

Let me ask you: Do you want freedom, too? Are we on the same page here? I sure hope so!

In this final part of the book, I'm going to emphasize something: You can be completely healed. You can *completely* offload that heavy burden and become free. True and total freedom is possible. And we're about to get into the "how" for that.

CHAPTER SEVEN

Independence and Interdependence

*"Brethren, if a man is overtaken in any trespass, you who are spiritual restore such
a one in a spirit of gentleness, considering yourself lest you also be tempted. Bear
one another's burdens, and so fulfill the law of Christ."*

—Galatians 6:1, 2 (NKJV)

*"In the progress of personality, first comes a declaration of independence, then a
recognition of interdependence."*

—Henry Van Dyke

Before I walk you through this final part, I want you to read this out loud to yourself:

A HEALTHY RELATIONSHIP IS POSSIBLE. I DESERVE TO HAVE A
HEALTHY RELATIONSHIP. I CAN HAVE A HEALTHY
RELATIONSHIP.

Repeat that to yourself till you're convinced of what you're saying.

Independence vs. Codependency

If you've been around for a while, you've almost certainly heard of America's Declaration of Independence. In the late 18th century, the North American colonies of Great Britain revolted against British rule to secure one thing: independence. They were tired of being controlled. They didn't want to be told what to do and what not to do by Britain, so they revolted.

Why would anyone want to be independent, and why would they fight with everything they have in order to get it? The primary motive behind every fight for independence is to be able to stand alone, make decisions without any external influence, be free of the control of others, and live life the way they think it should be lived. This makes independence sound like a sure deal for good living.

The longing for independence usually occurs when a relationship goes sour. The suffering party will seek to opt out and be left alone—as they should. That's what happens in codependent relationships and other forms of toxic relationship. In this book, I've discussed some steps you need to take to end and recover from toxic relationships, especially those involving codependency and narcissism. But the essence of taking you through that process isn't to lead you into another cycle of problems. Everything I've shared in this book to this point is to ensure you're free from toxicity. It's to liberate you from every emotional disorder that comes with toxic relationships. Most importantly, it's to lead you to be *free.*

Independence is a great thing to seek. A parallel can be drawn between codependency and independence; they're two ends of the relationship spectrum that can never blend. In codependency, you're obsessed with looking out for your partner, so much so that you allow their lifestyle to influence your emotions, attitudes, and behavior. In the process, you forget to take care of yourself because you believe that your self-worth comes from what you do for your partner. But independence is different. It's a phase in a relationship that's higher and better than codependency.

In an independent relationship, you don't feel responsible for what happens to the other person. You allow them to live their life while you live yours without remorse or guilt. As an independent partner, you're self-reliant and self-empowered. Your emotional, physical, and spiritual needs are your sole responsibility. You pride yourself on your ability to make independent choices and do things your way. And that's where your self-worth and self-esteem emanate from.

In recovering from a toxic relationship, independence is a comfortable haven to go to first. The reason to set healthy boundaries and be assertive in your decisions is so that you can be free from the control of the other person in the relationship. It's the same reason a colony fights to stand alone, to be able to self-govern the affairs of its domain. That's the first thing you need to learn to do as well. Your life is precious, and the person you'll eventually become hinges on the decisions you make about your relationships.

This book has been designed to equip you to make the right decisions for yourself. I've discussed the intricacies of toxic relationships and how to end them in the first two parts. If you've followed the book to this point, you'll know that you don't need someone else to steer your life anymore. Hopefully, you've begun to realize that it's time for you to take the reins and drive. That's being independent.

How to Become More Confident and Independent

One of the things that happened while you were in a toxic relationship is that your self-confidence was battered. But if you've gotten to this recovery phase, you'll need your confidence back to live life to the fullest.

Confidence comes as a result of a variety of factors. It's not one size fits all. Different people derive confidence from different things, but according to Bridges (2017), choices and accomplishments that make you feel happy and proud of who you are generally make great confidence boosters.

Here are a few things you can do to boost your self-confidence, independently:

Find Activities That Give You a Sense of Fulfillment

There's a feeling of happiness you get from doing things you like to do. For instance, I derive joy from sitting down at my laptop to write. It makes me happy that I can string words together to pass a concise message to people. I love to cook, too, even though I don't cook very often. Whenever I cook, I get this sense of satisfaction from it. That feeling of, "Boy, you just prepared a great meal" makes my heart leap for joy. The fulfillment derived from this accomplishment makes me eager to tell guests, "I cooked this meal."

Whatever you're interested in — a hobby, a passion, even chores — discover it and indulge yourself in doing it as frequently as you can. It'll help to add blocks of strength to your growing confidence.

Create a Daily Personal To-Do List

I've also tried this, and I recommend it to people as well. It has really helped me and those I've recommended it to. Think of everything you need to do today and write a list (you can write it on paper, a sticky note, or your phone). Let that list guide your day. Let it be your compass for engaging with the day, and ensure that regardless of the distractions you encounter, you stick to the items on the list.

There's usually a sense of accomplishment to be gained from ticking off each completed task. It makes you feel good about yourself, and it raises your level of confidence in accomplishing anything you set your heart on doing.

This is important: Don't just *think* about what you want to do today — *write it down.* It might come to you as a thought, but you need to be diligent enough to write it in a place where you can see it and tick it off. This creates a positive psychological effect.

Also, don't beat yourself up if, at the end of the day, you haven't completed a task on the list. A lot of things can come up during the day which may inhibit you from finishing the task. Just think of how you can make up for it tomorrow.

Be Committed to Making Wise Choices

Some time ago, I made a financial decision that didn't seem logical at the time. I committed myself to consistently saving a percentage of my income. I ensured I was faithful in doing so. It didn't make any sense at the time, but as I kept at it, I became proud of that habit — and it turned out to be one of the best financial decisions I ever made. I was so excited about it that I'm now confident enough to share it with just about anyone when the need arises. Making that choice increased my confidence in talking about financial management.

In the same vein, make a commitment to yourself to make wise career choices. Take a professional course. Plan to upskill. Make plans to attend conferences, workshops, and/or seminars. These are the kinds of choices that will boost your confidence. Make choices that'll make you a better partner, friend, leader, or colleague.

Exercise

Bridges (2017) notes that exercise isn't just for building a good physique and healthy body; it's also beneficial for memory retention, focus, stress management and preventing depression. With this in mind, create time in your daily schedule to exercise. Don't aim for perfection; the goal is to make small changes in your physical health that help you build your self-confidence.

Step Out of Your Comfort Zone

This strategy could be tough to apply, but it's one of the most effective ways of boosting your confidence.

What do you dread doing? Whatever it is, plan to give it a try. For instance, if you've never traveled far away from home and you feel a bit nervous about the idea—book a trip. Perhaps you've always dreaded the idea of hiking—why not try it out?

Once you're able to face your fears and you accomplish something, the confidence that comes with the exclamation of, "Yeah! I did it!" is always amazing. It can strengthen your confidence, and you may realize that avoiding that thing has been limiting your potential and fulfillment.

When you step out of your comfort zone, you might be setting yourself up for opportunities you've missed in the past. It could set you up for new business partnerships, relationships, client acquisitions, scholarships, etc.

Focus on Your Strength

The more you concentrate on the things you can't do, the more you'll feel bad about yourself. Learn to accept that there are some things you can't do; perhaps you just aren't wired for them, or perhaps you don't have the skills required to do those things at the moment. Don't beat yourself up about it. Instead, focus on what you *do* have the capability to do.

There are things you're exceptionally good at. Funnily enough, when people focus all their energy on the things they can't do, they tend to forget all about their potential. You're gifted. You might not be able to do certain things, but there are other things you can do. Concentrate your energy on those things.

Stop focusing on your errors. Celebrate your achievements and let them spur you on to work on the weak spots.

Stop Comparing Yourself

Comparison is an easy way to tank your confidence, especially when you focus more on the accomplishments of the other person and on your own failures.

Stop it! You're deflating your confidence.

Don't focus on other people's achievements—focus on your path. Of course, you could learn from the success stories of others, but don't use them as your yardstick for measuring your own success.

Balancing Independence with Interdependence

When you're recovering from a toxic relationship, especially a romantic relationship, one of the things we've discussed that you need to learn is how to set healthy boundaries. This will help you to regain your freedom and take charge of your life once again.

If you're in a situation where you don't have to leave the relationship but you need to stop being codependent, setting boundaries will allow you to live an independent lifestyle in that relationship. You won't need to depend on your partner for validation or to build your self-worth. You won't need the input of other people to make certain decisions; you'll be able to independently make those choices yourself. You won't feel responsible for anyone's life, and you'll focus on living your own life and pursuing your dreams.

Basically, you'll be able to say good riddance to toxicity. Sounds amazing, right? Yes, I agree—it is!

But let's look at the flip side of this coin:

In our society, we often view independence as an indication of being afraid to depend on other people (Khurana, 2017). The fear of being controlled or manipulated by others is the primary motivation for seeking independence. According to Khurana (2017), true independence doesn't mean simply freeing yourself from the yokes of all relationships, dusting your hands of all social responsibilities, and doing whatever you want without taking others into account whatsoever.

If independence is taken to the extreme in this way, a few things that will likely happen to your relationship include:

- Emotional detachment
- Declining communication
- Apathy
- Eventual death of the relationship

Independence is great, but there's a higher level of relationship you should know about. It's *interdependency*. Independence is not the ultimate goal. It's actually not the best kind of relationship—the kind that can guarantee lasting peace and joy.

Interdependence opens the possibility of bringing down your walls so that other people can access your true feelings and opinions. This should be done respectfully, without the other person trampling on you while you're vulnerable. Opening up to others enables you to be available for your partner to attend to their physical, emotional, and spiritual needs, while they also attend to yours, too. Interdependence is not a one-sided affair, but a mutual commitment.

Overcoming Barriers to Interdependence

Let's look at how a fundamental misunderstanding of the function of independence in a relationship can lead to problems.

Amanda and her husband, Mike, had been married for five years, and they both claimed that they were independent. They were happy that they had different careers and separate friend circles. However, Amanda sometimes got annoyed when Mike forgot about their plans to do things together. Instead of expressing how she felt to her husband, she would let off steam through other channels; she didn't want anyone to think of her as being "needy" or "weak." Whenever she wasn't happy with Mike's behavior, she threw herself into her work or talked to her friends to distract herself from the irritation.

Mike, on his end, didn't create time for Amanda either. He was always at work. After all, he was independent, right? Eventually, Amanda felt Mike was making his work his top priority while she came second. She started to feel insecure, but she still didn't tell him.

Soon afterwards, Amanda got pregnant. Mike was supposed to meet her at the doctor's office, but at the last minute he called her to say he would be late because he wanted to finish up a task at the office. And that was it! Amanda's temper flared. She called her husband a selfish person. Mike didn't understand why she was angry, and that made Amanda even angrier.

As you can see, complete independence doesn't really work out in relationships. Truth is, nature designed humans to function interdependently, not independently. You may have had a toxic relationship at some point, but that doesn't mean the next step for you is to live independently—not relating with anyone—for the rest of your life. You still need a network of relationships around you.

It's when people don't understand the true essence of independence that they take it to the extreme. Thus, the balance to our understanding of independence is knowing that the order of things in nature is interdependence: a mutual relationship, in spite of our individuality.

Interdependence doesn't rob you of your freedom or independence, it enhances it. While independence will make you a great individual boxer, single tennis player, or soloist, interdependence will make you an amazing football captain or team player. For the vast majority of things in life, we need to work with other people to achieve our goals.

But a lot of people still don't understand interdependence, and that constitutes one of the barriers to practicing interdependence. How do we remove these barriers?

Step out of your cocoon: You need to realize that you can't get too far in achieving your dreams when you're alone. So step out and embrace the possibility of a partnership.

Be open to talking: Good communication is one of the key elements of an interdependent relationship. Don't assume that your partner knows something. Talk about it. Talk about everything and hide nothing, including your grievances.

Create time to be with them: Being independent means that you have to build boundaries for your own benefits. But to enjoy a healthy, mutual relationship, you'll need to lower the fence and create specific times to interact with your partner. Don't shut them out totally. Now that you understand your individuality, you can spend better quality time with them.

Respect their boundaries: Just as you want other people to respect your boundaries, you should also respect theirs. If not, you'll step on each other's toes. The outcome won't be great.

Be sincere: Don't be suspicious of your partner. Trust is one of the most crucial characteristics of an interdependent relationship. If you're suspicious or distrusting of your partner, you'll create an environment for toxicity.

Please note that the knowledge you've gained about toxic relationships and the signs of each type should be able to guide you in avoiding getting into another one. It'll also prevent you from losing your individuality as you embark on an interdependent relationship.

Celebrating Independence

How is interdependence better than codependency? Write down three ways.

_____

_____

_____

_____

It is important to know the things that keep us busy and give us great joy. Trying new things also allows us to discover activities that can help reduce our tendency towards codependence.

Write down five activities that give you a sense of fulfillment.

Activity 1:

_____

Activity 2:

_____

Activity 3:

_____

Activity 4:

_____

Activity 5:

_____

Why haven't you been able to do some of those activities that give you joy and fulfillment?

_____

_____

_____

Which of the following have you done recently?

    A. Attended a conference or workshop

    B. Been on an excursion

    C. Gone on a road trip

    D. Exercised

    E. Attended a concert

    F. Visited an art gallery

Create a bucket list of things you're going to do (by yourself) before this year is over. Write those activities in the list below and set a date for them.

BUCKET LIST

- ☐ ....
- ☐ ....
- ☐ ....
- ☐ ....

BUCKET LIST

- ☐ ....
- ☐ ....
- ☐ ....
- ☐ ....

BUCKET LIST

- ☐ ....
- ☐ ....
- ☐ ....
- ☐ ....

BUCKET LIST

- ☐ ....
- ☐ ....
- ☐ ....
- ☐ ....

P.S. Learning to be independent is a major way to stop codependency. It helps if you can learn to enjoy life and do what makes you happy without depending on someone else or waiting for their permission.

Chapter Seven Takeaway

Healthy relationships are rare gifts. Such relationships create the right environment for us to become all the amazing things we've been created to be. We cannot afford to lose such relationships.

To keep these healthy relationships, do the following:

- Don't make a fuss about tiny issues
- Communicate with clarity
- Avoid assumptions
- Don't shy away from arguments—have healthy, respectful ones
- Always pay attention to the bright side of things
- Admit that your relationship is not immune to challenges
- Learn and practice trust
- Prioritize each other
- Be each other's biggest fan
- Respect your individualities

Interdependence is possible, and you can merge it with independence. You need people; people need you. It's a two-way street. Get that balance right and you'll be well on your way to healthy, happy relationships. You know I wouldn't mess with you—it really is that simple.

CHAPTER EIGHT

The Radical Self-Love Guide and Workbook

"You shall love your neighbor as yourself."

—Mark 12:31 (NKJV)

"The absence of self-love can never be replaced with the presence of people's love for you."

— Edmond Mbiaka

What Is Self-Love?

In an article for *Cosmopolitan*, actress Raveena Tandon shares the story of her two-decade journey to body acceptance. From the early years of her life, she had a love-hate relationship with her body. She hated herself as a young girl because she was overweight and everyone in her class teased her for it. Despite this, she went on to start her acting career at age 16. Her body was the same size, but in the early years of her career, she didn't feel insecure. Then the media came along, labeling and body-shaming her on a regular basis. Female journalists were the leader of the pack. They labeled her "Miss Thunder Thighs" and "Amazonian." These comments made her extremely conscious of her body.

Raveena is a tall woman with a big build. Since she wasn't slim, she tried to find clothes that suited her body type. Even as a public figure, she struggled to accept her body. The struggle continued in her twenties and thirties. It was until her forties that she began to feel comfortable with the way she was. She started dressing more confidently and resolved to focus on being a confident woman instead of trying to fit someone else's idea of a "perfect" body.

As Raveena discovered, loving yourself is the best thing you can do for yourself. This is regardless of your background, status, or age. There's no universal definition of what self-love is, but you can figure out whether you love yourself or not through reading these descriptions.

Martin (2019) and Borenstein (2020) each give a long list of descriptions of self-love. You love yourself if you:

- Always talk to yourself with love
- Always talk about yourself with love
- Forgive yourself every time you mess up
- Commit to meeting your own needs
- Take a break from self-judgment
- Are assertive
- Trust yourself
- Recognize your strengths
- Are true to yourself
- Value your feelings
- Are nice to yourself
- Prioritize your health and total wellbeing
- Set healthy boundaries
- Challenge yourself to be better

- Pursue your interests and goals
- Say positive things to yourself
- Accept your imperfections
- Spend time with the people who support you and believe in you
- Avoid toxic people
- Ask for help
- Make healthy choices most times
- Don't let other people take advantage of you
- Live according to your set values and principles
- Hold yourself accountable
- Release grudges or anger that holds you back
- Set realistic expectations
- Appreciate your effort to become a better version of yourself
- Notice and celebrate your progress
- Give yourself healthy treats

This list isn't exhaustive. There are many more. However, this description will give you a glimpse of what self-love means and allow you to assess yourself with it. You're beautiful only if you see yourself as beautiful. You're smart only if you regard yourself as smart. Whatever the quality or characteristic, you're a product of the way you see yourself. Your self-worth, self-esteem, and self-confidence hinge on your love for self.

Debunking Self-Love Myths

From my interactions with different people, I've realized that everyone has their own idea of what self-love is, but in truth, it's not what they think. In this section, I'll share a few misconceptions and try to show you the true side of it as well.

Myth 1: Self-love is self-centered

Self-love could sound like you're only focused on yourself without minding what goes on with other people. It could also sound like you're only taking care of yourself, but that's not what it's all about.

If self-love is viewed from the standpoint that you're better and more worthy than other people, you'll lose the moral heart to extend love to the people around you. The real essence of self-love is to embrace yourself with great compassion and earnest faith in yourself. And while doing so, you extend the same compassion to others as well.

In essence, self-love starts with you but it doesn't end with you. It makes you a better human with whom others can have a healthy relationship.

Myth 2: Self-love is a path to self-sufficiency

No! It's true that to love yourself properly, you need to set healthy boundaries. And such boundaries limit the access some folks have to you. It stands as a wall that wards off toxic people.

However, you should also remember what I told you about interdependence. To believe that self-love leads to self-sufficiency is to defy the law of nature. No one is self-sufficient. We need people around us in different contexts at different times. We cannot reach our goals alone. Any description of self-love that contradicts the principle of interdependence is wrong. Self-love makes you an independent individual who can have better relationships with other people without being intimidated into conforming to other people's opinions.

Myth 3: Self-love makes you complacent

When describing self-love to people, we tell them to take their eyes off their weaknesses, flaws, and mistakes and focus on their strengths. But we're not saying you should ignore your mistakes and never take responsibility for your life.

Self-love doesn't mean being irresponsible; in fact, it makes you take charge of your life and live your life to the fullest. You can't do that if you're complacent and you

Robert J. Charles, PhD, DMin

leave things to fate. Self-love doesn't mean that you should accept your flaws and say things like, "Well, that's just the way I am. I love myself this way. There's nothing I can do about it." It's actually quite the opposite—if you love yourself, you'll work on getting better. There's no form of work that's done complacently. It all requires a certain degree of diligence and commitment.

Myth 4: Self-love is about proving a point to other people

What point do you want to prove by loving yourself? The only person you need to prove anything to is yourself. That's what self-love is. Over the years, people have told you that you can't do certain things and you believed them. You tell yourself you can't do it, too. You refuse to attempt anything worthwhile because you've failed at it once. The only person affected here is you—your self-esteem, self-worth, and self-confidence have been shattered.

When you begin to love yourself properly, you'll tell yourself that you can do what people said you couldn't. You can succeed in the things you've failed at before. You're pushing yourself to believe in possibilities. That's how to love yourself.

Will people see your progress and evolution? Of course! Nothing good can be hidden for too long. But your real intention for doing the amazing things you do for yourself isn't to make a statement or prove a point to anyone.

Myth 5: Self-love is only for those who struggle to believe in themselves

As much as this may sound true, it doesn't reveal the whole truth about the practice of self-love.

Although people who are experiencing an identity crisis or relationship problems might need it more than other people who feel confident in themselves, we all need to love ourselves unconditionally. Life isn't a bed of roses. There are days when life will toss challenges our way. The way we handle those challenges shows how much we've invested in our minds. Anyone who doesn't love themselves lives by chance, but those who love themselves and want to continue on the path of success invest in themselves and enrich themselves mentally, spiritually, and physically. You don't need to have an identity or relationship crisis to love yourself.

333

Myth 6: Self-love says all you need to excel is within you

Self-love teaches you to look within and appreciate the great gifts you've been endowed with, but it certainly doesn't teach you that all that's within you is sufficient to take you to your destination. Your innate abilities are enough to sustain you, but self-love also teaches you to recognize the gifts in others and appreciate them for the things they contribute to your existence and the existence of the human race.

The most important thing to remember about self-love is that you're living from the inside out. This means that if you're healthy within, you can have healthy relationships with other people. If you love yourself, you can give the same love to others.

How to Start Loving Yourself

Now that you know what self-love is and what it's not, the next most pertinent question is: How do I start loving myself? Self-love may come in the form of eating healthy, exercising, or having healthy relationships.

Here are a few ways you can start:

Be committed: The best way to start learning how to love yourself is to commit yourself to doing so. It must be an intentional learning process. The results might not come as quickly as you want, but your commitment to learning will keep you at it until you begin to get the desired result.

Control your impulses: Our impulses and desires can be weird at times. For instance, there are times we crave certain foods. If we respond to and overindulge in our desires, the aftermath of such a response is that a feeling of condemnation washes over us. To start practicing self-love, you must learn to distinguish between the things you need and the things you want. Focus on the things you need only. Reduce the control your impulsive desires have over you.

Practice healthy habits: Decide within yourself to practice healthy habits like eating right and exercising. Commit to doing valuable things during the day, spend time with your family, have healthy conversations with friends and colleagues, etc. Don't do these things out of compulsion or necessity; do them because you want to.

Be patient: Don't expect these things to begin to yield immediate results. If you're coming from a point where you don't treat yourself well enough, you'll need time to adjust and adapt to this new learning scheme. Therefore, be patient with yourself. Just as a baby learns to walk, learn to take one step at a time. Don't be in haste to become perfect at once. Love is patient.

Have dialogues with yourself: It helps a lot if you can create time to have honest conversations with yourself. This could look like a moment of reflection or self-evaluation. The most important thing is that you're questioning beliefs you have perhaps held for years and have allowed to define you.

Ask yourself about your values, beliefs, emotions, behavioral patterns, habits, etc. The things you find out will help you to make necessary adjustments to begin to live right.

The benefits that come with loving yourself are enormous. It will improve everything in your life—your self-esteem, relationships, self-worth, self-confidence, health, and wellbeing. Fulfilling your dreams will become possible.

A Special Note: What Does the Bible Say about Codependency?

God created man and all other creatures to function in perfect harmony. God's structure of creation was simple: man would be in control of the entirety of creation, while everything would work together for man (Genesis 1:26-30). At another time, God created a helper for the man because of the nature of his tasks (Genesis 2:18).

This shows that God's template for the whole of creation was interdependence. God intended the world to function by mutual relationship.

Unfortunately, after the great fall (Genesis 3:1-19), man became an arrogant, self-seeking, deceptive, and murderous being (Genesis 4:3-10) who would do anything to preserve his ego and remain the center of attention. That was the beginning of toxic relationships according to these scriptural records.

Jesus the True Model

Jesus had a great relationship with His disciples. The force behind all His actions was love. As a leader, He demonstrated love for all of humanity by releasing himself to be punished and sacrificed on behalf of the entire human race. This makes sacrifice the highest form of demonstrating love.

Contemporary Christians

Two millennia after the departure of Jesus, contemporary Christians are still expected to follow in the footsteps of Jesus–to walk in love (Ephesians 5:2). But Jesus made it clear that the extent to which you love your neighbor shows the extent to which you love yourself (Mark 12:31).

Love is the sole law that guides the Christian community. But what does this love mean? Going by the example in the Bible:

- Love is sacrifice (John 15:13)
- Love is selfless service (Matthew 20:26-27)
- Love is giving (John 3:16)
- Love is genuine interest in others (Philippians 2:4)

Does This Love Make Me Foolish?

Love is not foolish. A lot of Christians misunderstand what it means to love genuinely. But gleaning wisdom from the life of Jesus will show the truth. If love is patient and kind, then Jesus, being the perfect example of a lover, was patient and kind. But despite His patience and kindness, He never allowed anyone to take advantage of Him. He went wherever He chose to go, not where the people wanted Him (Mark 1:37-38). He visited the places He wanted to visit whether people approved of it or not (Luke 19:1-10). He was in charge of His life.

Love makes you compassionate, but you shouldn't run into debt because you're trying to help another Christian. We have been exhorted to bear each other's burden (Galatians 6:2), but how can you bear another's burden when your own needs your attention?

Ultimately, to sacrifice something valuable for someone in the name of love has to be by choice, not out of self-pity. Jesus said that He laid down His life willingly; He wasn't compelled to do so (John 10:18). He was an independent leader who didn't derive His sense of fulfillment from doing what people would have Him do, but from doing whatever He knew was best for Himself and others.

A Closing Statement

In closing, self-love is not about shutting yourself out of the world while you create a utopic space for yourself alone, a space where all that matters is you. Rather, it's an opportunity to create a healthy and serene space within in order to accommodate new relationships. It's a powerful way of finding your feet again and walking on the path of fulfillment. And as you do so, you release the fragrance of love to those you meet on your path.

Exercise One

Fill in the blanks with words of self-love showing who you are and what you now believe about yourself. For example, "I am intelligent."

1 I am

_____

2 I am

_____

3 I am

_____

4 I am

_____

5 I am

_____

6 I am

_____

7 I am

_____

8 I am

_____

9 I am

_____

10 I am

_____

How you view yourself matters. All these words you've written about yourself aren't mere writing exercises. Read them aloud daily, and you'll see how much more you'll begin to respect yourself and fall in love with your being.

Exercise Two

This activity will help you ascertain things you love and hate about yourself. When you're done filling in the boxes, work on the things you hate about yourself. This will help you have more things you love about yourself. The more things you have on your love list, the more you'll love yourself.

WHAT YOU LOVE ABOUT YOURSELF	WHAT YOU HATE ABOUT YOURSELF

Chapter Eight Takeaway

A popular disinfectant brand that I love has a slogan along these lines: "If I don't take care of you, who will?"

Well, let's invert that now, shall we? If you don't take care of yourself, who will?

Take care of yourself. You get the drift.

Conclusion

M y husband and I were married for 16 years and had two beautiful daughters. Our lives couldn't have been better. Until they got worse. He met a woman at the gym, and I was suddenly "too old." When he served me divorce papers, I thought I was in a nightmare. My life fell apart in two weeks as one thing led to another and we finalized the divorce. I thought I would die.

I'm telling this story now, five years later, and I'm fine because I've moved on. What I want to share is this: My happiness now is not automatic. I'm happy because I'm doing well for myself, and also because I've got wonderful people around me who support me.

If one human makes you sad, another human will make you happy. If you had a toxic relationship, you can have a new, non-toxic one. If you were codependent and had to break free, you can become interdependent and begin to love healthily. You need people, even if you've been hurt by humans in the past.

—*Story by Serena*

As early as the late third century AD, there was a group of individuals—men and women—who lived in different times and places in history, but had similar experiences. Common to their experiences is the fact that they all wanted to attain a higher level of spiritual perfection. They wanted to be morally upright and holy. Therefore, they committed themselves to asceticism. Some took their practice to the extreme; they isolated themselves from civilization and people and began living alone in the ancient Egyptian deserts. They're known as "desert fathers and mothers."

Although a few of them achieved their goals, this is not the best path forward for most people in this modern age. Humans might be flawed and damaged, but how can we live out our dreams and explore our potential if we're not living in this flawed space together as a society?

You may have had some nasty experiences in your relationships, and that could be one of the main reasons you chose to read this book. But your past experience doesn't change the fact that you still need to live your life in the human community. The question, then, is: How do you live in a society filled with all different kinds of humans and still be fulfilled and happy?

That's one of the questions to which I hope this book has provided a robust answer. Primarily, my aim with this book has been to focus on specific types of relationships: those that are toxic and dangerous for your wellbeing. Having interacted with a lot of people, I can confidently say that codependency and narcissism are both toxic in relationships, and many people are silently suffering in their relationships as a result.

Being in such a relationship is proof that humans are still flawed, including you—but the good news is that humans can change and become better. We can all become better partners, live happily with our family members, and have healthy work relationships with our colleagues at the office.

This book has offered practical steps to help anyone who seeks to become a better human. I didn't stop there, though. The first port of call is to become an independent individual who doesn't need to depend on others to live a good life. One of the things a toxic relationship does is make you dependent on someone else's evaluation of you (often, these are demeaning and devastating evaluations that make you feel bad and even, in some cases, unworthy of living).

When you take the steps I've shown in this book, you'll begin to realize that there's more to life than what someone you were in a relationship with has told you. Therefore, having an independent opinion of yourself is the first step to becoming a better human.

However, to have a good opinion of yourself, you need to love yourself unapologetically. It's only then you'll be able to wash off the negative labels and toxic perspectives you've held about yourself due to what others have said.

Being an independent individual in relationships is only the start of your journey to becoming a better human in society. You'll still need other people to live a fulfilled life; no one is self-sufficient. You need other people—healthy people—in your circle. In this way, you'll achieve a higher level of relationship whereby you retain your individuality, but you're still a great partner, and you enjoy your life to the fullest.

I trust that this book has taken you on a journey of self-realization, healing, and recovery. From the first page to the last, I hope there have been moments of truth and revelation. I know you're ready for a change. It's your time to face that fear. You're ready to meet the new you.

So, don't hesitate—go start applying everything you've learned so far, if you haven't already.

BOOK #4

Happiness Returns - The Self Care and Self Compassion Workbook

15 Easy Techniques to Strengthen Your Mind, Master Emotional Regulation, Embrace Self-Acceptance to Step Into Your New and Happy Life

"I'm back! What did I miss?..."

Introduction

Whate can you expect from a group of people caught in the crossfire of what started as a cry for justice but soon descended into a full-blown civil war—people whose families were torn apart and their homes reduced to rubble, their nation in ruins and their lives forever changed?

Happiness? I doubt that...

Yamen is one of the young people caught in the crossfire in Syria and is now a refugee who has faced enormous challenges after arriving in the United States.

With little knowledge of the English language, Yamen took it upon himself to learn. He pored over books, listened to podcasts, and practiced speaking with anyone who would lend an ear. His dedication paid off, and he passed his GED, thanks to the support of a nonprofit school for refugee children.

Yamen's commitment didn't stop there. He began volunteering at the very same school that helped him on his educational journey. Through his tireless efforts, he gained a reputation as a reliable and helpful worker. And then, by a stroke of luck, an incredible donor decided to sponsor him for college.

Curious about how Yamen had managed to find happiness amidst these stark realities, Hugo Huijer (2020), founder of the blog Tracking Happiness, asked him for his secret. His answer was amazingly profound. Yamen said with a smile,

"Happiness is about how you're raised to view things."

Yamen went on to say that despite their struggles, his parents instilled in him and his siblings the belief that they had everything they needed to be happy and taught them to find satisfaction in what they had, rather than yearning for what they lacked. It was a mindset that carried Yamen through times of crisis and uncertainty.

He explained that even now, in the midst of upheaval and challenges, he strives to focus on the present and embrace what he does have—not to dwell on the elusive possibilities of the future, but rather to find contentment in the here and now.

In an age where so many things, including our daily lives, are defined by social media, we often find ourselves striving for happiness, seeking fulfillment in external accomplishments and possessions. However, true happiness isn't something we can find outside of ourselves. It resides within us, waiting to be discovered and nurtured.

This book, *Happiness Returns: The Self-Compassion and Self-Care Workbook,* is a guide that will lead you towards unlocking the secrets to a truly contented and fulfilling life.

Each chapter is a treasure chest that takes you deeper into the core of your being—meaning, we're not necessarily embarking on a utopic journey to a fabulous future, where all things are perfect; rather, we're diving deep into the depths of our being, exploring the profound connection between self-compassion, self-care, emotional wellbeing, and happiness.

This journey begins in Chapter 1, where we lay the foundation by understanding the essence of self-compassion. We explore the transformative power of being kind to oneself, fostering a gentle and understanding relationship with our inner selves. This leads us to discover that self-compassion is not only an act of kindness but also a catalyst for personal growth and happiness.

Taking a step further, we explore the fascinating world of happiness in Chapter 2. We're not just talking about the superficial experience here; we're diving into the psychology behind it all. We want to understand what truly makes us happy—is it just a temporary mood or something more profound? We'll debunk some common misconceptions and unravel the key elements that contribute to a deep sense of joy. By delving into the intricacies of happiness, we'll equip ourselves with the knowledge and insights to create a life that's brimming with authentic contentment.

With the wisdom of self-compassion and a solid understanding of true happiness, Chapter 3 introduces us to the practice of mindful self-compassion. This mindfulness helps us approach ourselves with kindness and understanding. By embracing mindful self-compassion, we're setting ourselves on a powerful path towards happiness. It's a journey that nurtures our wellbeing in the present moment, embraces our imperfections, and fosters personal growth.

In Chapter 4, we'll explore the intriguing connection between self-esteem and happiness. There's a complex dance between these two forces, and we want to understand how having a healthy sense of self-worth can impact our overall wellbeing and long-term happiness. There are proven practices that can boost our self-esteem and empower us to lead lives filled with confidence, authenticity, and a genuine appreciation for who we truly are.

Emotional health plays a vital role in our pursuit of happiness, and that's exactly what Chapter 5 is all about. We're going to explore strategies to nurture our emotional wellbeing, enhance our resilience, and cultivate positive emotions. Life throws challenges our way, but by mastering the skills of emotional wellbeing, we'll have the tools to stay in a happy state even when the going gets tough.

Chapter 6 tackles a common roadblock on our path to happiness: depression. Depression is often one of the reasons for the loss of amazing souls in our communities. It isn't a plague against one person, but against an entire race. And it doesn't respect status, background, color, or tongue. Therefore, it's important to deal with the plague of depression before it robs us of our brightest minds.

In Chapter 7, we're all about strengthening our minds. Your mind is the center of the action. That's what this whole book is targeting. It's also the place from which negativity emanates, if we let it. To have a negative mentality is to be toxic and pessimistic and not even try to live happily. This chapter, therefore, aims at reprogramming our mentality to discover the incredible inner strength within each of us. We'll share practical techniques to cultivate a resilient mindset. With these tools, we can face adversity with courage and come out stronger on the other side.

The last chapter, Chapter 8, brings us to the crucial pillar of self-care. We'll uncover the transformative impact of nourishing our minds, bodies, and spirits. This chapter reveals the practices and rituals that promote a happier and more fulfilling existence. By embracing self-care as an integral part of our lives, we'll create a solid foundation for sustained happiness, ensuring that our wellbeing remains a top priority.

As you embark on this incredible internal journey through the pages of *The Self-Compassion and Self-Care Workbook*, always remember that true happiness isn't some far-off destination—it's a way of being and living. By embracing self-compassion and self-care, and by understanding the psychology of happiness, you will give yourself the power to transform your life and experience the joy that you deserve.

Don't try to rush to finish this book as quickly as possible. I recommend you take each chapter a week at a time, or read one part over the span of a week, whichever one works for you. Just ensure you get the most from these pages.

So, let's embark on this transformative adventure together and cultivate a life filled with happiness, purpose, and a deep love for ourselves.

I'm ready whenever you're ready to flip to the next page.

Robert

PART 1

Self-Compassion and Its Link to Happiness

Happiness is abstract, and it means different things to different people.

As abstract as it is, though, virtually everyone is in search of happiness. Everyone wants a share of it. Our search for happiness takes us to different places. Unfortunately, many people are usually frustrated and met with disappointment when they don't find happiness in the places their search takes them.

So, where does happiness reside? How can you possibly handle something as abstract as happiness?

As I guide you through the first part of this book, you'll realize that what we seek isn't lost. Happiness is naturally attracted to another abstract phenomenon: love. So, to be happy, you need to understand love first. And before anything or anyone else, you need to be able to love yourself.

In this part, you'll also learn that happiness goes beyond superficial appearances. There's a psychological dimension to it. The objective of this part is to help you see and understand that dimension so that you won't be tossed about by transient emotional outbursts.

Are you ready for a mental paradigm shift? Then this is for you. Let's get started.

CHAPTER 1

Being Kind to Self

"Love your neighbor as yourself."

—Matthew 19:19

"Be nice to yourself… It's hard to be happy when someone is mean to you all the time."

—Christine Arylo

During my undergrad studies, I had an amazing friend named Maya. She was a sweet young woman, the kind you always love to have in your circle. She always put everyone else's needs before her own. She was a loving and supportive friend who went above and beyond to make sure everyone around her was happy and taken care of.

However, amidst all her selflessness, I noticed that Maya wasn't giving herself as much care as she gave to others. In fact, she rarely took time for self-care and would dismiss her own needs and desires, believing that they were not as important as those of others. Over time, this self-neglect started taking a toll on her wellbeing. She felt drained, overwhelmed, and constantly stressed.

Although it took time for her to reevaluate her priorities, she eventually had a moment of realization. She began to realize that in order to be truly there for others and make a positive impact, she needed to start being kind to herself as well. She had always thought it was selfish to look out for herself, but now she knows better. Looking out for herself was the realest act of self-compassion and self-preservation.

As a step toward reinventing herself and living a truly happy life, Maya told me then that she now sets aside some time each day just for herself. She admitted that there was a limit to what she could do for people. This helped her learn how to set boundaries. Of course, these changes didn't happen as swiftly as waving a magic wand. It took some time for her to make these adjustments. But in those moments of transformation, she evolved into a happier friend.

—Olivia

Taking a cue from Maya's story, I'd consider this the golden rule for being truly happy in life: love yourself first.

"Hey, don't give me that look!"

Self-Compassion: Crucial to Happiness

Does anyone deserve to be happier than you?

I can imagine your hesitation in responding to that question. Your piety and generous mind kicked in the moment you read that question because you want people around you to be happy too—even happier than you are, perhaps. Well, I don't dispute that. Every well-meaning person deserves to be happy.

But should they be happier at your expense?

Do you deserve to be happy?

Those questions are not intended to undermine your intention to do the things you do for other people; rather, they're intended to make you reflect—an introspective reflection of your actions, ideals, and perspectives in relation to your total wellbeing.

You, my reader, are the focus of this book, not the other person you care so much about (although you can recommend the book to them as well, and I encourage you to do so). But at this moment, I see you alone. And you are the focus of my long hours at my writing desk.

Self-compassion is crucial to your happiness, yes! But who is this self, and why does it need compassion?

Using *self* as an affix is pretty common today. Because of this, many people use *self-this* and *self-that* casually without thinking about what "self" actually means. I'm telling you right now, "self" is not just a word. It is a reference to a living entity.

Let's take a quick look at **what or who this self is**. I'm going to be a bit analytical in trying to help you understand the self.

The ancient Greek philosopher Aristotle believed that when it comes to the self, it's all about the combination of the body and soul. He called this idea "hylomorphic." Basically, you can't separate the two—they're always connected. So, talking about the self means considering both the body and the soul. Aristotle believed that the self is essentially a harmonious blend of the physical and immaterial aspects (Admin, 2022).

In summary, according to Aristotle, the self is a combination of the body and the soul. This is the first point.

Another philosopher whose perspective I'd like us to consider is Socrates. I love his view on this. Socrates had a different take on the true self. He didn't think it was about what we owned, our social status, our reputation, or even our physical bodies. According to Socrates, our true self is actually our soul. This means that the essence of who we really are goes beyond material possessions or external factors. Socrates became famous for emphasizing the importance of our inner being, our soul, as the core of our true selves (Academy of Ideas, 2015).

On this point, Socrates and Aristotle seemed to agree about the soul being the true self.

Do you have a soul?

Two more definitions, and then you'll see what I'm trying to paint vividly.

The philosopher Plato, who was Socrates's student, takes a step further to explain the essence and composition of the self. He had an interesting idea about the nature of the self. He believed that the self is primarily an intellectual entity and that its essence exists independently of the physical world.

In other words, according to Plato, who we truly are goes beyond our physical body and is rooted in our intellectual capabilities. This means that our true selves are not limited or defined by our physical surroundings but are instead connected to a deeper realm of knowledge and understanding (Valerio, 2019).

And finally, the Merriam-Webster Dictionary expounds on what the self consists of through its definition. According to Merriam-Webster, we're referring to the unique combination of different elements that make us who we are. These elements include things like our "body, emotions, thoughts, and sensations" (Merriam-Webster, 2023). It's the coming together of all these aspects that form the very essence of a person.

So, essentially, the union of these various elements shapes a person's individuality and identity.

What are the commonalities?

1. Self is not external; it is internal.
2. Self is not material; it is immaterial.
3. Self is not only your body but a combination of your soul and your body. Therefore, if you're hurting within and you're trying to feign happiness physically, you're hurting yourSELF.

What does this have to do with your happiness?

Socrates specifically explained that only when we truly know ourselves can we learn how to take care of ourselves. Without being aware of the "self," we'll always be in the dark about what we really need (Academy of Ideas, 2015). So, according to Socrates, getting to know ourselves is the first step toward living a fulfilling life.

You can't be truly compassionate toward yourself if you don't know who you are. So here it is, dear reader—the first step to being happy is: **Know yourSELF, and you'll know what you need**.

When you fail, what do you need?

When you make a mistake, what do you need?

When you couldn't meet a deadline, what do you need?

Self-compassion and happiness

When people around you are in need of love, a companion, comfort, or encouragement, you know what to do or say to make them feel better. You show compassion to them because you know what they need in that moment.

But when you find yourself in the same boat as those people, can you recognize what you need?

Recognizing your needs—physical, intellectual, and emotional—and serving yourSELF is being compassionate to yourSELF. That's the pathway to being happy.

But remember, to recognize your needs, you'll have to recline in your seat a bit and spend some time with yourself regularly to get to know yourself. You'll find out so many amazing things you didn't know about YOU before.

Try this short exercise:

Set aside about 20–30 minutes to be with yourself for the next seven days. During this time, ask yourself, "Who am I?" Document everything you discover in a journal.

The Importance of Self-Compassion

Is self-compassion important? I can almost hear my inner being screaming, YES! After reading the previous section, you've probably deduced the importance of self-compassion.

Here are 15 benefits of self-compassion:

1. **Emotional wellbeing:** It nurtures positive emotions and reduces negative ones, leading to greater overall emotional wellbeing.

2. **Resilience:** It helps build resilience by providing a supportive and understanding inner voice during challenging times.

3. **Self-acceptance:** It fosters self-acceptance, allowing us to embrace our imperfections and recognize our inherent worthiness.

4. **Reduced self-criticism:** It decreases self-critical thoughts and reduces the tendency to be overly hard on oneself.

5. **Improved mental health:** It contributes to improved mental health outcomes, such as lower levels of anxiety and depression.

6. **Increased motivation:** It encourages self-motivation and the pursuit of personal growth and goals without harsh self-judgment.

7. **Healthier relationships:** By cultivating self-compassion, we develop healthier and more compassionate relationships with others.

8. **Stress reduction:** It helps to alleviate stress and promotes a greater sense of calm and relaxation.

9. **Enhanced self-care:** It encourages self-care practices, as we recognize the importance of attending to our own needs and wellbeing.

10. **Boosted self-confidence:** It boosts self-confidence and self-esteem, as we learn to treat ourselves with kindness and understanding.

11. **Improved decision-making:** It fosters a non-judgmental attitude, which supports clearer and more rational decision-making.

12. **Empathy for others:** By extending compassion to ourselves, we also develop greater empathy and compassion for others.

13. **Increased self-awareness:** Self-compassion cultivates self-awareness, allowing us to better understand our emotions, thoughts, and behaviors.

14. **Authentic self-expression:** It enables us to express ourselves authentically and embrace our true selves without fear of judgment.

15. **Happiness and life satisfaction:** Ultimately, self-compassion contributes to increased happiness and overall life satisfaction.

What Self-Compassion Is and Isn't

I've explained what self-compassion is, but just a little addition here. According to Dr. Emma Seppälä (2021), the Science Director of Stanford University's Center for Compassion and Altruism Research and Education, self-compassion means treating yourself with the same kindness and understanding that you would show to a friend who made a mistake or didn't meet expectations.

Instead of criticizing or berating your friend, you would likely offer a listening ear and remind them that mistakes are a normal part of life, right? Self-compassion is about extending that same gentle and supportive approach to yourself. It means acknowledging your own imperfections and being understanding, just as you would be with a friend.

Self-compassion is not...

Self-pity

It is not about wallowing in self-pity or constantly seeking sympathy from others.

Self-indulgence

It is not about indulging in unhealthy behaviors or making excuses for harmful actions.

Selfishness

It does not promote selfishness or disregard the needs and feelings of others.

Self-criticism

It is not about engaging in self-criticism or harsh self-judgment.

Self-esteem

While related, self-compassion is not the same as self-esteem. It doesn't rely on external validation or comparisons to others.

Self-denial

It is not about denying your own needs or sacrificing your wellbeing for the sake of others.

Self-isolation

It does not encourage isolating oneself or avoiding social connections.

Self-absorption

It is not about being self-absorbed or solely focused on one's own needs without considering others.

Self-deception

It does not involve deceiving oneself or avoiding responsibility for one's actions.

Self-judgment

It is not about judging oneself or engaging in a constant evaluation of one's personal worth based on achievements or failures.

Self-comparison

It is not about constantly comparing oneself to others or striving for unrealistic standards.

Self-doubt

It is not about harboring self-doubt or undermining one's own abilities and potential.

Self-righteousness

It is not about adopting a self-righteous attitude or feeling superior to others.

Self-ignorance

It is not about ignoring or neglecting self-awareness and personal growth.

There's this balanced outlook to self-compassion. It's just a nurturing way of relating to yourself and fostering kindness, understanding, and acceptance without falling into these misconceptions or extremes.

The Three Main Components

Dr. Kristin Neff, a psychologist and associate professor in the department of educational psychology at the University of Texas, did some groundbreaking research on self-compassion. In the course of her research, she came up with three components of self-compassion (Frank Porter Graham Program on Mindfulness & Self-Compassion, 2023). The three components of self-compassion are:

Self-kindness

Common humanity

Mindfulness

Being self-compassionate is being kind to self

Being self-compassionate means treating ourselves with kindness instead of being overly critical when things go wrong. It's about understanding that it's normal to make mistakes and face difficulties in life. Rather than getting angry or ignoring pain, self-compassionate people show themselves gentleness and acceptance.

Being self-compassionate is accepting our humanity

When we're frustrated, it's easy to think we're the only ones going through tough times or making mistakes. But self-compassion reminds us that suffering and imperfection are part of being human. It's about recognizing that we're not alone in our struggles and that everyone experiences challenges and setbacks.

Being self-compassionate is being mindful of our situation

Self-compassion means finding a good balance when it comes to dealing with our negative emotions. It's about having a healthy approach and not letting them overwhelm us. It means neither suppressing nor exaggerating them. We achieve this by connecting our own experiences of suffering to the experiences of others, gaining a broader perspective. It also requires being mindful, which means observing our thoughts and feelings without judgment* or denial. Mindfulness helps us hold our pain with awareness, without getting overwhelmed by it or carried away by negative reactions.

* Do you want to become Your Own Best Friend? Check out the Worksheet #1 in the BONUS #2 at the beginning of the book.

Understanding Self-Esteem

There's this folktale about a certain oak tree that I heard some years ago. The oak tree was majestic and stood tall in the midst of the forest. With its towering height and strong branches, the tree commanded admiration from all the surrounding trees. However, deep within, the tree had a secret struggle—it doubted its worth and felt insignificant compared to the other grand trees in the forest.

One day, a powerful storm swept through the forest. Fierce winds blew, rain poured, and thunder roared. The forest was in chaos. While other trees bowed, and some were uprooted, the oak tree stood tall, its roots firmly grounded. As the storm subsided, the oak realized something remarkable—it had weathered the tempest with resilience and strength.

Word of its unwavering presence during the storm spread throughout the forest. Other trees, once envious of the oak's stature, began seeking its guidance and protection. The oak humbly shared its knowledge, offering shelter and support to those in need.

This made the oak realize the significance of its unwavering presence. It understood that its unique qualities and strength were valuable contributions to the forest ecosystem.

What does this mean for our discussion of self-esteem? Well, sometimes you don't know how much you're worth until your strength is put to the test.

What is self-esteem?

Cherry (2022) describes self-esteem as how you see yourself and how much you value yourself. It's like having a personal measure of how much you respect and believe in your own abilities and qualities. In a nutshell, it's about how confident you feel about yourself.

Your self-esteem has an impact on various aspects of your life. It can influence:

How much you like and appreciate yourself as an individual

Your ability to make decisions and confidently express your thoughts and opinions

Your recognition of your own strengths and abilities

Your willingness to step out of your comfort zone and tackle new or challenging tasks

The level of kindness and compassion you show yourself

How you handle mistakes without unfairly blaming and criticizing yourself

Your ability to prioritize and take time for self-care and personal wellbeing

Your belief that you are important and worthy, just as you are

Your belief that you deserve happiness and fulfillment in life

According to Trzesniewski et al. (2003), self-esteem usually starts off lower in childhood and then tends to grow as we become teenagers and adults. Eventually, it reaches a point where it becomes relatively steady and consistent. It's kind of like how our personality traits also tend to stay fairly stable over time. So, just like our personalities, our self-esteem develops and solidifies as we grow older.

When You Have Low Self-Esteem

As a teen, I used to struggle to air my opinions in class. Even when I knew the answer to a question, at best, it stayed in my head and I kept quiet because I was always afraid of what others would think if I got it wrong.

I was in a chemistry class one day and our chemistry teacher asked a question. Not even the brightest students in the class could answer it, but I knew the answer. The answer kept dancing somewhere in my head but couldn't step out of my mouth. I doubted myself. If the best students in the class couldn't answer the question, who was I to do so?

The teacher had a mix of disappointment and frustration written on her face. After waiting for someone to answer her question (no one did), she answered it herself. Fortunately for me, I was correct, but only in my head. The guilt of not being bold enough to say the answer that day lingered with me for a while. Later on, I criticized myself for not being brave enough to answer.

I'm a better adult now. But the scars from not believing in myself while growing up remain.

—*Lucas*

Low self-esteem is like having a little voice in your head that constantly puts you down. It tells you things like "You're no good," "You're overweight," "What's the point?", or "You're not capable of doing this." It's that negative chatter that undermines your confidence and makes you doubt yourself.

What happens when you have low self-esteem?

Persistent self-doubt

Feelings of worthlessness or inadequacy

Fear of judgment or rejection by others

Difficulty in asserting oneself or setting boundaries

Always needing validation and approval from others

Avoidance of new challenges or opportunities due to fear of failure

Negative self-talk and self-criticism

Lack of self-confidence and self-belief

Tendency to compare oneself unfavorably to others

Vulnerability to anxiety, depression, or other mental health issues

Difficulty in maintaining healthy relationships

Reduced motivation and ambition

Social withdrawal or isolation

Increased susceptibility to peer pressure or manipulation

Limited belief in one's own abilities and potential

What causes low self-esteem?

From my personal experience and reflection, I know that low self-esteem can be caused by one or more of the following:

Bullying or experiencing abuse

Prejudice, discrimination, or stigma (e.g., racism)

Job loss or difficulty finding employment

Work or study-related challenges

Physical health issues

Mental health challenges

Relationship difficulties, separation, or divorce

Financial or housing problems

Concerns about appearance and body image

Feeling pressured to meet unrealistic expectations (e.g., from social media)

Childhood experiences of neglect or emotional/physical abuse

Critical or unsupportive parenting

Academic or athletic failures

Chronic stress or trauma

Unhealthy or toxic relationships

Social isolation or loneliness

Feeling like a failure in achieving personal goals

Cultural or societal pressure to conform

Internalizing negative messages from media or society

Perfectionism and fear of making mistakes

Unresolved past traumas or emotional wounds

Chronic illness or disability

Feelings of unworthiness due to past mistakes or regrets

You may have gone through some of these things, or you might have faced challenges that aren't mentioned here. It's also possible that there isn't just one specific cause for your low self-esteem.

If you're dealing with low self-esteem, making a change might seem hard. But don't worry, there are things you can do to improve it. There's hope for you.

Here are some simple actions you can take:

Be mindful of negative thoughts. Pay attention to those sneaky negative thoughts that affect how you see yourself. Recognize them and challenge their accuracy.

Question negative thinking patterns. When negative thoughts arise, challenge them by replacing them with more realistic and positive ones.

Embrace positive self-talk. Repeat positive affirmations to yourself, like a mini pep talk that uplifts your spirits (Cascio et al., 2015).

Cultivate self-compassion. Practice forgiveness for past mistakes and accept yourself as a whole, including your flaws and imperfections. Move forward with kindness and understanding.

The Role of Self-Compassion in Self-Esteem and Overall Wellbeing

Self-compassion plays a crucial role in shaping one's self-esteem. By cultivating self-compassion, you can develop a healthier and more positive relationship with yourself, which in turn positively impacts your self-esteem and overall sense of wellbeing. Self-compassion involves treating yourself with kindness, understanding, and acceptance, particularly in times of difficulty or self-judgment. It means acknowledging that everyone makes mistakes and experiences challenges, and extending the same compassion and support to yourself as you would to a close friend or loved one.

Practicing self-compassion has been shown to have a multitude of benefits. Here are some key points to consider:

1. **Enhances self-esteem:** Self-compassion helps individuals develop a kind and nurturing inner voice, counteracting the negative self-talk that often accompanies low self-esteem. By treating oneself with compassion, individuals can foster a greater sense of self-worth and appreciation.

2. **Reduces self-criticism:** Engaging in self-compassion practices helps individuals let go of harsh self-judgment and self-criticism. It encourages self-acceptance and self-forgiveness, leading to a more positive and nurturing mindset.

3. **Cultivates emotional resilience:** Self-compassion allows individuals to acknowledge and validate their emotions without judgment. By practicing self-compassion, individuals build emotional resilience, allowing them to navigate life's challenges with greater ease and bounce back from setbacks.

4. **Supports overall wellbeing:** Self-compassion contributes to a sense of overall wellbeing by promoting self-care, stress reduction, and positive self-regard. It encourages individuals to prioritize their physical, mental, and emotional needs, leading to improved overall health and happiness.

Common Self-Compassion Misconceptions

Earlier in this chapter, I told you what self-compassion isn't. As I close this chapter, I want to emphasize again some misconceptions you might have about self-compassion—and these come from the pioneer of the concept itself, Dr. Kristin Neff.

Dr. Neff (2020) shares the five top myths about self-compassion:

Myth 1: Self-compassion is equivalent to self-pity.

Myth 2: Self-compassion is a sign of weakness.

Myth 3: Self-compassion leads to complacency.

Myth 4: Self-compassion is narcissistic.

Myth 5: Self-compassion is selfish.

In reality, it's not any of those. Dr. Neff concludes by stating that self-compassion taps into our ability to love, be wise, show courage, and be generous. It's a state of mind and heart that knows no boundaries and doesn't require a specific path. It's accessible to every individual just by being human.

Chapter Takeaway

This chapter has given us a solid foundation for the whole essence of this book. If you've skipped any section in this chapter, you've missed a foundational building block in this book, so please make sure you've read through the entire chapter.

Our starting point in this book stressed the importance of understanding the self. Since the core message of this book is directed towards just one person, YOU, it's essential to have an understanding of yourself before you can direct any form of care towards yourself. An understanding of yourself will help you know what you need and how to cater to those needs.

Also, don't forget that the value you place on yourself has an effect on your wellbeing. Prioritize self-compassion and cultivate self-esteem, and you'll be signing yourself up for happiness.

CHAPTER 2

The Psychology of Happiness

"To the person who pleases him, God gives wisdom, knowledge and happiness."

—Ecclesiastes 2:26

"One of the secrets of a happy life is continuous small treats."

—Iris Murdoch

Emily, a typical millennial young woman who had always believed that external achievements and material possessions were the keys to happiness, worked tirelessly to climb the corporate ladder. She accumulated a lavish lifestyle and chased after societal ideals of success.

Despite her accomplishments, Emily felt a lingering sense of emptiness and dissatisfaction. She constantly yearned for more, believing that the next promotion, bigger house, or luxury purchase would finally bring her the happiness she sought.

Unfortunately, that vacuum kept expanding with each new accomplishment. She kept craving more. Frustrated, Emily began to wonder why, despite all she had acquired, that vacuum within her hadn't been filled yet.

She asked questions. She kept looking for answers. Finally, she found one in the most unlikely of places. She stumbled upon an old classmate from college at a mall and the two of them stopped to catch up. Emily discovered something that day: her old classmate wasn't living an exotic life like she was, yet she was happy and felt fulfilled. Emily had been looking for happiness in all the wrong places all this time.

I dare say that everyone longs to be happy, but obviously, not everyone *is* genuinely happy. As I delve into this discussion on happiness, please indulge me for a moment and respond to this question:

What can give you (not us) the happiness you long for? Have you found it yet?

Happiness: A Mood or a Feeling?

What do you associate with happiness?

Christmas is a special time of the year that many people look forward to. Oh, how they love the Yuletide season and that giddy sensation that grows larger in their hearts as Christmas approaches. Having loved ones around and being able to share the love and joy of the season with other people is usually the high point of the holiday.

Would you call that sensation during the Christmas season a feeling of happiness or a mood of happiness?

Well, you wouldn't be wrong if you called it a mood or a feeling. But whether you call it a mood or a feeling, I'd like you to bear in mind that both of these descriptions are temporal and imply that happiness is subject to external factors, like events, occasions, and seasons.

Is happiness a mood?

Foster (2013) states that researchers in anthropology and psychology have identified six primary emotions commonly experienced by humans: joy, distress, anger, fear, surprise, and disgust. Foster adds that some people also include happiness and sadness in this list, while others consider these to be moods rather than emotions.

However, Foster's stance on happiness is that when it comes to defining happiness as either an emotion or a mood, she personally finds it more sensible to consider it a mood. For instance, when she's in a happy mood, she tends to experience the emotion of joy more frequently, and it takes a lot to bring about the emotion of distress.

Is happiness a feeling?

Cherry (2022), in contrast, calls happiness a feeling—usually, happiness is when we feel joyful, satisfied, content, and fulfilled. She agrees, however, that although happiness can have various meanings, it's often described as having positive emotions and feeling satisfied with life.

Ackerman (2019) adds that happiness is often associated with experiencing pleasure and contentment. It's important to note that happiness is different from intense feelings like joy, ecstasy, or bliss.

Another school of thought says that happiness is *a state of mind*. Kashyap (2022) writes in the *Hindustan Times* that happiness is all about feeling good and having a positive mindset. It's something we can work on and develop within ourselves. The best part is that we get to choose whether we want to be happy or not. It's like having a remote control for our emotions! We have the power to decide how we feel. Remember, what we focus on tends to shape our experiences, so it's important to direct our attention towards the things that bring us joy and positivity.

My take

Whether you believe that happiness is a mood, a feeling, a state of mind, or a choice you're poised to make daily, I'd say whichever you go for, ensure you don't settle for anything transient.

If you think it's a mood or a feeling, you'll be inclined to believe that your happiness is tied to certain events, people, circumstances, or occasions. You don't expect those external factors to always happen, do you? And you don't expect them to always produce the same emotional energy, do you?

So think it through before you stick with an opinion. Stick with a definition that's not subject to time and seasons.

What Is True Happiness?

Purohit (2022) states that no one in this world has the exact answer to what true happiness really means because true happiness can mean different things to different people; we all have unique definitions and experiences of what makes us truly happy. And I think he's right.

Some people have emphatically proclaimed that happiness doesn't rely on what's happening around us or the circumstances we find ourselves in. It's not just a state of mind, either, but rather an attitude that comes from deep within the heart. It's about how we choose to approach life and the perspective we adopt.

So, *happiness is an attitude that flows from deep within*. I do concur!

In line with this thought, Julia Roberts, who starred as Elizabeth Robert in the biographical drama *Eat, Pray, Love*, says that happiness is something that doesn't just fall into our laps. It's the result of our personal efforts. We have to fight for it, work hard for it, and never give up on it.

Sometimes, we may even go on adventures and explore the world in search of it. We need to actively engage in the things that bring us joy and appreciate the blessings that come our way. Once we've found happiness, we can't become complacent. It's essential to continuously strive to maintain happiness. We must keep putting in the effort to stay afloat and keep swimming towards happiness.

This also means that *true happiness is an attitude that must be cultivated and nurtured over time*.

To achieve this, here are a few practical tips for you:

Be your own best friend: Treat yourself with love and kindness, just like you would treat a prince or princess.

Surround yourself with positivity: Stay away from people who bring negativity into your life.

Let go of negative emotions: Avoid feelings of envy, jealousy, fear, and anger as much as possible.

Take care of your wellbeing: Nourish your body and soul by eating nutritious meals and practicing meditation.

Enjoy your own company: Set aside time for yourself to engage in activities like reading, writing, or watching a movie at home. Embrace the opportunity to be alone without fearing it.

Make a pact with yourself: Commit to treating yourself in the best possible way, with love, respect, and self-care.

Practice kindness and humility: Start by being kind and humble towards yourself, and then extend that same kindness and humility to others.

Engage in small acts of selflessness: Spread positivity by smiling at strangers or offering your seat to someone in need on public transport.

Remember, happiness starts from within, and by taking these small steps, you can create a more joyful and fulfilling life.

The Role Our Brain Plays

Our brain plays a significant role in shaping our happiness and wellbeing (Hanson, 2013; Nesse, 2000). As human beings, we have inherited a complex brain that has evolved over millions of years and has shaped our thoughts, emotions, and behaviors in various ways.

One key aspect of our brain's role in happiness is its ability to regulate our emotions (Siegel, 2007). The limbic system, which includes structures like the amygdala and hippocampus, is responsible for processing emotions and forming memories. These brain regions help us experience and process both positive and negative emotions, which ultimately impact our overall happiness.

Furthermore, our brain is wired for social connection and belonging (Hanson, 2013). The prefrontal cortex, a part of the brain involved in social cognition and decision-making, allows us to form and maintain relationships, empathize with others, and experience feelings of love and belonging. These social connections and a sense of belonging are crucial for our happiness and wellbeing.

The brain is also equipped with a phenomenon called the "negativity bias" (Hanson, 2013). This means it has a tendency to pay more attention to negative experiences or threats in order to ensure our survival. While this bias helped our ancestors avoid danger, in today's world, it can lead to a greater focus on negativity and a reduced emphasis on positive experiences. Understanding this bias can help us consciously shift our attention toward positive aspects of life, cultivating happiness in the process.

It's important to note that our brain's influence on happiness is not fixed or predetermined. Through neuroplasticity, our brain has the remarkable ability to adapt and change throughout our lives (Davidson & Begley, 2012). We can actively engage in practices like mindfulness, positive affirmations, gratitude, and acts of kindness, which can reshape the neural pathways in our brain, fostering greater happiness and wellbeing.*

*Explore the self-care wheel and practice your perfect self-care day. Look for Worksheet 7 when you download the <u>BONUS #2</u>.

"Uhhh, Sir, I don't want to interrupt your meditation but we're live on air."

Why We Feel the Way We Do: The Psychology of Moods

Have you ever wondered why you feel the way you do in a given situation? Our moods are complex and can be influenced by various psychological factors. Let's take a closer look at the psychology of moods and why they occur.

1. Moods are often described as prolonged emotional states that can last for hours or even days. They are different from emotions, which are shorter-lived and more specific in nature. Moods tend to be less intense and have a broader range of emotional experiences.

2. One of the factors that influence our moods is our thoughts and beliefs. Our interpretation of events and situations can shape how we feel. For example, if we perceive a situation as threatening, we may experience anxiety or fear. On the other hand, if we view a situation positively, we may feel happiness or excitement.

3. Our behaviors and actions also play a role in our moods. Engaging in activities that we enjoy or that align with our values can boost our mood. Similarly, negative behaviors or situations can contribute to negative moods. For instance, if we constantly engage in self-critical thoughts or surround ourselves with negative influences, it can lead to feelings of sadness or frustration.

4. Social factors are another important aspect of our moods. Our interactions with others, such as receiving social support or facing social rejection, can impact how we feel. Positive social connections and a sense of belonging can enhance our mood, while loneliness or conflicts can lead to negative emotions.

5. Biological factors, including our brain chemistry and hormones, also play a role in our moods. Neurotransmitters like serotonin and dopamine influence our emotional wellbeing. Additionally, hormonal changes, such as those during menstruation or menopause, can affect mood stability.

6. Environmental factors, such as our physical surroundings and the weather, can influence our moods as well. For example, being in a pleasant environment or experiencing sunny weather can boost our mood, while a gloomy or stressful environment can contribute to negative feelings.

7. It's important to remember that our moods can fluctuate throughout the day and are influenced by a combination of these factors. Understanding the psychology of moods can help us become more aware of our emotional experiences and develop strategies to manage and improve our overall wellbeing.

Factors That Influence Your Mood

I'm sure you've experienced having your mood take a sudden dip and become negative. There are several factors at play that contribute to why this can happen, including biological, psychological, and environmental influences (Monitoring-your-mood, n.d.).

Let's take a closer look at some common factors that affect our moods.

Stress

We all know that stress can weigh us down and put us in a sour mood. Whether it's work deadlines, relationship issues, or financial pressures, stress has a way of casting a shadow over our emotions.

Poor sleep, fatigue, and overwork

When we're running on empty, lacking sleep and feeling exhausted, it's no wonder our mood takes a hit. Burning the candle at both ends can leave us feeling irritable and cranky.

Hangry moments

Ever experienced that sudden shift in mood when you're desperately in need of food? When your stomach starts rumbling, your mood can quickly plummet. It's amazing how a satisfying meal can turn things around.

Social interactions

Our encounters with other people can have a surprising impact on our mood. A rude comment, a friendly gesture, or an awkward encounter can all contribute to how we feel in the moment.

The news

Oh, the power of the media! Sometimes, getting bombarded with negative news stories can leave us feeling down and disheartened. It's hard to stay upbeat when the headlines are constantly filled with doom and gloom.

The weather

Nature has a way of influencing our mood. Rainy days can make us feel a bit gloomy, while sunny weather can lift our spirits. It's like our mood takes a cue from the sky.

Hormonal rollercoaster

We can't forget about the influence of hormones on our mood. From the ups and downs of puberty to the hormonal shifts that occur during a woman's menstrual cycle, pregnancy, and menopause, our mood can go for a wild ride.

Lack of exercise

When we've been sitting around like couch potatoes for too long, our mood can suffer. Getting our bodies moving and engaging in physical activity can do wonders for our mental wellbeing.

Lack of break time

Sometimes, we're just in dire need of a break, whether it's from the daily grind at work or responsibilities at home. Taking some time off and rejuvenating can work wonders for our mood.

And let's not forget these factors as well:

Colors

Believe it or not, certain colors can affect our mood. Bright and vibrant colors can uplift us, while dull and muted tones may have a more negative impact.

Dehydration

Our body's cry for water can also impact our mood. When we're not drinking enough water, it can leave us feeling sluggish and irritable.

Social media

Ah, the double-edged sword of social media. While it can connect us with others, it can also contribute to negative emotions. Comparing ourselves to others' highlight reels or getting caught up in online drama can definitely put a damper on our mood.

Posture

Yes, even our posture can influence how we feel. Slouching and hunching can make us feel down, while standing tall and confidently can give us a mood boost.

Partner's mood

The vibes from our significant other can have a ripple effect on our own mood. When our partner is in a grumpy mood, it can be contagious and bring us down too.

Physical space

The environment we're in can impact our mood. Cluttered spaces or a lack of organization can create a sense of chaos and negatively affect our emotions.

Temperature

Believe it or not, the temperature around us can play a role in our mood. Being too hot or too cold can leave us feeling uncomfortable and affect our overall wellbeing.

Menstrual cycle

Ladies may experience mood swings or changes in emotional wellbeing as a result of their monthly cycle.

Diet

What we eat can have an influence on our mood. A poor diet lacking in essential nutrients can leave us feeling sluggish and less than cheerful.

So, the next time you find yourself in a funk, remember that there could be a whole range of factors at play. From stress and sleep to the weather and even colors, the world around us has a funny way of shaping our mood.

The Link Between Your Feelings and Actions

The relationship between our feelings and actions is a complex and intertwined one. Have you ever responded poorly to a simple question such as, "Excuse me, where's the restroom?" because you were angry?

Did you know you could have responded to certain inquiries differently if you were feeling differently?

Obviously, our emotions can significantly influence the way we behave and the choices we make. Here are some key points to consider:

Positive emotions, such as joy, contentment, and love, have a tendency to drive pro-social behaviors and acts of kindness. When we feel happy and fulfilled, we are more likely to extend that positivity to others.

Negative emotions, like anger, sadness, or fear, can sometimes lead to impulsive or aggressive behaviors if not effectively managed. It is crucial to recognize and regulate these emotions to avoid any harmful actions.

Our feelings of motivation and enthusiasm can serve as powerful catalysts for action, propelling us toward our goals and prompting us to engage in activities that bring us fulfillment. When we feel inspired and driven, we are more likely to take steps towards personal growth and achievement.

Emotions like guilt or remorse can act as signals for us to reflect on our actions and behaviors. They prompt us to take responsibility, apologize, make amends, or change our behavior to rectify a situation. These emotions can serve as a catalyst for personal growth and learning.

Finally, it is important to note that the relationship between feelings and actions is not one-sided. While emotions can influence our behaviors, our actions can also impact our emotions. Engaging in positive actions can generate positive emotions, creating a positive feedback loop.

Common Happiness Misconceptions

Humans are naturally inclined to think negatively. I believe that our negativity contributes to a lot of the misconceptions prevalent in our society.

There are many misconceptions surrounding the concept of happiness. People often have preconceived notions about what it takes to be happy and what happiness truly means. Here are some of those misconceptions about happiness:

The more money you have, the happier you'll be.

True happiness is found in the act of giving alone, not in receiving.

Having too much freedom of choice can reduce happiness.

Happiness is the only way to find joy.

Happiness is a destination.

Happiness conflicts with a mature sense of purpose.

Happiness is all about selfishness.

No one can recreate happiness.

The best times are over for us.

Happiness is solely about goals.

Longer vacations aren't always worth it.

No one should try to be happy all the time.

Misconceptions such as these are sometimes the product of fear and ignorance. The only way to debunk them is to know the truth! The truth sets us free.

Will I Ever Find Happiness?

I won't dive into a long discussion about this—the outright answer is a resounding YES!

Remember, you can't find happiness in anything external. You'll have to look within. That's the attitude you need to cultivate and nurture daily.

You deserve to be happy.

Chapter Takeaway

I hope this chapter has been truly enlightening for you in redefining concepts, debunking myths, and realigning you to the true meaning of things.

In this chapter, we've explained that happiness is not transient. It's something we can experience every day as an attitude. But it needs to be cultivated and nurtured. We're not inherently wired to live that way, but we can reprogram ourselves to live a happy life every day.

Don't rely on feelings and moods to determine your happiness because they're subject to external factors themselves. If you feel you really need to settle on a particular definition of happiness, at least don't settle for anything transient.

PART 2

Improving Emotional Health

I invite you to explore with me the incredible power of mindful self-compassion. It's one of the super keys to having stable emotional health.

Are you wondering how treating yourself with kindness and understanding can lead to greater happiness? Well, that's one of the things you're about to discover in this part of the book.

Although we had a discussion on self-esteem and its impact on your wellbeing in the previous part, we'll expound on it more deeply in Chapter 4 and discover how it is connected to your happiness. Just so you know, strong positive self-esteem paves the way for a happier and more confident existence. You don't want to miss out on these strategies for building your self-esteem.

Throughout the fifth chapter, we will explore practical ways to boost emotional health and enhance our mood. You'll learn the intricacies of emotional regulation and how to apply it to enhance your emotional wellbeing.

The final chapter in this part addresses a sensitive issue: depression. Depression is a bane in our society today, and I can tell you that it's so real. Dealing with depression can be incredibly challenging, but it is important to remember that there is hope and support available. There are diverse techniques outlined in this chapter that you can apply. You could also recommend them to someone that you know has been having a difficult time in their life.

I would describe this part of the book as a redemptive and curative section where you'll receive instructions that will guide you to receive healing and restoration for your soul. By delving into these topics, you will be equipped with valuable knowledge and practical tools to navigate life's challenges and cultivate a profound sense of happiness and wellbeing.

The wisdom in this part is bubbling forth; let's sit and drink together, shall we?

CHAPTER 3

Mindful Self-Compassion

"I rejoice in following your statutes as one rejoices in great riches. I meditate on your precepts and consider your ways. I delight in your decrees;I will not neglect your word."

—Psalms 119: 14-16

"Healing takes self-compassion."

—Juansen Dizon

Recently, I a new friend of mine unexpectedly canceled our meetup for the third time. I felt a wave of hurt, sadness, and disappointment wash over me. It wasn't easy, but I knew this was an opportunity to practice mindfulness and emotional healing.

So, I settled down in a comfortable place and took a moment to check in with myself. Instead of seeking distractions, I chose to sit with these emotions and explore their underlying messages.

As I turned my attention inward, I noticed the extent of the hurt within. I felt scared, abandoned, neglected, and rejected. I couldn't discard those feelings—they were valid. And I couldn't suppress them because to do that would be to aggravate the hurt. I didn't take it out on my new friend either; rather, I chose to look within and offered myself compassion and support.

My new friend was going through her own struggles. Allowing her situation to keep influencing my emotions would only expose me to more pain. So, I stopped getting my hopes up when it came to her. This affected our relationship, but it was worth it. I needed to heal from the series of emotional wounds first. And I had to protect my mind as well.

Through this experience, I grew as a person and learned to take better care of my inner self. I'm still on a journey of learning and growth, knowing that when things become painful, mindfulness and self-compassion are more essential than ever.

Mindfulness in the Self-Compassion Context

Mindfulness and self-compassion are the latest trends in self-improvement. But here's what's more fascinating about them: there's actually a number of ongoing studies all around the world that are exploring how these practices can seriously improve your mental health (Turow, 2023).

So far, the results of that research have made it pretty clear that mindfulness and self-compassion really do work and have some amazing benefits. It's pretty awesome to see how and why these practices make such a positive impact, don't you think?

My emphasis, however, is not on how these practices work together to enhance your wellbeing, but on how one of the practices enhances the other. What role does mindfulness play in making self-compassion more effective? That's the question in this section.

We should start with an understanding of mindfulness. ***What is mindfulness?***

Scott (2022a) defines mindfulness as being fully aware of the present moment without any judgments or distractions from the past or future. It involves tuning in to your senses and paying attention to things like your breath or the sensations in your body. The main idea is to be fully "in the now" and not let your mind wander.

Crumpler (2022) adds that mindfulness is all about consciously and gently directing one's attention to the present moment—essentially, reminding yourself to stay focused on what's happening right now. By contrast, having a mind full of divergent thoughts means you're not fully rooted in the present moment.

How can I be mindfully self-compassionate?

Through mindfulness, you can quickly identify negative, critical thoughts about yourself when they arise. This quick identification will help you to:

- Gather your thoughts and focus on the issue at hand, not the past or what is yet to happen.

- Respond to your thoughts and feelings in a non-judgmental way.

- Respond with kindness and compassion to release negative thoughts and emotions before they escalate and have a negative effect on you.

"I'd be more convinced we weren't lost if the map wasn't upside-down."

Overcoming Barriers to Self-Compassion

Did you know that being kind to yourself can have some amazing benefits for your health? It turns out that self-compassion is linked to things like having better relationships, improved physical health, and the ability to bounce back during tough times (MacBeth & Gumley, 2012). Even though lots of research has shown how great it is for our wellbeing, many people still find it hard to actually practice self-compassion (Gilbert et al., 2011).

Here are a few reasons some people find it hard to practice self-compassion.

1. **Feeling "not good enough" and being too hard on ourselves:** Sometimes we get caught up in negative thoughts and criticize ourselves too much. We may strive for perfection and constantly feel unworthy, which makes it difficult to show ourselves compassion.

2. **Struggling with overwhelming emotions:** When we're dealing with intense emotions like sadness, anger, or fear, it can be hard to offer ourselves

kindness. We may get stuck in the grip of these emotions and forget to be gentle and understanding toward ourselves.

3. **Feeling like self-compassion is pointless:** Some people might question the purpose of self-compassion. They may think it's selfish or unnecessary to focus on caring for themselves when there are so many other things to worry about. This mindset can prevent them from practicing self-compassion.

4. **Difficulty with the concept of "self-compassion":** The term "self-compassion" itself can be confusing or off-putting to some individuals. They might associate it with self-indulgence or view it as a sign of weakness. This misunderstanding can create a barrier to actually embracing self-compassion.

5. **Being trapped in a cycle of harsh self-judgment:** Many of us have a habit of being overly critical and harsh towards ourselves. This inner voice of self-judgment can be relentless, making it hard to show ourselves the kindness and understanding we truly deserve.

6. **Believing self-compassion is too touchy-feely or weak:** Some people perceive self-compassion as something overly sentimental or soft. They may think it goes against being strong and resilient. This misconception can make them hesitant to practice self-compassion.

7. **Feeling overwhelmed by the idea of self-compassion:** For some individuals, the idea of showing themselves compassion can feel overwhelming. They may not know where to start or how to integrate it into their lives. This overwhelm can hinder them from embracing self-compassion.

8. **Lack of experience receiving compassion from others:** If someone has had limited or no experience receiving compassion and understanding from others, they may find it difficult to extend the same kindness to themselves. They may not have a reference point for what self-compassion looks or feels like.

How can you overcome these barriers to self-compassion?

1. **Recognize your worth and challenge self-criticism:** Remind yourself that you are deserving of kindness and understanding, just like anyone else. When self-critical thoughts arise, question their validity and replace them with more compassionate and realistic self-talk.

2. **Embrace and validate your emotions:** Instead of pushing away or suppressing your emotions, allow yourself to feel them without judgment. Practice self-compassion by acknowledging your emotions, offering yourself comfort, and seeking healthy ways to cope with them.

3. **Find meaning in self-compassion:** Understand that self-compassion is not selfish but rather a vital component of overall wellbeing. Recognize that taking care of yourself allows you to be more present and available to help others in a meaningful way.

4. **Reframe the concept:** If the term "self-compassion" feels off-putting, reframe it in a way that resonates with you. Think of it as self-care, self-kindness, or simply treating yourself with the same understanding and support you would offer a friend.

5. **Challenge the inner critic:** Whenever your inner voice becomes harsh or judgmental, consciously choose to counteract it with self-kindness. Treat yourself with the same compassion and encouragement you would extend to a loved one facing similar challenges.

6. **Understand the strength in self-compassion:** Recognize that self-compassion is not a sign of weakness but rather a display of inner strength and resilience. It takes courage to acknowledge your vulnerabilities and offer yourself the care and support you need.

7. **Take small steps and be patient:** Overcoming barriers to self-compassion can be a gradual process. Start with small acts of self-kindness and build from there. Remember, it's okay to take it one step at a time and be patient with yourself along the way.

8. **Seek out compassionate support:** Surround yourself with individuals who demonstrate compassion and understanding. Engage in conversations or

seek guidance from supportive friends, family, or professionals who can help you navigate and cultivate self-compassion.

How to Practice Self-Compassion

Self-compassion is all about being kind to ourselves, even when things feel tough. It's not just about feeling good; it's about showing ourselves goodwill. When we practice self-compassion, we acknowledge that the present moment may be painful, but we choose to be mindful and respond with kindness and care. We also remind ourselves that it's okay to be imperfect because that's something all human beings experience (Neff, 2019).

Here are a number of ways I believe you can practice self-compassion:

Treat yourself like a friend

Start by imagining how you would treat someone you care about. We can't always take away their pain, but we can acknowledge it and offer support to help them through it. So, let's apply the same kindness to ourselves. It's okay to make mistakes and be human. Just like you wouldn't judge a friend for being lazy or missing a call, give yourself the same understanding and cut yourself some slack. Remember, imperfection is part of being human, and you're not alone in that.

Take care of yourself as you would others

This tip goes hand in hand with the previous one. Just like you would comfort a friend in need, show the same care and empathy towards yourself. When a friend is feeling down, you might give them a pat on the back or hold their hand to provide comfort. Well, guess what? You can do those things for yourself too! It may feel a bit strange at first, but try using tender and forgiving language with yourself, like calling yourself "darling" or "sweetheart."

These small gestures can activate your caregiving system and release oxytocin, which has positive effects on your heart. Don't worry if it feels a bit awkward; you can adjust the endearing terms to something that feels more natural to you. The key is to treat yourself with kindness and understanding.

Quiet your inner critic

Did you know that you are most likely your own toughest critic? Have you ever had those negative thoughts like, "I dressed nicely today, but I still don't look as good as those guys in GQ magazine" or "I got a pay raise, but it's just not enough"? We often fall into the trap of constantly wanting more and comparing ourselves to others, which leads to negative thinking.

Negativity is the enemy of self-compassion. It's easy to be negative, but it's not helpful. We're often kind and supportive to our close friends, yet we can be so hard on ourselves, creating a downward spiral of self-criticism.

So, how do you break free from this negative thought loop?

Silence that self-critical voice.

Boost your emotional awareness

A great way to cultivate self-compassion is learning to identify and label your emotions. By doing this, you can understand what they're trying to tell you about the things that truly matter in your life.

Try journaling

Writing in a journal can be a helpful practice in developing a better understanding of your inner experiences. It gives you a chance to expand your vocabulary and gain insights into your emotions.

Recognize feelings and needs in others

As you become more comfortable with acknowledging your own feelings and needs, you'll start noticing them in the people around you too. Whether it's your manager, colleagues, partner, or family members, developing this awareness of their emotions is an important part of self-compassion.

Remember that shared humanity matters

Connecting with others and recognizing our shared humanity is crucial for cultivating self-compassion. When we understand that others have similar desires and struggles, it becomes easier to extend compassion and empathy toward them.

Try "releasing statements"

Positive affirmations may not resonate with everyone, and that's okay. If you find them unnatural or ineffective, you can try something called "releasing statements." These statements are like exercises in self-forgiveness and detached non-judgment. When you catch yourself thinking a negative thought, like, "I'm such a horrible person for getting upset," try flipping it around and "releasing" yourself from that feeling. For example, say to yourself, "It's okay that I felt upset."

Embrace self-acceptance

Self-acceptance means embracing both your perceived shortcomings and your character strengths. Self-compassion involves not blowing up these shortcomings to define who you are. Instead, remember that thoughts and feelings are simply behaviors and states.

Practice mindfulness

Mindfulness practices are a great way to stay present in the moment. They are not only core components of self-compassion but can also be done anytime and anywhere. Activities like deep breathing, body scans, and the "self-compassion break" can help you cultivate mindfulness.

Avoid quick judgments

Don't assume that you will always behave a certain way. For example, instead of thinking, "I always get grumpy and antisocial on flights," give yourself the benefit of the doubt. Treat yourself* as you would treat others, and be open to the possibility of acting differently in different situations.

Do you want to host a "Compliment Shower" for yourself? **Check out** *the exercises of Worksheet #3 when you download the BONUS #2.*

The Role of Self-Acceptance

To be kind to ourselves, we must learn to accept who we are—but it's easy to get confused about what it really means to "accept" oneself. When someone tells us to accept something, we might think they're telling us to just tolerate it or deal with it.

But acceptance is actually a much stronger and more helpful tool than that. It doesn't mean giving up or surrendering. Acceptance is about recognizing where we are right now, which is crucial in figuring out how to move forward from that point (Hannan, 2020).

Sakhaee (2019) notes that acceptance ought to be accompanied by a genuine willingness to evolve, contribute, and focus on one's values, strengths, and interests. The truth is that when we accept ourselves as we are, we shift from being our own adversary to our own ally. Carl Rogers (cited by Sakhaee, 2019), a key figure in humanistic psychology, observed that true self-acceptance leads to personal change. It is a transformative process.

What's really interesting is that the initial step towards change isn't about judging ourselves—it's about accepting who we are. That's the crucial part, even though it might go against what we usually think. Embracing our imperfections actually helps us be more genuine and authentic. When we practice acceptance, we don't feel the need to defend or deny our flaws, which tends to happen when we're not accepting. This opens the door to more effective change as we examine our flaws with acceptance, compassion, and curiosity.

It all begins with a simple act of self-love, even in moments when you're angry, scared, confused, or tired (Fahkry, 2017).

I'll give you a few indicators that you're not accepting yourself as you ought to:

Always feeling discouraged

Dealing with depression

Experiencing anxiety

Experiencing fear, particularly social fears

Avoiding people and situations that may trigger negative emotions

Struggling with self-loathing

Overachieving or underachieving

Having difficulties with setting healthy relationship boundaries and experiencing relationship problems

Engaging in negative self-talk

You wouldn't be experiencing all of these if you took the bold step to embrace yourself and work on yourself to become better.

4 ways to practice self-acceptance

Practice self-compassion:

Be kind to yourself

Be mindful of your feelings

Permit yourself to have flaws

Be non-judgmental:

Recognize judgmental thoughts about yourself and others

Increase awareness of these thoughts

Label them as "just thoughts" without treating them as facts

Be balanced in your thinking:

Acknowledge that difficulties arise from a combination of your own mistakes (and strengths), other people's mistakes (and strengths), and circumstances

Acknowledge both strengths and weaknesses

Be open about all sides of yourself

Share both your strengths and weaknesses with yourself and others

Avoid definitive language:

Refrain from using terms like "always," "should," and "never"

Embrace the middle ground and acknowledge the nuances of reality

Replace definitive words with "often" or "sometimes" to reflect a more accurate perspective

Cultivating a Positive Self-Image

In our society, there is a strong emphasis on always wanting more. Simply being ourselves is often considered insufficient. We're constantly bombarded with messages that suggest we can improve ourselves or our lives by acquiring or achieving something new.

However, according to Scott Bea, a Doctor of Psychology, it is essential to recognize the importance of self-acceptance in order to truly accept who we are (Cleveland Clinic, 2020). To embrace our true selves, we must practice self-compassion and accept our inherent human nature. It's important to remember that having flaws doesn't make us inherently bad individuals.

Self-image is all about how we see ourselves—our thoughts, emotions, and beliefs about who we are as individuals. It encompasses our personality traits, abilities, and physical appearance (Shethna, 2023).

Many things contribute to our self-image, both from within us and from the world around us. Factors like genetics, life experiences, relationships, culture, and societal norms all play a role in shaping how we perceive ourselves.

I've curated *12 ways you can cultivate your self-image*:

1. Stop criticizing yourself

Avoid self-criticism for minor mistakes

Embrace your imperfections and learn from them

Practice self-forgiveness and focus on personal growth

2. Experience and express gratitude

Practice gratitude journaling or activities

Recognize your role in positive aspects of your life

Foster a positive self-view through gratitude

3. Smile when you look in the mirror

A simple smile can boost your self-image and confidence

Even a fake smile can improve your mood

Radiate positivity to others and yourself

4. Make a list of things you like about yourself

Recognize and appreciate your positive qualities

Include both small and significant aspects of yourself

Boost your confidence and self-perception

5. Praise others liberally

Acknowledge and praise the strengths and successes of others

Celebrate the wellbeing and positive experiences of others

Building others up contributes to a healthier self-image

6. Prioritize quality sleep

Get enough sleep for a refreshed and positive mindset

Adequate sleep improves mood, confidence, and focus

Start the day with a positive self-image

7. Engage in activities you enjoy

Pursue hobbies and interests that genuinely interest you

Prioritize your own desires and passions

Embrace new experiences to boost self-confidence

8. Have a plan for self-growth and enact it with determination

Dedicate effort to personal growth and development

Pursue activities for self-improvement

Actively engage in actions that contribute to a positive self-image

9. Take social media breaks

Temporarily disconnect from social media platforms

Reduce social comparisons and negative self-perception

Eliminate judgmental thoughts and foster a healthier self-image

10. Be authentic and true to yourself

Embrace your unique qualities and personality

Avoid trying to meet others' expectations of perfection

Be comfortable in your own skin and let your true self shine

11. Dress in clothes that make you feel good

Choose outfits that flatter your body and make you feel confident

Prioritize comfort and personal style over trends

Enhance your self-image through your fashion choices

12. Express yourself through hairstyles and/or makeup

Experiment with hairstyles that make you feel good

Wear makeup if it boosts your confidence and self-expression

Embrace your personal style without worrying about others' opinions

Cultivating a positive self-image is an ongoing process that requires consistent effort and self-reflection. Resist hastiness. Allow yourself to grow and evolve over time.

Elements of Mindfulness

Non-judging

Cultivate a non-judgmental attitude towards yourself and others, letting go of critical thoughts and embracing acceptance.

Acceptance

Acknowledge and accept the present moment, including both the things within your control and those outside of it, to foster problem-solving and intentional living.

Patience

Embrace the understanding that personal growth and change take time, allowing yourself to experience the journey without rushing or forcing outcomes.

Beginner's mind

Approach each moment with curiosity and openness, seeing the world with fresh eyes and finding joy in the simple wonders of everyday life.

Trust

Develop trust in yourself by listening to your feelings and intuition, allowing them to guide your mindful awareness and decision-making.

Non-striving

Practice being present without striving for specific outcomes, observing and experiencing things without the need to constantly fix or achieve.

Letting go

Release attachments to past memories and future worries, observing and accepting your experiences in the present moment without clinging or aversion.

Gratitude

Cultivate an appreciation for the simple things in life, expressing thanks and acknowledging the positive aspects that contribute to happiness and wellbeing.

Generosity

Extend generosity towards yourself and others, offering gifts of time, acceptance, and support without expecting anything in return.

Mindfulness Self-Compassion Theory

Mindful self-compassion (MSC) is all about blending the skills you gain from mindfulness with the practice of being kind and compassionate toward yourself (Mead, 2019). It's a powerful combination that allows you to bring awareness to the present moment while also nurturing a sense of warmth and understanding toward yourself.

MSC helps you cultivate a compassionate attitude toward your own struggles and challenges, treating yourself with the same kindness and care you would offer to a close friend. By merging mindfulness and self-compassion, you can experience greater inner peace, resilience, and a greater capacity to navigate life's challenges with kindness and understanding.

Here are some practical MSC tools you can apply in your daily life:

Self-compassion break

Pause during difficult moments.

Acknowledge pain and suffering.

Recognize shared humanity.

Offer words of kindness and understanding to yourself.

Loving-kindness meditation

Direct kindness to yourself and others.

Extend well-wishes to loved ones, acquaintances, and even difficult individuals.

Self-compassion journaling

Write down thoughts and emotions related to self-compassion.

Reflect on self-criticism and challenging situations.

Explore ways to offer yourself more compassion and develop a supportive inner dialogue.

Body scan meditation

Bring mindful awareness to different parts of the body.

Observe sensations and tensions without judgment.

Cultivate connection and kindness towards your own body.

Informal mindfulness

Incorporate mindfulness into your daily activities (e.g., brushing your teeth, eating, or taking a walk).

Pay attention to the present moment.

Approach tasks with a non-judgmental attitude.

P.S. You don't need to apply all of these tools. Just find the ones that resonate with you and make them a regular part of your life.

Mindfulness Exercises for Self-Compassion

1. Loving-kindness meditation

Spend a few minutes each day sending loving-kindness and compassion to yourself, using phrases like, "May I be happy, may I be healthy, may I be safe, may I live with ease."

2. Self-compassion break

When you're feeling stressed or struggling, take a moment to acknowledge your pain and offer yourself words of kindness and understanding. Remind yourself that suffering is part of being human.

3. Self-compassionate journaling

Write down your thoughts and feelings without judgment. Treat yourself with kindness and understanding as you reflect on your experiences.

4. Self-compassion affirmations

Create positive affirmations that promote self-compassion and repeat them to yourself regularly. Examples include, "I am worthy of love and compassion" or "I forgive myself for my mistakes."

5. Mindful walking

Take a mindful walk, paying attention to the sensation of each step, the movement of your body, and the sounds and sights around you. Practice self-compassion by offering yourself kind words as you walk.

6. Gratitude practice

Cultivate gratitude by focusing on the things you appreciate in your life. Each day, write down three things you're grateful for and reflect on why they bring you joy and gratitude.

7. Self-compassionate visualization

Imagine yourself in a peaceful and safe place where you feel loved and supported. Engage your senses to make the visualization vivid, and use it as a source of self-compassion.

8. Compassionate touch

Place your hand over your heart or give yourself a gentle hug to provide comfort and reassurance. Use touch as a physical reminder of self-compassion and care.

9. Self-compassionate letter

This exercise will help you cultivate self-compassion by offering yourself kind and supportive words, just as you would to a friend in need.

Instructions:

1. Think back to a time when you were overly harsh towards yourself or briefly felt inadequate or insecure.

2. Envision yourself composing a letter for a close friend who is experiencing similar circumstances.

3. Start the correspondence with "Dear [Your Name],".

4. Jot down the encouraging, kind, and understanding phrases you would typically use to comfort a friend. Treat yourself with compassion and patience, acknowledging your own difficulties.

5. Take your time and express compassion for yourself by writing as much as you need to.

Reflection:

Did it feel weird writing a compassionate letter to yourself? Did any insights come up during this exercise? Write down your reflections.

10. Self-compassion affirmations

This exercise will help you reinforce self-compassion by repeating positive affirmations that promote self-acceptance and kindness.

Instructions:

1. If possible, look at yourself in a mirror. If you don't have a mirror available, find a comfortable place where you can sit quietly.

2. Take a few deep breaths to center yourself.

3. Repeat the following affirmations out loud or in your mind:

I am deserving of love and compassion.

I accept myself as I am, flaws and all.

I am enough, just as I am at this moment.

I treat myself with kindness and understanding.

I am worthy of self-care and self-compassion.

4. Repeat each affirmation several times, allowing the words to sink in and resonate with you.

Reflection:

How did repeating the self-compassion affirmations make you feel? Did any particular affirmation resonate with you more than others? Write down your reflections.

11. Gratitude journaling

Another way to foster self-compassion is by focusing on the positive aspects of your life instead of the negatives and expressing gratitude for them.

Instructions:

1. Get a journal or some paper ready.

2. List three things in your life for which you are grateful at the moment, no matter small they might seem.

3. Think about how each of them makes you happy or brings you joy.

4. For each thing for which you are grateful, compose a little essay in which you express your gratitude and describe how it has improved your life.

5. If you're feeling inspired, continue writing in your journal about other aspects of your life that you're grateful for.

Reflection:

How did practicing gratitude make you feel? Did it shift your perspective and help you appreciate the present moment more, or are you still worried about all the bad things going on? Write down any reflections or insights.

Chapter Takeaway

The emphasis of this chapter has been on helping you live your life optimally without fear or any other negative emotions that make you hang your head in defeat.

Every exercise in this chapter is meant to help you cultivate self-compassion, self-acceptance, and mindfulness in your daily life. Feel free to modify them to suit your preferences and needs.

CHAPTER 4

The Self-Esteem Boost

"I praise you because I am fearfully and wonderfully made."

—Psalm 139:14

"If you hear a voice within you say 'you cannot paint,' then by all means paint, and that voice will be silenced."

—Vincent Van Gogh

Whenever I'm preparing to give a speech or write about the significance of self-esteem, I always remember a story Dr. Denny Coates, an expert in parent-child communication and author of several books including *Connect With Your Kid*, shared once about a young lad named Jason. I read the story long ago, but it has stuck with me.

Jason grew up in a large Christian family with parents who were good people. His dad served in the Navy, which meant he was often away from home, and his mom focused on taking care of the younger children. It was an environment where most kids would thrive, but Jason had a different path.

In high school, Jason played golf—and, boy, he was so good. Unfortunately, despite his talent, he constantly cheated during games. It wasn't just golf; he had a habit of lying about many things. His older brother, Mark, was an accomplished student, excelling in academics and popularity. Jason, on the other hand, seemed to feel bitter and inadequate compared to his brother.

Jason's actions only worsened his situation. He engaged in reckless behavior like starting a forest fire, getting caught shoplifting, and damaging the family car. Graduation day was marked by a destructive outburst, symbolizing his anger and desire for approval that he didn't receive. His low self-esteem fueled a destructive cycle.

Jason grew malicious and highly temperamental. He later enlisted in the Navy, but his struggles with alcoholism led to a Dishonorable Discharge. He became an outcast in his own family after seducing his younger brother's wife and was tragically gunned down in Miami.

Don't forget that Jason started out a talented golfer, but he didn't focus on that; rather, he allowed the successes of others to define his life—a symptom of low self-worth—leading to destructive choices.

"WOOOH! I'm awesome! ...Although I do believe I left my keys in the car."

Are You Your Worst Critic?

Why do you do that to yourself?

Why do you put the blame on yourself whenever you feel inadequate?

Yes, it's important to have high standards and strive towards your goals and dreams. But sometimes, these self-imposed expectations can backfire and lead you to criticize yourself harshly. Without realizing it, you become your own worst critic, constantly belittling yourself with negative self-talk (Nasir, 2019).

For those with low self-esteem, our entire world exists within the bubble we have created for ourselves. In this bubble, we hold ourselves to an immeasurable standard of perfection. When that standard fails to be met, our carefully crafted image begins to crumble, piece by piece. It feels like the world is collapsing around us, and we start questioning our worth.

We replay scenarios, imagining different outcomes, and negative thoughts like "I'm not good enough" spiral in our heads. This self-deprecating dialogue tears us down and sabotages our progress, stripping us of our self-esteem.

Here's the thing: the standards by which we measure ourselves, our self-worth, and our value are not even real. We created them ourselves. These benchmarks that we desperately want to attain, that feel like a matter of life or death, were created by us.

But what happens when we believe these self-imposed labels and standards?

We make heartache, regret, and disappointment a norm in our lives.

We feel undeserving and unworthy, constantly seeking approval from others.

We try to prove ourselves to the world, desperately grasping at any form of flattery to feel good.

We fear being exposed as flawed and believe our failures are the logical outcome of who we really are.

The self-critiquing and hatefulness we carry within ourselves erode our self-esteem, robbing us of joy and self-acceptance.

While others may see our successes and accomplishments, we struggle to believe in ourselves. We attribute our achievements to luck or chance because we don't truly believe we have the power to make great things happen. We become our own worst critic, doubting our abilities and undermining our self-worth.

It's time to break free from this cycle and cultivate a healthier self-image.

You have the power to shape your self-worth and define your own standards.

Mistakes and setbacks do not define you; they are opportunities for growth.

Focus on your strengths and celebrate your achievements, no matter how small.

Surround yourself with positive influences and supportive people who uplift you.

Practice self-compassion and kindness towards yourself, replacing self-criticism with self-love.

Recognizing and Addressing Negative Self-Talk

Everyone has experienced that inner critic, the little voice that offers critiques of what we're doing (Scott, 2022b). Sometimes it can actually be useful, like when it nudges us to make healthier choices or think twice before doing something risky.

But can I be real with you? That little voice can also be a real pain. It starts whispering all these negative things, and before we know it, we're trapped in a spiral of self-doubt and self-criticism. Yeah, it's called negative self-talk, and it's a real mood killer.

The Mayo Clinic (2022) identifies different forms of negative self-talk, including:

1. **Filtering:** This happens when we focus solely on the negative aspects of a situation and disregard any positive elements (e.g., ignoring a productive day at work and compliments from coworkers and choosing to dwell on unfinished tasks).

2. **Personalizing:** This involves blaming ourselves for things that aren't our fault (e.g., assuming that plans with friends got canceled because nobody wanted to be around us).

3. **Catastrophizing:** This is the tendency to anticipate the worst-case scenario without any supporting evidence (e.g., receiving an incorrect drive-through order and immediately beginning to catastrophize, believing the rest of the day will be an absolute disaster).

4. **Blaming:** Instead of taking responsibility, we shift the blame onto others. We fail to acknowledge our own role and attribute our experiences to external factors.

5. **"Should" statements:** This refers to constantly imposing unrealistic expectations on ourselves. We repeatedly remind ourselves of all the things we "should" be doing, which leads to feelings of guilt and inadequacy.

6. **Magnifying:** This occurs when we blow minor problems out of proportion, making them seem much bigger than they actually are. It amplifies stress and creates unnecessary distress.

7. **Perfectionism:** This is setting unattainable standards for ourselves. Striving for flawlessness leads to constant disappointment and a sense of failure.

8. **Polarizing:** This refers to viewing things in absolute terms, without considering any middle ground. It's a rigid thinking pattern where situations are either completely good or completely bad, leaving no room for nuance.

How to Address Negative Self-Talk

Become aware of it

Take a time out to reflect on your thoughts and inner voice.

Try journaling to improve your awareness of negative thinking.

Challenge negative self-talk

Recognize negative thinking patterns and challenge irrational beliefs.

Use positive affirmations to retrain your mind and shift your perspective.

Practice positive self-talk

Focus on your blessings and shift your attention to the positive.

Practice gratitude through reflection, thankfulness, or a gratitude journal.

Step outside of yourself

Shift perspectives by asking how your best friend would view the situation.

Develop self-talk rooted in self-love and compassion.

Talk it out

Seek support from loved ones or a therapist to challenge negativity.

Discuss your thoughts to gain clarity and separate reality from negative thinking.

Put it on the shelf

When negative thoughts become overwhelming, visualize setting them aside.

Revisit those thoughts at a later time that better serves you.

Focus on the present moment

Practice mindfulness techniques to refocus your mind and break free from negative thoughts.

Engage in breathing exercises, grounding, or meditation to stay present and find relief.

Self-Criticism and Your Self-Esteem

Self-criticism and self-esteem are two interconnected aspects of our self-perception and inner dialogue.

Sometimes, without even realizing it, we carry around a sense of discomfort within ourselves. We have a habit of criticizing our own thoughts, feelings, and actions before anyone else gets the chance to criticize us. This is a manifestation of low self-esteem (Gilbertson, 2010). It stems from past experiences where we felt unworthy, and it continues to affect us through a never-ending cycle of self-criticism.

Self-criticism can be fueled by negative self-talk, where we engage in a constant stream of self-deprecating thoughts. It can hinder our progress, diminish our self-confidence, and create a cycle of negativity and self-doubt.

Balancing self-criticism and self-esteem

1. It's important to find a balance between self-criticism and self-esteem to foster personal growth without falling into a pattern of excessive negativity.

2. Acknowledge areas for improvement without harshly judging yourself, and use self-criticism as a constructive tool rather than a source of self-sabotage.

3. Cultivate self-compassion and supportive inner dialogue, treating yourself with kindness and understanding during challenging times.

4. Practice self-reflection and self-awareness to recognize when self-criticism becomes excessive, and consciously shift your focus towards nurturing self-esteem.

Exploring Possible Causes of Low Self-Esteem

In the first part of this book, I listed numerous things that cause low self-esteem. In this part, however, I'll focus on a few of these and expound on them.

1. Authority figures in conflict

Witnessing parents or caregivers engage in constant conflict can make a child feel scared, overwhelmed, and responsible for their pain.

These intense conflicts can create a sense of being "tainted" or to blame, leading to low self-esteem that may persist into adulthood.

2. Bullying

Experiencing bullying can leave lasting emotional scars, especially if there is a lack of support from a safe and responsive family environment.

Bullying can make a child feel undeserving of attention and abandoned, and eventually develop a sense of self-loathing.

In the absence of a supportive home life, the effects of bullying can continue to impact self-esteem well into adulthood.

3. Academic challenges

Struggling with academics and feeling incapable of understanding classroom material can deeply impact self-esteem.

Falling behind without support or intervention can lead to feelings of inadequacy and internalization of a belief in one's own lack of intelligence.

Challenged learners may become excessively self-conscious about sharing thoughts and opinions, doubting their own intelligence and abilities.

4. Trauma

Experiencing physical, sexual, or emotional abuse can profoundly affect self-esteem.

Victims may struggle with displaced guilt and blame themselves, leading to deep shame and self-loathing.

Difficulty trusting others due to trauma can further contribute to low self-esteem.

5. Society and the media

Unrealistic standards of physical beauty perpetuated by media images and depictions can negatively impact self-esteem.

Exposure to unfair physical comparisons from a young age can lead to negative self-image and the development of eating disorders.

Feeling inadequate based on societal and materialistic standards can have long-lasting effects on self-esteem into adulthood.

Developing a Healthy Sense of Worth

Self-worth plays a significant role in many aspects of our lives. Among other things, it influences our relationships, work performance, self-perception, and even how others perceive us (Gupta, 2023).

According to Sabrina Romanoff, PsyD, a clinical psychologist and professor at Yeshiva University (cited by Gupta, 2023), self-worth is a subjective concept that can be influenced by various factors. These factors include core beliefs and values, thoughts and feelings, emotions and mental wellbeing, experiences and interactions with others, relationships, health and physical fitness, career and profession, activities and hobbies, community and social status, financial position, and physical appearance.

All of these aspects can have an impact on how individuals perceive and assess their own self-worth.

Here are some strategies suggested by Dr. Romanoff to enhance your self-worth (cited by Gupta, 2023):

1. Engage in activities you enjoy and excel at

Finding activities that bring you joy and allow you to showcase your skills can boost your self-worth. Recognizing your talents and strengths reinforces feelings of competence and confidence, which can positively impact other areas of your life.

2. Embrace challenges and push your limits

Research indicates that physical exercise is linked to higher self-worth. By challenging yourself physically and setting progressively more ambitious goals, you can demonstrate your capabilities and expand your belief in your own potential. Exercise also has the added benefit of improving your mental wellbeing.

3. Challenge negative thoughts

Remember that your thoughts are not always accurate reflections of reality. Negative self-talk often arises from internalized criticism, stress, or external pressures. Whenever you catch yourself engaging in negative self-talk, try replacing those thoughts with more realistic and positive alternatives.

4. Seek support

If you find that low self-worth is impacting your relationships, work, or overall emotional wellbeing, it may be beneficial to seek the guidance of a therapist. Low self-worth can limit your perspective and lead to complacency, making it crucial to seek professional help to overcome these challenges. A therapist can offer a neutral perspective and provide effective strategies for building self-worth.

Mindful Strategies to Boost Your Self-Esteem

Rachael Kable, host of The Mindful Kind podcast, shares some mindfulness strategies you can apply to boost your self-esteem. Below is a summary of her practical tips, which you can read more about on her blog (Kable, 2016):

1. Be your own supporter

Instead of seeking validation from others, take time to reflect on your worthiness. Make a list of your positive qualities, from acts of kindness to traits you appreciate about yourself. Embrace and believe in these attributes wholeheartedly.

2. Practice positive self-talk

Whenever you consciously choose to believe in yourself and acknowledge your efforts, reward yourself. Commend yourself for recognizing your own abilities and doing your best.

3. Engage in activities that uplift your mood

When facing a tough day or pursuing your dreams, remind yourself that it's temporary and take a break to boost your spirits. Listen to uplifting music, visit your favorite restaurant, spend time with loved ones or pets, participate in rejuvenating activities or self-care—do whatever brings you joy and makes you feel good.

4. Step outside your comfort zone gradually

If public speaking terrifies you, for example, don't rush into speaking in front of large audiences right away. Take small steps to build your confidence. You could start by creating a podcast, then practice speaking in front of family members, and gradually work your way up to speaking at events. After each step, practice self-care to reinforce feelings of safety and security, strengthening your confidence for the next challenge.

5. Practice mindfulness when overwhelmed

Stress, fear, and overwhelm can undermine your confidence. When you notice your confidence wavering due to these emotions, practice mindfulness techniques to regain calm, focus, and clarity. This can include breathing exercises, mindful walks, or engaging your senses by noticing things around you.

6. Embrace confidence without fear

Many people mistake confidence for arrogance and feel afraid of appearing overly confident, but these are two different things. Confidence inspires others and fosters a positive environment, while arrogance is intimidating and drains the confidence of those around you. Confidence is genuine and open to feedback, while arrogance often stems from insecurity seeking external validation.

7. Practice kindness

Kindness is a powerful confidence booster. When you choose to be kind to others, it not only benefits them but also enhances your own confidence. You can show kindness by simply smiling at others, actively listening, or reaching out to loved ones to check in on them.

8. Believe in your own confidence

It's crucial to see yourself as a confident person. If you continue to tell yourself that you lack confidence, it becomes a self-fulfilling prophecy. Challenge your self-perception by asking yourself what actions you can take to strengthen your self-belief and which thoughts you need to change to genuinely embrace your confidence.

Chapter Takeaway

The primary focus of this chapter is to prod you to shift your gaze from the negativity that seems to engulf your mind and help you recognize the goodness locked within you.

Until you begin to say some really nice, positive things to yourself, you won't be able to attempt anything great in life. You'll be a shadow of yourself and live in mediocrity, trapped by lack of self-worth.

Before you allow your imagination and negative thoughts to consume you and sentence you to a life of unhappiness, dare to practice the mindfulness skills that have been recommended in this chapter to gradually step out of that dark box of low self-esteem.

P.S As you continue your voyage through these pages of discovery, we invite you to share your thoughts, feeling, and impressions with us. That will illuminate the path of all seekers of knowledge.

Before you venture into the next chapter, we encourage you to **pen down your impressions below.** Your contributions breathe life into the ongoing dialog and inspire fellow seekers of knowledge,

Thank you for being part of this journey.

With appreciation,

Click HERE to leave your review! Or Scan the QR code.

CHAPTER 5

Your Emotional Health

"He heals the broken hearted and binds up their wounds."

—Psalms 147:3

"When our emotional health is in a bad state, so is our level of self-esteem. We have to slow down and deal with what is troubling us so that we can enjoy the simple joy of being happy and at peace with ourselves."

—Jess C. Scott

At 16 years old, Alex seemed to have it all together. He excelled in school, had a supportive group of friends, and participated in various activities. From the outside, everything seemed perfect, but deep down, Alex was struggling with his emotional health.

Alex often felt overwhelmed by the pressure to succeed and meet everyone's expectations. He put on a brave face, but inside, a whirlwind of emotions was brewing. Anxiety, self-doubt, and sadness frequently crept in, leaving him feeling trapped and confused.

This continued until Alex mustered the courage to reach out for help. When he finally talked to one of his trusted friends, he realized he wasn't the only one with emotional struggles. Together, they started researching and discovered the power of self-care, mindfulness, and self-compassion. Alex and his friend began implementing small changes in their daily routine. They set aside time each day to practice mindfulness exercises, like journaling their thoughts and feelings. They also made sure to engage in activities they enjoyed, such as painting, playing an instrument, or going for walks in nature.

As time went on, Alex and his friend noticed a positive shift in their emotional health. They started to understand that it was okay to prioritize their wellbeing and that their worth wasn't solely based on external achievements.

With newfound tools and a support system, Alex continued to navigate the ups and downs of life with a greater sense of emotional balance.

"You were right - that was a terrible idea."

The Complexity of Our Emotions

Emotional complexity refers to the way we understand and handle our emotions. It's about our ability to tell the difference between pleasant and unpleasant feelings and how we see them in relation to each other. Everyone has their own unique way of dealing with emotions and figuring out what makes them feel good or bad (Ong & Bergeman, 2004).

Someone who is "emotionally complex" might have a unique ability to see both the positive and negative aspects of situations. They can describe their feelings in great detail and accuracy, and they're able to predict which emotions will arise in different circumstances. They can remember experiencing multiple emotions simultaneously.

However, that's just one description of this term. The concept of emotional complexity is quite diverse and can be understood in various ways within the field of psychology—meaning that there are numerous ways a person can be considered "emotionally complex."

Dr. Colleen Cira (cited by Hill, 2021), a clinical psychologist, notes that when we talk about emotional complexity, it's like saying someone is a bit of a puzzle when it comes to their feelings, thoughts, behavior, or reactions; it's not easy to predict how they will respond in different situations.

Before we delve into this further, here are some key facts about human emotion:

Our emotions are fascinating and complex aspects of being human.

Emotions go beyond simple black-and-white categories and exist on a spectrum.

Emotions can be influenced by various factors, such as our experiences and circumstances.

We can feel multiple emotions simultaneously or have conflicting emotions about a situation.

Emotional complexity involves the ability to identify, understand, and express a range of diverse emotions.

Some individuals have a higher level of emotional awareness and can articulate their feelings with precision.

Developing emotional intelligence through self-reflection, mindfulness, and connections with others can enhance our understanding and management of our emotions.

Understanding Your Emotional Health

Emotional wellbeing encompasses our thoughts and emotions, reflecting our overall state of being. It involves our capacity to navigate life's challenges, acknowledge and manage our own emotions, as well as empathize with others. It's important to note that emotional wellbeing is not synonymous with constant happiness (Miller, 2020).

Being emotionally healthy means having the ability to accept and effectively handle our feelings, even in the face of adversity and change. It entails being able to process and understand our emotions in a constructive manner, promoting a balanced and healthy mindset.

Brennan (2021) adds that emotional health is a part of mental wellbeing. It's all about being aware of your emotions, both the good and the bad, and how you handle them. When it comes to negative emotions, emotionally healthy individuals have effective coping strategies in place and also recognize when it's necessary to seek professional support.

The following are the qualities of an emotionally healthy life:

1. **Self-awareness:** An emotionally healthy person has the ability to recognize and redirect their emotions when necessary to navigate both distress and elation. This skill develops throughout childhood but can be strengthened in adulthood through practice.

2. **Self-acceptance:** Emotionally healthy individuals accept themselves and are capable of handling adversity with clarity. They might allow themselves space to express and process emotions, such as having a "behind closed doors" temper tantrum to release anger in a healthy way.

3. **Self-care:** Those with good emotional health prioritize self-compassion and take care of their physical wellbeing. They intentionally and regularly practice self-care to ensure their overall wellbeing.

4. **Emotional agility:** An emotionally healthy person is not immune to setbacks or adversity. However, with an open mind and a curious thought process, they have the ability to thrive through difficulties and adapt to challenging circumstances.

5. **Coping skills:** Emotionally healthy individuals possess strong coping skills. By practicing these skills during calm times, they build resilience, which helps them navigate turbulent periods. It's like preparing for battle—adversity is inevitable in real life, and emotional capital is built during peaceful moments.

413

6. **Kindness and integrity:** An emotionally healthy person treats others with kindness and integrity, without expecting anything in return. They approach interactions with curiosity and compassion, fostering positive connections with those around them.

7. **Living with purpose:** Having a sense of purpose is another characteristic of an emotionally healthy person. They focus less on their inner experiences and more on how their experiences can serve others. They acknowledge their emotions but prioritize the bigger picture, allowing emotions to pass and embracing their purpose.

8. **Stress management and serenity:** An emotionally healthy person manages stress effectively and regularly practices moments of serenity. Just as good leaders remain calm during chaotic circumstances, self-mastery requires the same ability to find inner peace amidst external challenges.

You're most likely unhealthy emotionally (and could also be dealing with a mental illness, such as depression) if you consistently experience the following:

- Social isolation from friends, family, or coworkers
- Neglecting personal hygiene and self-care routines
- Decreased energy levels
- Disrupted sleep patterns, either excessive or insufficient
- Changes in appetite, either overeating or undereating
- Increased reliance on substances
- Racing thoughts
- Heightened interpersonal conflicts
- Feelings of irritability, guilt, hopelessness, or worthlessness
- A decline in work performance or productivity

Create an Emotional Reset

There is a powerful tool you can use when you're feeling overwhelmed by stress and anxiety. It's called the Emotional Reset Technique, or ERT, and it was created by therapist and author Jacqui Olliver (Olliver, 2023).

Whenever you're faced with overwhelming feelings or triggers, this amazing method comes to the rescue, preventing your mind from getting trapped in a whirlwind of thoughts and overthinking. Instead, it empowers you to shift your focus and regain control over your emotions.

By doing so, you can foster a sense of inner calm and clarity, allowing you to communicate more confidently and say goodbye to mental turmoil. Here is a simple five-step emotional reset process that can help you connect with your emotions:

Step 1: Pause and take three deep breaths, consciously allowing your body to relax. Release any tension you feel, letting each breath loosen your muscles.

Step 2: Ask yourself, "What am I feeling right now?" Embrace the emotion and fully experience it. Are you feeling sadness, happiness, resentment, gratitude, loneliness, excitement, frustration, peace…?

Step 3: Let go of any negative self-talk that arises. As you continue to breathe, practice self-acceptance. Inhale acceptance, exhale judgment. Inhale peace, exhale stress.

Step 4: Reflect on how you want to feel. It's okay if you're not ready to let go of your current emotions just yet. You may need to fully experience your anger or sadness before moving forward. Remember, whatever you feel is valid and okay. When you're ready, ask yourself again how you want to feel.

Step 5: Take a proactive step towards improving your emotional state. If you're feeling lonely, consider reaching out to a friend for a meaningful conversation or engage in self-care at home. If you're harboring resentment, have a calm conversation with the person involved and express your need for a positive change. Take action aligned with how you want to feel.

Understanding Emotional Regulation

According to Thompson (1994), emotional regulation involves both internal and external processes, including monitoring, evaluating, and adjusting our emotional responses to achieve our goals. Gross (1998) defines emotional regulation as the way we influence and express the emotions we experience. Additionally, a crucial part of emotional regulation is aligning with societal expectations and our own needs (Cole, Michel, & Teti, 1994).

Lebow and Casabianca (2022) provide perhaps a simpler definition: emotional regulation refers to the skill of recognizing, controlling, and effectively dealing with your emotions. It plays a crucial role in how you interact with yourself, others, and the world around you. Without proper regulation, emotions can easily take control and affect various aspects of your life.

Emotional regulation is a skill that we must learn and develop, and it is a fundamental aspect of emotional intelligence. It involves being able to process information, maintain a composed response that aligns with the situation, and effectively communicate our needs to others.

Practicing emotional regulation requires creating a sacred space between experiencing an emotion and reacting to it. It could mean taking a pause to gather your thoughts before responding. It can also involve waiting until you are in a supportive environment before you begin processing difficult emotions.

Emotional regulation is essential for overall mental wellbeing and for establishing healthy relationships. When we master this skill, it empowers us to:

- Maintain a sense of balance and control over our emotional reactions
- Stay composed and calm in challenging situations
- Effectively manage and cope with stress
- Preserve and nurture important relationships
- Actively listen to and understand the needs of others
- Express our own needs in a constructive manner
- Demonstrate professionalism in work-related situations
- Avoid taking things personally and maintain objectivity

The Three Emotional Regulation Systems

According to Gilbert's theory, our emotional system can be divided into three parts that interact with each other. These systems play a role in mental health issues.

1. The first system is focused on threat and self-protection. It reacts to signs of danger and triggers negative emotions like anxiety, anger, and disgust. Its purpose is to keep us safe from threats and harm.

2. The second system is focused on drive-seeking and acquisition. It drives us to seek resources necessary for survival and reproduction. It responds to signs of reward and generates positive emotions such as vitality and excitement. However, excessive activation of this system can lead to a constant search for resources and increase the risk of mental health problems.

3. The third system is focused on soothing behaviors. It is connected to our attachment system and aims to suppress the threat and drive systems, creating a sense of calm and safety. It responds to signs of warmth and affiliation, leading to positive emotions like calmness, contentment, and feelings of social connection.

Emotional Regulation and Self-Compassion: The Interrelation

Emotional regulation and self-compassion are closely interconnected and play a significant role in our wellbeing and mental health.

Emotional regulation, as we have discussed, refers to the ability to recognize, understand, and manage our emotions. Self-compassion, on the other hand, involves treating ourselves with kindness, understanding, and acceptance, especially in times of difficulty or failure. It entails being supportive and nurturing toward ourselves, just as we would be toward a close friend or loved one. Self-compassion allows us to acknowledge our pain and suffering without judgment or self-criticism.

The interrelationship between emotional regulation and self-compassion becomes apparent when we consider how they influence each other:

1. **Emotional regulation enhances self-compassion:** When we develop effective emotional regulation skills, we can respond to our emotions with compassion and understanding. Instead of being overwhelmed or harshly judging ourselves for experiencing certain emotions, we can approach ourselves with kindness and self-care.

2. **Self-compassion supports emotional regulation:** Practicing self-compassion provides a nurturing and safe space to explore and regulate our emotions. By accepting our emotions without judgment, we can better understand their underlying causes and respond to them in a healthy and constructive manner.

3. **Both contribute to overall wellbeing:** Emotional regulation and self-compassion are vital for promoting mental health and wellbeing. When we regulate our emotions effectively and show ourselves compassion, we cultivate emotional balance, reduce stress, and foster resilience.

Compassion Focused Therapy

Compassion focused therapy (CFT) was created by Paul Gilbert, a professor of clinical psychology, to help people deal with mental health issues involving feelings of shame or self-blame. It's specifically designed for those who find it hard to connect their thoughts with their emotions, which is often called "head-heart lag" (Lee, 2005; Stott, 2007).

In CFT, the focus is on developing compassion for oneself and others. The therapy aims to help individuals cultivate a kinder and more understanding attitude toward themselves, especially during tough times. It encourages people to acknowledge their struggles without judgment and to treat themselves with care and kindness (Alavi, 2021).

The goal of CFT is to bridge the gap between knowing something logically and truly feeling it deep inside. It helps individuals develop a sense of emotional connection and empathy towards themselves and others, leading to greater emotional wellbeing and improved mental health.

CFT is a valuable approach for anyone who finds it challenging to show themselves compassion or who tends to be self-critical. By learning to be kinder to yourself and developing a compassionate mindset, you can find relief from shame, self-attack, and self-blame, and move towards a healthier and more balanced mental state.

How does CFT work?

Compassion focused therapy is based on the idea that our brain has three different systems that help us survive and feel good. These systems developed a long time ago and still affect how we feel, act, and think today.

1. **Threat system:** This system helps us sense and respond to threats. When we encounter something scary or dangerous, we might feel fear, anxiety, or anger. Our body may react by wanting to fight, run away, or freeze. Sometimes we may also experience biased thoughts or jump to conclusions when we feel threatened.

2. **Drive system:** The drive system is all about pursuing important goals and finding resources. It gives us motivation and pleasure when we achieve something we want. However, if this system becomes too strong, it can lead to risky behaviors like using drugs and alcohol.

3. **Contentment system:** This system is connected to feelings of happiness and calm. It's not just about seeking pleasure or avoiding threats, but about feeling connected to others, cared for, and safe. The contentment system helps regulate the threat and drive systems, keeping them in balance.

CFT techniques and exercises

In CFT, therapists use a variety of techniques to help clients develop compassion for themselves and others. Here are some common ones:

1. **Appreciation exercises:** These activities focus on the things that bring you joy and pleasure. You might make a list of things you like, take time to enjoy

the moment when something good happens, or engage in positive, rewarding behaviors.

2. **Mindfulness:** This is about paying attention to the present moment without judging it. It helps you become aware of your thoughts, feelings, and sensations in a non-judgmental way.

3. **Compassion-focused imagery exercises:** These exercises use guided memories and fantasies to create a mental image that stimulates the contentment system. The goal is to evoke feelings of warmth, safety, and care.

4. **Exploring self-attacks:** If you struggle with self-criticism, the therapist can help you understand why it happens and where it comes from. They might ask you to visualize your self-attacking thoughts as a person and describe what that person looks like and how they make you feel. This helps you better understand and address your self-criticism.

5. **Developing compassion:** If you find it hard to show compassion to yourself or others, the therapist will ask you questions to explore any barriers or reasons why it might be difficult for you. They can help you work through these blockages and find ways to express compassion.

CFT Worksheet

Emotion Carousel

Instructions:

1. Spend a moment getting comfy before getting ready to examine the complex tapestry of your emotions.

2. Think about the feelings stated below. Write down one emotion that is very important to you at this time and write it down.

Emotions to choose from:

Joy

Anger

Sadness

Fear

Excitement

Guilt

Disgust

Surprise

Anxiety

Love

3. Complete each section based on the prompts given, allowing your creativity to shine.

4. Remember, this exercise is a gentle exploration of your emotions, fostering self-compassion and growth.

Emotion Carousel Worksheet:

1. Emotion: _____

2. Word Association:

Take a moment to reflect on your chosen emotion. Write down five words or phrases that come to mind when you think of this emotion, and write those words down.

a. _____

b. _____

c. _____

d. _____

e. _____

3. Physical Sensations:

Take a breather and pay attention to your body. What bodily sensations do you experience when you have this feeling (tingling, sweating, etc.)? Please explain in the space provided.

4. Triggers:

Examine the various situations, occasions, or ideas that usually cause you to feel this way. Spend some time writing down or elaborating on some examples.

5. Cultivating Self-Compassion:

Think of yourself as a close friend who is presently experiencing this. What comforting and motivating things would you say to them? Fill the space below with the comforting words you'd say.

6. Perspective Shift:

Let's examine a few alternative viewpoints on this feeling that can be empowering or lead to a positive shift. Write down a fresh perspective or an affirming statement that can help reframe this emotion for you.

7. Healthy Coping Strategies:

List three effective coping or management techniques for this feeling as it arises. Any relaxing activities are acceptable as part of these strategies.

a. _____

b. _____

c. _____

8. Gratitude:

Specify a feature of this emotion for which you are grateful. It might be a chance to learn something valuable, advance personally, or develop stronger relationships. Write it down below.

9. Reflection:

Take a moment to reflect on the insights you've made about yourself and this emotion throughout this exercise. Are there any action steps you'd like to embrace moving forward? Write them below.

Chapter Takeaway

Taking care of your mental health is crucial for your overall wellbeing. By practicing mindfulness techniques, learning emotional regulation skills, and exploring compassion focused therapy (CFT), you can effectively manage negative emotions and reduce stress and anxiety.

These tools are valuable resources that can significantly improve your mental wellbeing. Don't hesitate to explore and embrace them to nurture your mind and live a happier, healthier life.

CHAPTER 6

Dealing with Depression

"The Lord is close to the brokenhearted and saves those who are crushed in spirit."

—Psalms 34:18

"A big part of depression is feeling really lonely, even if you're in a room full of a million people."

—Lilly Singh

A Wandering Mind and Depression

Have you ever caught yourself daydreaming and noticed that your thoughts tend to lean toward the negative? It's common to think about the future or remember past events, but sometimes those thoughts can become a bit gloomy.

Scientists are still trying to unravel the mysteries of our thoughts and how they shape our consciousness. One interesting aspect they're studying is the tendency for negative thoughts to cycle and repeat in our minds (Seth, 2018). Understanding this pattern could give us valuable insights into mental health.

So, the next time you find yourself lost in your thoughts, pay attention to whether they tend to be more negative or positive. It's an important clue that can help you better understand your mind and how you can cultivate a healthier thought process.

There's a lot of research out there about how overthinking and dwelling on negative thoughts can contribute to feelings of sadness and depression. But when it comes to simply letting our minds wander, there's not as much information available (Chaieb et al., 2022).

So, here's the thing: we're not quite sure yet if the way our minds wander is different when we're feeling down or depressed. And if there are differences, we're still trying to figure out how they're connected to those repetitive negative thoughts. It's an open question that researchers are still exploring.

But *what is a wandering mind?*

A wandering mind is when your thoughts start drifting away from what you're supposed to be focusing on and into unrelated stuff. It's like your mind decides to take a little detour and think about things that don't really matter in that moment (Smallwood & Schooler, 2006).

Research has shown that a wandering mind is not a happy mind. In a study conducted by Matthew Killingsworth and Daniel Gilbert, it was found that almost half of the time, people's thoughts were focused on something other than what they were currently doing. Interestingly, it didn't matter whether these thoughts were positive or negative; the more time people spent thinking about things unrelated to the present moment, the more unhappy they felt (Killingsworth & Gilbert, 2010).

With a growing number of people experiencing depression and other mood disorders, it becomes important for us to learn ways to interrupt and redirect our wandering minds. By doing so, we can improve our overall happiness and wellbeing.

"OK. All downhill from here!"

How Depression Influences the Body-Mind Connection

Depression affects more than just your mood. It can also have physical symptoms. Here are a few of the most common:

Increased aches and pains: Approximately two out of three people with depression experience increased physical pain.

Chronic fatigue: Feeling constantly tired and lacking energy is a common symptom.

Decreased appetite: Many people with depression experience a decrease in their appetite and may have difficulty eating.

Sleep disturbances: Insomnia, difficulty sleeping deeply, or oversleeping are common sleep problems associated with depression.

But what causes these physical symptoms of depression? Changes in the brain can have an impact on various systems in the body. For example, abnormal functioning of neurotransmitters like serotonin, which affects mood, can also influence pain perception. This means that you may become more sensitive to pain, especially back pain. Serotonin also plays a role in sleep and sexual drive, and it's not uncommon for individuals with depression to experience difficulties in these areas.

Unfortunately, the physical symptoms of depression are often overlooked by those suffering from depression, their families, and even healthcare professionals. In spite of the fact that sleep problems, fatigue, and concerns about health have been found to be reliable indicators of depression in some older adults, these signs are often dismissed as a natural part of aging.

It's important to note that depression also increases your risk of developing other physical illnesses. It can raise levels of stress hormones like cortisol and adrenaline, which have negative effects on the body over prolonged periods. It can weaken the immune system, making it harder for your body to fight infections.

Additionally, some vaccinations, such as the shingles vaccine, may be less effective in older adults with depression. Depression has also been linked to heart disease and an increased risk of substance abuse.

426

The physical changes caused by depression, such as sleep disturbances or a weakened immune system, can worsen existing illnesses as well. Similarly, physical changes caused by chronic diseases or depression itself can trigger or worsen depressive symptoms.

This creates a cycle that can be challenging to break without proper treatment for both depression and any other coexisting medical conditions. It's important to address both aspects to improve overall wellbeing and break the cycle.*

Boost your Mental Health with Worksheet #6. Download BONUS #2 to check it out.

Detaching for a Happier Life

Sometimes, we get really attached to things, goals, dreams, or even people. We feel like if we don't have them, we won't be complete. This attachment can bring up all sorts of emotions like anxiety, fear, anger, jealousy, and sadness. It can make us feel disconnected from ourselves and others. But here's the thing: we don't need to be attached to anything to be whole.

Attachments can be to relationships, money, social status, or even our jobs. We use these things to define ourselves and who we are. But the truth is, we are more than just those labels. If something changes or we lose something we're attached to, it doesn't change who we are deep down.

So how do we let go of unhealthy attachments? Here are five steps to help:

1. **Pay attention to your thoughts:** Notice the thoughts that come up regularly. What labels do you identify with the most? This awareness can help you understand where your attachments lie. Attachments often come with strong emotions, so pay attention to how your body feels when you think about them.

2. **Separate your ego from reality:** Sometimes our ego makes us believe that not getting something we want is the end of the world. But the reality is, it's just a disappointment. The situation hasn't changed, only our thoughts about it. You can still move forward and achieve your goals.

3. **Embrace uncertainty:** Security doesn't come from holding on to things. It comes from accepting the unknown and being open to new possibilities. Let go of the need for certainty, and you'll find true happiness and fulfillment.

4. **Try meditation:** Meditation is a great way to quiet your mind and let go of old thought patterns that no longer serve you. Spend some time each day in meditation and you'll start to see positive changes in your life.

5. **Be kind to yourself:** Changing old habits takes time and effort. Instead of being hard on yourself when you slip back into old patterns, celebrate the fact that you're aware of them. Awareness is the first step toward transformation.

Self-Compassion and Depression

It can be tough to show yourself kindness and compassion when you're dealing with depression, but making some small changes can actually make a big difference in how you feel.

Here's the thing: nobody is perfect. We all have our own quirks, flaws, and complexities. Compassion helps us show kindness and forgiveness to others, but somehow, we often forget to treat ourselves with the same understanding.

So, the first step to practicing self-compassion is to recognize that you're human, just like everyone else. It's okay to struggle, and even though it may not always come naturally, you deserve your own compassion and understanding.

1. Remember, depression isn't your fault

When you're living with depression, it's easy to blame yourself and wonder why you can't just be happier. But here's the truth: Depression is not a choice you make. You're not waking up each day and deciding to feel down or isolated. It's important to practice self-compassion and remind yourself that you're not to blame for your depression symptoms.

2. Change your perspective

When practicing mindfulness while dealing with depression, try shifting your perspective. Instead of being hard on yourself, imagine you're talking to a friend going through the same situation. You wouldn't say harsh things to them, so why say them to yourself? Changing your perspective can help you be kinder and more understanding towards yourself.

3. Take it one step at a time

Breaking the habit of negative self-talk can be challenging. If practicing self-compassion feels difficult, start small. Find ways to be kind to yourself through self-care activities. Treat yourself to something special, indulge in a relaxing bath, or enjoy a favorite beverage. Self-compassion and self-care go hand in hand, both helping you show kindness towards yourself.

4. Use reminders to stay on track

Sometimes, we're not even aware of how harshly we're treating ourselves. Placing reminders around your home can be a great way to encourage self-compassion. Sticky notes with messages like "Be kind" on your mirror, refrigerator, or even bookmarks can help interrupt negative self-talk and remind you to practice self-compassion.

5. Connect with others who understand

Joining support groups or online communities or reading blogs about living with depression can remind you that you're not alone. It's important to realize that what you're going through is not a failure on your part. By sharing in the journeys of others, you can cultivate compassion for them and recognize that it applies to your own experiences as well.

Practicing the RAIN Techniques

Have you ever heard of the "RAIN" strategy? It's a simple and helpful technique used in mindfulness to navigate your emotions and cope with stressful situations (Verastegui, n.d.).

It's a simple way to practice mindfulness and compassion in these four steps:

1. **R**ecognize: Notice what's happening and acknowledge your feelings.
2. **A**llow: Allow the experience to be there without judgment or resistance.
3. **I**nvestigate: Curiously explore your thoughts and emotions with care.
4. **N**urture: Treat yourself with kindness and self-compassion.
1. You can use RAIN as a meditation practice or apply it whenever you're facing difficult emotions. Take your time and give it a try.

Managing Depression with ACT

Have you heard of acceptance and commitment therapy (ACT)? It's a type of therapy that combines mindfulness and cognitive-behavioral techniques. It has been shown to be really effective in helping people with various health issues (Nash, 2022).

ACT was created by clinical psychologist Steven C. Hayes, who developed it as a way to manage his own panic disorder. He has shared his personal story and how it led to the development of ACT in a TED Talk (TEDx Talks, 2016).

This therapy has proven helpful in managing chronic pain, addictions, anxiety, depression, obsessive-compulsive disorder, and psychosis. There's a lot of scientific evidence supporting its effectiveness.

ACT focuses on accepting your thoughts and feelings instead of fighting them.

It helps you to identify your values and set goals that align with what's important to you.

ACT teaches you to be present in the moment and not get caught up in negative thoughts about the past or worries about the future.

It encourages you to take committed action toward your goals, even when you're feeling down or unmotivated.

ACT can be used alongside other treatments for depression, like medication or talk therapy.

Many people have found ACT helpful in reducing their symptoms of depression and improving their overall wellbeing.

ACT Worksheets for Depression

Worksheet 1: The Power of Acceptance

1. List three things about yourself or your life that you've been struggling to accept.

2. Imagine what your life would look like if you fully accepted those things. How would it feel? How would it change your perspective? Write it down.

3. Write down three actions you can take to start accepting these aspects of your life. Remember that it doesn't mean you have to like everything; it means you're acknowledging and making peace with reality instead.

Worksheet 2: Showering Yourself with Self-Compassion

1. Make a list of five things you love about yourself.

2. Write a kind, compassionate letter to yourself, as if you were talking to your best friend. Remind yourself of your strengths, your resilience, and your unique quirks.

Worksheet 3: Defusing the Funk

1. Write down three negative thoughts that often pop up when you're feeling down. Be specific! What's that inner critic whispering in your ear?

2. Imagine those thoughts as characters or objects.

3. Come up with a funny, quirky way to respond to each thought. Remember, we're defusing the funk here! Make those thoughts lose their power with humor.

Worksheet 4: Dancing with Values

1. List five values that are important to you in life. Think about what makes your heart sing, what gets you fired up, and what brings you joy.

2. Rate your current level of alignment with each value on a scale of 1 to 10. Be brutally honest with yourself. Where are you slacking? Where are you rocking it?

3. Choose one value that you want to focus on right now, and identify one small action you can take today to bring you closer to that value.

Chapter Takeaway

This chapter is sensitive because of the nature of the topic we discussed. I wrote this chapter with special care because I don't want you to join the number of people whose lives have been cut short due to depression.

Depression isn't a life sentence—don't forget that. And it isn't your fault. You can come out of it by practicing any of the techniques that I have highlighted in this chapter, and with the support of a professional therapist if needed.

P.S As you advance through the chapters of this book, your thoughts and reflections may be a guide for many. Your feedback will shape the path and enrich fellow readers' experience.

Before you dive into the next chapter, we invite you to take a few seconds to share your feedback below. **Your review** ignites the conversation and encourages an ongoing narrative to help others.

Thank you for being an active part of this ongoing quest for knowledge.

With gratitude,

Click **HERE** to leave your review! Or Scan the QR code!

Robert J. Charles, PhD, DMin

PART 3

Working on Your Mental and Physical Health

You can't be happier than your own mind is. What happens when you try to put up a little act to feign happiness when you're hurting within?

Personally, I know that's an extra pound of pain.

Anyway, the emphasis here is that your mind is pivotal to all you'll ever become and experience in your short time on planet Earth. When you've lost the fervor of happiness, but still feign happiness, your efficiency scorecard will betray you. Thus, it's essential to look after the mind.

Ensuring your mental state is healthy is more important than ever, especially during difficult times. A healthy mind can still pivot you out of a bad situation because it'll keep hope alive.

Thus, the last two chapters of this book focus on the wellbeing of your mind and body in reference to how they influence your happiness and attitude toward living.

Do you know you can remain at peace and happy during a chaotic season? You'll find out more in the following pages of this book.

CHAPTER 7

Controlling Your Mind

"Don't be like the people of this world, but let God change the way you think.
Then you will know how to do everything that is good and pleasing to him."

—Romans 12:2

Have you heard about the reporter who had a panic attack while doing a live broadcast on national TV?

His name is Dan Harris. He was a young, ambitious reporter who was striving to make a mark in the industry. When Dan was in his twenties, he was really focused on his work, but, as he has since explained while reflecting back on the panic attack, he also had a negative voice inside his head that made him doubt himself.

After reporting on the Iraq War, he started using drugs to help him cope with his depression.

One day in 2004, while getting ready to do a news update on *Good Morning America*, something unexpected happened. As the cameras were rolling and millions of people were watching, Dan suddenly couldn't breathe. His heart was racing, his mouth was dry, and his palms were sweaty. It was a panic attack.

This panic attack was a major turning point for Dan. He decided to quit using drugs and started exploring mindfulness—something he learned about while working for ABC News.

According to Dan, mindfulness is a skill you can keep getting better at. It's all about being present, focusing your attention, and being kind to yourself and others. Dan admits that he isn't perfect and still has moments of being not-so-great, but affirms that practicing mindfulness has made a big difference in his life.

"Hey! I'm happy you found inner peace and all, but put me down!"

Self-Compassion and Your Cognitive Functioning

This book started with a discussion about self-compassion with an emphasis on *self*. But now, let's go a bit deeper by looking at the impact of self-compassion on cognitive function. Although we're moving outside of the self, we're still staying within the confines of the emphasis of this book — the soul (mind).

What is cognitive functioning?

Fisher et al. (2019) explain that cognitive functioning is all about how our minds work and our different mental abilities. The term covers a whole range of things, like learning, thinking, reasoning, remembering, solving problems, making decisions, and paying attention. Basically, it's everything that goes on in our head when we're using our brain to do things. It's how we process information, come up with ideas, remember things from the past, figure out solutions to problems, make choices, and stay focused on what we're doing.

Our cognitive functioning plays a big role in how we learn new things, how we make sense of the world around us, and how we navigate through life. It's like the engine that powers our thinking and helps us make sense of the world.

What will happen to your performance if your cognition fails? A stressed mind cannot perform optimally, and neither can a depressed mind. This is where practicing self-compassion comes in handy.

One factor that can have a positive impact on cognitive function is self-compassion, which, as you know by now, is how we treat ourselves with kindness and understanding, especially during difficult times. Research suggests that self-compassion is linked to better cognitive function, and here are some key points to understand this relationship:

Self-compassion helps reduce stress and negative emotions, which can improve our ability to think, learn, and remember things.

By being kind to ourselves, we create a positive internal environment that supports cognitive processes.

Self-compassion enhances our attention and focus, allowing us to better concentrate on tasks and absorb information.

It promotes a positive mindset and helps us approach challenges with resilience, leading to more effective problem-solving and decision-making.

Practicing self-compassion cultivates a healthy and balanced mindset* that supports our cognitive abilities.

Unlock easy strategies to foster a joyful mindset and activate your happiness boosters. Get started with Worksheet #2 by securing BONUS #2 at the start of this book.

Being Grounded for Mental Clarity

Grounding means tuning in to the present moment and becoming more aware of what's happening around you. It's a way to connect with your surroundings, understand how they fit into the bigger picture of your life, and become more in touch with your own emotions. It's all about being present and aware in the here and now (The Light Program, 2019).

Grounding is a technique that taps into your five senses to help you calm and comfort yourself when you're feeling overwhelmed. Essentially, you can use what you see, touch, hear, smell, and even taste to bring yourself back to the present moment and find a sense of stability. Focusing on your senses will anchor you, allowing you to find a sense of relief during challenging times.

Jacquelyn Van Zile, a licensed professional clinical counselor (LPCC), has recommended the following grounding techniques (General Health Team, 2022):

Mental grounding

Mental grounding techniques are helpful for shifting your thoughts away from negativity and stress. Here are some examples:

Categories game: Think of as many things as possible within a specific category. (You may have played a similar game with friends while growing up.) For instance, name as many mammals as you can think of, or as many countries as you can think of.

Describe your surroundings: Take a moment to look around and describe your environment to yourself. Be as detailed as you can, but stick to the reality of what you see and avoid adding emotions or opinions to your description.

Physical grounding

Physical grounding techniques involve focusing on something you can touch or a sensation. Here are a few examples:

The five senses: Stimulate one of your senses. For example, if you're using the sense of smell, take a whiff of something strong, like peppermint or coffee beans. For the sense of taste, you can take a bite of something with a strong flavor, like a grapefruit or licorice. Whatever you choose, pay attention to the feedback your senses give you.

Music: Pick some neutral music to listen to—it should be something that doesn't bring up strong emotions for you.

Soothing grounding

Soothing grounding techniques are all about finding comfort in the things that you like and that give you a sense of identity. Here are a couple of examples:

Your favorite things: Just like the song from *The Sound of Music*, think about all your favorite things—whether that's your favorite season, song, book, food, etc. Think about all the reasons you like those things.

Comforting photos: Keep photos that soothe you nearby, like a picture from a memorable trip you took, or a photo of yourself with family or a good friend.

It can be helpful to have someone else practice these techniques with you. Why? Believe it or not, just being in someone else's presence and hearing their voice can make a difference in grounding yourself.

The Neuroplastic Effect of Mindfulness

The neuroplastic effect of mindfulness refers to the changes that occur in the brain as a result of practicing mindfulness. Here's what you need to know:

Brain plasticity: The brain has the remarkable ability to change and reorganize itself throughout life. This is known as neuroplasticity. Mindfulness has been found to have a positive impact on brain plasticity.

Structural changes: Research suggests that regular mindfulness practice can lead to structural changes in the brain, particularly in areas associated with attention, emotional regulation, and self-awareness. These changes can enhance cognitive function and emotional wellbeing.

Increased gray matter: Mindfulness has been linked to an increase in gray matter volume in certain brain regions, such as the prefrontal cortex and the hippocampus. These areas are involved in executive functions, memory, and emotional regulation.

Strengthened connections: Mindfulness practice can strengthen the connections between different regions of the brain, improving communication and integration. This can enhance cognitive abilities, emotional resilience, and overall mental wellbeing.

Regulation of stress response: Mindfulness has been shown to modulate the brain's stress response, reducing activity in the amygdala (the brain's fear center) and increasing activity in the prefrontal cortex (responsible for rational thinking and decision-making). This helps in managing stress and promoting a sense of calm.

Long-term benefits: The neuroplastic effects of mindfulness are not just temporary. Regular and sustained practice can lead to long-term changes in the brain, resulting in improved cognitive functioning, emotional regulation, and overall mental health.

Resilience and Healthy Coping with Self-Compassion

Resilience and healthy coping are essential for navigating life's challenges, and self-compassion plays a crucial role in developing these qualities. Here's how self-compassion can contribute to resilience and healthy coping:

Acceptance of imperfections: Self-compassion involves recognizing and accepting our own imperfections, acknowledging that everyone makes mistakes and faces difficulties. This mindset helps us bounce back from setbacks and view them as opportunities for growth rather than personal failures.

Kindness towards oneself: Self-compassion encourages treating ourselves as we would treat a friend who is going through a tough time. By offering ourselves compassion and support, we develop a nurturing inner voice that helps us cope with stress and adversity.

Emotional regulation: Self-compassion helps us regulate our emotions effectively. Instead of suppressing or ignoring difficult emotions, we acknowledge them with kindness and non-judgment. This allows us to process and manage our emotions in a healthier way, which promotes resilience in the face of challenges.

Reduced self-criticism: Self-compassion helps to counteract self-critical thoughts and self-blame. When faced with difficulties, we tend to be our own harshest critics. However, self-compassion allows us to respond to setbacks with encouragement and understanding, fostering resilience and motivating us to keep going.

Building a support network: Self-compassion enables us to cultivate healthy relationships and seek support when needed. When we value ourselves and our wellbeing, we are more likely to reach out to others for help and build a supportive network. This social support is crucial for coping with stress and enhancing resilience.

Self-care practices: Self-compassion encourages self-care, which involves prioritizing our physical, emotional, and mental wellbeing. Engaging in activities that promote self-care, such as exercise, relaxation techniques, hobbies, and enjoyable experiences, enhances resilience by providing us with the necessary resources to cope with stress.

Applying Self-Compassion to Challenging Situations

Applying self-compassion to challenging situations can help us navigate difficulties with greater understanding, resilience, and kindness toward ourselves. Here are my recommendations for applying self-compassion in challenging situations:

Recognize common humanity

Remind yourself that everyone faces challenges and struggles at some point. You are not alone in experiencing difficulties. Recognizing our shared humanity helps us feel connected to others and reduces feelings of isolation.

Practice self-kindness

Treat yourself with kindness, care, and understanding, just as you would treat a friend in need. Offer yourself words of comfort and encouragement, acknowledging that it's okay to make mistakes and face obstacles. Be patient and gentle with yourself as you navigate the challenges.

Validate your emotions

Acknowledge and validate your emotions without judgment. It's normal to feel upset, frustrated, or overwhelmed in challenging situations. Instead of suppressing or denying your emotions, allow yourself to fully experience them while offering yourself compassion and understanding.

Reframe negative self-talk

Notice any negative self-talk or self-critical thoughts that arise during challenging situations. Challenge and reframe them by replacing them with kind, supportive, and realistic thoughts.

Don't isolate yourself

Reach out to trusted friends, family, or professionals who can provide support and guidance during challenging times. Sharing your experiences and seeking assistance is an act of self-compassion and shows that you value your wellbeing.

Learn and move on from setbacks

View failures as opportunities for growth and learning. Embrace the lessons that challenging situations offer and see them as stepping stones towards personal development and resilience. Remember that mistakes and difficulties are a normal part of life, and they do not define your worth or capabilities.

Engage in self-care

Prioritize self-care activities that nurture your physical, emotional, and mental wellbeing. Take breaks when needed, engage in activities you enjoy, practice relaxation techniques, exercise, get enough sleep, and eat nourishing foods. Taking care of yourself supports your overall resilience and helps you better cope with challenges.

If you act on each of these recommendations, you will be better able to develop a compassionate, perceptive, and resilient mindset toward yourself—thereby empowering you to face difficulties with greater compassion and navigate them in a healthier and more supportive way.

Mindfulness Exercises for Improving Focus and Clarity

Let's take a look at a few more mindfulness exercises to enhance your focus and clarity.

Slow down and be present

In our busy world, it can be challenging to slow down and truly notice things. Take the time to engage your senses and fully experience your environment. Pay attention to the sounds, sights, smells, and perhaps tastes around you. For example, when you eat your favorite food, savor the moment by smelling, tasting, and enjoying it.

Embrace the now

Make a conscious effort to live in the present moment. Approach each activity with an open, accepting, and attentive mindset. Find joy in the simple pleasures that surround you, whether it's the warmth of sunlight on your skin or the sound of birds chirping.

Practice self-acceptance

Treat yourself with the compassion you give to your close friends. Accept yourself as you are, embracing both your strengths and imperfections. Remember that it's okay to make mistakes and that self-acceptance is an important part of personal growth.

Resilience Worksheet

Section 1: Reflect on Your Past Triumphs

1. Remember That Time You Conquered a Challenge:

Think back to a time when you overcame a difficult situation—maybe getting through a difficult exam, conquering a fear, or overcoming a personal setback. Detail your experience, including how you felt, what you did, and how it affected your personal development. Relive your accomplishment to bolster your confidence.

2. Your Resilience Recipe:

Identify the traits and strategies that helped you get through the challenge. Was it your perseverance, your upbeat outlook, the encouragement of your loved ones, or a special strategy? List the key ingredients in your recipe for resilience. They will serve as reminders of what works best for you when times are tough.

Section 2: Supercharging Your Resilience

3. Embrace the Power of Gratitude:

Make a list of at least five items in your life for which you are grateful at the moment. They could be significant or insignificant, from loved ones to small pleasures that make you happy. Gratitude practice aids in shifting your focus to the positive aspects of your life and boosts resilience.

4. Your Support Squad:

As a superhero, no one takes on life alone! Find out who in your life is always there for you and offers unflinching support. It may be close relatives, close friends, mentors, or even online communities. List their names and the ways they have previously assisted you. In trying times, reaching out to your support network is a sign of strength, not weakness.

5. Flex Your Resilience Muscles:

Resilience is like a muscle that needs regular exercise to grow stronger. Identify an area in your life where you can challenge yourself and step out of your comfort zone. It could be trying a new hobby, setting a fitness goal, or learning a new skill. Write down your chosen challenge and outline the steps you'll take to achieve it. Remember, even small steps count!

Section 3: Building Resilience in Daily Life

6. Taming the Inner Critic:

Everybody has that inner voice that likes to criticize them. Make a note of the phrases you use the most often to criticize yourself. Now, respond to those statements with positive, empowering affirmations. If your inner critic tells you, "You're not good enough," for instance, respond, "I am capable of anything I set my mind to!" Daily repetition of these affirmations will retrain your brain to be resilient.

7. The Power of Play:

Being robust does not necessitate being solemn all of the time! Find activities that you enjoy and that make you feel carefree. It could be as simple as playing with your pet, singing in the shower, dancing, or going on a walk. Make a list of fun things to do and commit to doing at least one of them every day. Remember that having fun and laughing are essential for building resilience.

8. Learning from Setbacks:

It is more important to bounce back stronger from setbacks than to avoid them. Write down the lessons you learned from a recent setback or failure. How can you use those lessons to advance your development?

Section 4: Cultivating Resilience in Relationships

9. Building Empathy Bridges:

Being resilient involves more than just bouncing back; it also involves supporting and understanding others. To develop empathy, try to imagine yourself in another person's position. List three ways you might show support and empathy for a person in your life who is struggling. It might be done by listening attentively, offering a helping hand, or just by being present.

Section 5: Your Resilient Future

10. Vision of Resilience:

Think of your future self as a tough superhero. Give specific examples of how this version of yourself solves issues, keeps a positive outlook, and motivates others. Make a list of the traits, actions, and mindset that your resilient future self will possess. This vision will act as a source of inspiration and optimism for daily resilience building.

11. Your Resilience Toolkit:

Create a list of resources, strategies, and activities that you can turn to when you need an extra boost of resilience. It could include inspirational books, uplifting podcasts, meditation exercises, or motivational quotes. Refer back to this toolkit whenever you need a reminder of the tools at your disposal to overcome any obstacle.

Chapter Takeaway

A few things I'd like you to remember in this chapter include:

Your mind is pivotal to everything you'll ever become. Therefore, guide and care for your mind well.

Self-compassion is a practice that can optimize your cognition. It can enhance your performance even when you're performing below par.

Self-compassion can also help you scale mountains and go through the tempestuous moments of life without drowning.

The practice of self-compassion can build resilience in you to survive difficult seasons of life.

Self-compassion takes time and patience. Therefore, don't rush through the steps in an attempt to get instant results. This is a lifelong practice that promises to yield life-transforming results.

CHAPTER 8

Self-Care for Happiness

"Are you tired? Worn out? Burned out…? Come to me. Get away with me and you'll recover your life. I'll show you how to take a real rest… Learn the unforced rhythms of grace. I won't lay anything heavy or ill-fitting on you. Keep company with me and you'll learn to live freely and lightly."

—Matthew 11:28-30

While I was putting this book together, the story of a particular young man caught my attention. This young man was multi-talented; he led a group of young religious people and was also a professional sign language interpreter, a wedding photographer, a radio host, a husband, and a father. Wow!

As an interpreter, he attended all of his students' after-school activities. On top of that, he had a radio show on Tuesday and Friday nights, church functions on Wednesday nights and on the weekend, and Sundays were filled with photographing weddings or youth group activities. His days were long, and he barely had any time to himself.

In his righteous mind, he believed that his constant busyness was making his wife proud. After all, he was doing so much for the church! However, in his lack of personal boundaries, he was unintentionally building walls between himself and the people who loved him the most. He didn't know it was okay, and even necessary, to say "no" to others, to take a day off, to switch off his phone, and to spend quality time with those who longed for his affection and attention.

As his personal relationships crumbled, he began to feel trapped and lost, drowning in shame and panic attacks that seemed to be happening more and more frequently. Eventually, the stress became too much for him to bear, and he reached a point of desperation, feeling utterly defeated.

But amidst the darkness, he found a glimmer of hope. He realized that he needed to prioritize his own wellbeing and recovery. He embarked on a journey of self-care, learning invaluable tips and tricks along the way to nurture his mental and emotional health. That's when he discovered the importance of self-care and the power it holds in maintaining a balanced and fulfilling life.

The truth remains: nothing is worth giving up your self-care for. When you cease to exist, those things will continue to exist. Someone else will continue where you left off. So why the stress?

Finding Happiness Through a Self-Care Routine

Self-care is all about consciously and intentionally taking care of our mental, physical, and emotional wellbeing. It involves engaging in activities that nourish and support our overall health (Adam, 2023). I'd like to emphasize that taking care of yourself is not selfish but is, in fact, essential for cultivating deeper connections with yourself and those around you.

You can try these self-care routines:

1. **Daily reflection:** Take a few moments each day for quiet reflection or meditation. This can help calm your mind and bring a sense of inner peace.

2. **Pursuing joy:** Engage in activities that bring you joy and happiness. It could be reading your favorite books, baking, listening to music, or engaging in any hobby that uplifts your spirits.

3. **Exercise:** Regular physical activity is important for your overall health. Find an exercise routine that you enjoy, whether it's going for a walk, dancing, or playing a sport.

4. **Healthy eating:** Pay attention to your diet and nourish your body with nutritious foods. Eating a balanced diet can have a positive impact on your energy levels and overall wellbeing.

5. **Sufficient sleep:** Make sure you get enough restful sleep each night. Establish a bedtime routine that promotes relaxation and creates a conducive environment for quality sleep.

6. **Setting boundaries:** Learn to set boundaries with others. It's okay to say "no" when you need time for yourself or when something doesn't align with your wellbeing.

"Are you sure you don't want to use it for yourself?"

The Role of Self-Care in Overall Wellbeing

Sometimes, when things get tough, we tend to forget about taking care of ourselves. We may prioritize work, money, or dealing with difficult situations. But it's important to remember that self-care should be a priority, especially during challenging times (Glowiak, 2022). It shouldn't be an afterthought, but rather, something we keep in mind every day. When we take care of ourselves, it can make a big difference in how we feel and how we handle tough situations. It's like giving ourselves a boost to stay strong and resilient.

According to Dr. Kaylee Crockett, a clinical psychologist who works in the UAB Department of Family and Community Medicine (cited by Jones, 2022), self-care can mean different things to different people. It could be making sure you eat nutritious meals and get enough sleep. It could be finding activities that bring you joy and help you relax, like reading, painting, or playing a sport. It could also mean taking breaks when you need them, setting boundaries with others, and asking for help when you need it.

Regardless of what self-care means to you, it prods you toward just one goal: your happiness and wellbeing.

What role does self-care play in your wellbeing?

Improved physical health

Self-care involves prioritizing your physical wellbeing. By taking care of your body through activities like regular exercise, proper sleep, and practicing good hygiene, you can enhance your overall physical health.

Reduced stress and anxiety

Engaging in relaxation techniques, such as taking a warm bath or listening to music, is an important aspect of self-care. These activities help reduce stress and anxiety, promoting a more positive mood.

Boosted self-esteem

Taking time to relax and care for yourself can have a positive impact on how you view yourself. Treating yourself with kindness and practicing self-care can improve your self-esteem, making you more resilient in the face of setbacks and more likely to achieve personal goals (Breines & Chen, 2012).

Protection of mental health

Prioritizing self-care can help manage and prevent the worsening of mental health issues. While self-care is not a substitute for professional help, it plays a crucial role in supporting your mental wellbeing. If you are experiencing mental health challenges, it's important to reach out to a professional for assistance.

Improved relationships

When you prioritize self-care and focus on your own happiness and health, it positively impacts your relationships with others. By taking care of yourself, you have more to give to your loved ones, fostering healthier and more fulfilling connections.

Self-Care, Self-Love, and Self-Compassion

These three are essential components of our wellbeing and how we relate to ourselves. They form the foundation of a healthy and fulfilling life.

When we practice **self-love**, we embrace ourselves with kindness, recognizing our worth and inherent value and accepting ourselves for who we are.

Self-care, as we have just discussed, is the intentional act of tending to our physical, mental, and emotional needs. It involves listening to our bodies, nurturing our minds, and engaging in activities that bring us joy and relaxation. By prioritizing self-care, we create space for rejuvenation and renewal, allowing us to show up fully in our lives and relationships.

Self-compassion goes hand in hand with self-love and self-care. As we explored in a previous chapter, it is about being gentle with ourselves when we face challenges or make mistakes. Instead of harsh self-judgment, we offer ourselves understanding, forgiveness, and encouragement. Self-compassion allows us to embrace our imperfections, knowing that they are a natural part of being human.

Together, self-love, self-care, and self-compassion form a powerful trio that nurtures our wellbeing. By cultivating these practices, we honor ourselves, recognize our needs, and create a solid foundation for a life filled with happiness, resilience, and meaningful connections.

Although these three work together and may appear similar on the surface, there are also some subtle differences between them (Gurwitz, 2019). Let's examine them together, shall we?

Self-love:

Focuses on cultivating a positive and unconditional regard for oneself.

Involves developing a deep sense of self-worth and self-acceptance.

Involves treating oneself with kindness, respect, and empathy.

Self-care:

Refers to the intentional actions taken to meet one's physical, mental, and emotional needs.

Includes engaging in activities that promote wellbeing, such as exercise, healthy eating, restful sleep, and practicing stress-reduction techniques.

Involves setting boundaries, saying no when necessary, and prioritizing self-nurturing activities.

Self-compassion:

Involves being kind, understanding, and forgiving toward oneself during times of difficulty, failure, or suffering.

Requires acknowledging and validating one's own emotions and experiences without judgment.

Involves treating oneself with the same compassion and care one would extend to a close friend or loved one.

The Seven Pillars of Self-Care

To maintain a well-rounded self-care routine, it's important to incorporate practices that align with the seven pillars of self-care: mental, emotional, physical, environmental, spiritual, recreational, and social. By engaging in activities from each pillar, you can better nurture your overall wellbeing. Here's a breakdown of each pillar with examples of how to practice them:

1. Mental self-care:

Engage in stimulating activities like reading, doing puzzles, or learning something new.

Take time to meditate to calm your mind and improve focus. In Joshua 1:8 and Psalms 1:1-3, God says you will have success in life when you meditate on His Word daily.

Set goals and challenge yourself intellectually.

2. Emotional self-care:

Express your feelings through journaling or creative outlets like art or music.

Seek therapy or counseling to process emotions and gain emotional support.

Engage in activities that bring you joy and make you feel emotionally fulfilled.

3. Physical self-care:

Prioritize regular exercise or physical activities that you enjoy.

Get enough restful sleep to recharge your body.

Maintain a balanced and nutritious diet for optimal physical health.

4. Environmental self-care:

Create a clean, organized, and clutter-free living space.

Spend time in nature, go for walks, or practice gardening.

Surround yourself with positive and uplifting environments and people.

5. Spiritual self-care:

Engage in activities that align with your beliefs and values.

Practice meditation, prayer, or mindfulness to connect with your inner self.

Spend time in reflection and gratitude, or engage in acts of kindness and compassion.

6. Recreational self-care:

Engage in hobbies or activities that bring you joy and relaxation.

Take breaks and enjoy leisure time to recharge and rejuvenate.

Plan outings, adventures, or trips to explore new experiences.

7. Social self-care:

Cultivate and maintain healthy relationships with family and friends.

Seek social support when needed and engage in meaningful connections.

Participate in social activities, or join clubs or organizations.

Self-Care Practices for Happiness

I've mentioned something similar to this before, but here I'll share some more detailed practices recommended by Dr. Crockett (cited by Jones, 2022):

Maintain a balanced diet

Consume a variety of fruits, vegetables, seafood, and nuts to boost energy levels and enhance focus throughout the day.

Stay hydrated

Drink at least 60 ounces of water daily (more during the hotter months!).

Engage in physical activity

Aim for at least 30 minutes of exercise (e.g., walking) each day, which not only improves mood but also enhances overall health. Remember, even small bursts of movement can make a difference.

Schedule relaxation time

Dedicate a part of your day to activities that reduce stress, such as meditation, deep breathing exercises, listening to music, journaling, or exploring new hobbies. Hobbies can keep the mind engaged and provide opportunities to learn new skills.

Prioritize sleep

Get seven to nine hours of quality sleep each night. Avoid using electronic devices before bedtime, as the blue light can disrupt sleep. Instead, opt for uplifting books or inspiring podcasts.

Cultivate meaningful relationships

Build strong connections with supportive family members and friends. Consider participating in activities that allow you to meet new people, such as classes or support groups. Reach out to loved ones who can offer emotional support and practical assistance.

Are you ready to enjoy even more self-care practices?

I've curated lots of them here for you. Try them at your leisure.

Take a relaxing bath

Create something—a painting, a poem, or anything that sparks your creativity

Spend time in nature, go for a walk in the park, or explore hiking trails

Enjoy some laughter—watch a comedy show or spend time with funny friends

Write your future self a letter expressing your hopes and dreams

Take a day trip to a new place and explore

Treat yourself to a spa day or indulge in a massage or facial

Wake up 15 minutes early and savor your morning routine

Spend quality time with a pet, playing and bonding with them

Reflect on your accomplishments and celebrate your achievements

Cook your favorite meal and savor each bite

Take a break from technology, disconnect, and focus on mindfulness

Dance to your favorite music and let yourself go

Go over your finances and create a budget that aligns with your goals

Volunteer and give back to your community

Write self-love affirmations and repeat them daily

Plan a trip, even if it's just a local exploration

Enjoy your tea or coffee in a cozy spot, savoring the moment

Try a new hobby or learn something new, expanding your horizons

Take a nap and prioritize rest and relaxation

Spend time with friends, family, or colleagues you haven't talked to in a while

Plant something and nurture it as it grows

Create a self-care kit with comforting items and activities

Watch the sunrise or sunset, appreciating the beauty of nature

Practice gratitude by making a list of things you're thankful for

Read a good book and immerse yourself in a different world

Clean up your space and create a clutter-free environment

Have a spa day at home—pamper yourself with a facial, manicure, or bubble bath

Buy yourself new sheets or pillows for a cozy and comfortable sleep

Contribute to a cause you care about

Write out your five-year plan, setting goals and aspirations

Take a relaxing shower and enjoy the warm water on your skin

Enjoy a movie marathon, binge-watching your favorite films or TV series

Fix something that's broken, whether it's a household item or a personal project

Be a child again and engage in playful activities or visit an amusement park

Make a gratitude jar and fill it with notes of appreciation

Take a self-care day and prioritize your wellbeing above all else

Explore your creativity by decorating your home with items that bring you joy

Write down your thoughts and feelings to process and reflect

Make a positive impact

Smile at yourself in the mirror, embracing self-love and acceptance

Engage in recreational activities that bring you joy and relaxation

Practice deep breathing exercises or meditation to calm your mind and reduce stress

Engage in mindful eating by consuming a balanced diet and savoring each bite

Engage in regular physical activity to improve energy levels and overall health

Engage in social activities and build strong relationships with supportive individuals

Indulge in hobbies that bring you joy and help you learn new skills

Write your first entry in a journal and begin the journey of self-reflection

Go through old photos and reminisce about happy memories

Enjoy a soothing music playlist that helps you relax and unwind

Take time to plan and organize your tasks to reduce stress and increase productivity

Fix or replace items that are worn out or no longer serving their purpose

Take a moment to express gratitude to someone who has made a positive impact on your life

Take care of your physical health by scheduling regular checkups and medical appointments

Integrating the Self-Compassionate Lifestyle

As this book draws to a close, it's important for you to know that integrating self-compassion into your life requires honesty and a commitment to seeking the truth. By uprooting misbeliefs and replacing them with self-acceptance and understanding, you can develop self-compassion and transform various aspects of your life.

Implement these three things to integrate self-compassion into your daily life.

1. Cultivate awareness of your internal dialogue

Take time to listen to your silent self-talk and identify any self-critical or negative thoughts.

Notice patterns of self-judgment and self-criticism, such as feeling like a failure or believing you are unlovable or unworthy.

Be mindful of the triggers that evoke these self-critical thoughts and the emotions associated with them.

2. Analyze and challenge your thoughts

Analyze your thoughts and beliefs, looking for irrational or unhelpful patterns.

Rate the strength of your belief in the self-critical thoughts on a scale of 0 to 100%.

Identify the tone of voice used in your self-talk and recognize the impact it has on your emotions.

Reflect on the triggers that activate self-critical thoughts and examine their validity.

3. Reconstruct your thinking with compassion

Replace distorted self-beliefs with more realistic and compassionate statements.

Use a softer and more understanding tone of voice when addressing yourself.

Imagine how you would offer support and guidance to a friend facing a similar situation.

Explore alternative perspectives that are kinder, more helpful, and aligned with reality.

Develop coping strategies and self-care practices to nurture yourself in challenging moments.

Embrace a compassionate and empowering conclusion that counteracts self-criticism.

Reassess the strength of your belief in the self-critical thoughts and the intensity of the associated emotions.

Practicing Self-Care Worksheets

Worksheet 1: Your Self-Care Bucket List

1. For a moment, visualize your ideal self-care activities. What practices or activities make you happy, content, and fulfilled?

1. Make a list of at least five ideas for activities.

2. Select a task from your list that you can complete today or this coming week.

3. Be practical and pick an activity that you can fit into your schedule.

4. Choose a time and date for the activity you want to do.

5. Put the time in your calendar and make it a priority.

4. Imagine yourself engaging in this activity; consider how it will impact you; consider the benefits it will provide for your overall wellbeing.

Worksheet 2: Embracing Daily Self-Care Rituals

1. Consider your existing daily routine. Are there any opportunities for self-care that you could be missing?

Look at all times of day (morning, afternoon, and evening).

2. List at least three self-care practices or rituals you can incorporate into your daily schedule.

It may be as simple as having a cup of tea or taking a stroll through the forest.

3. Establish a routine for your new self-care practices.

Set aside specific times of the day and stick to them for each activity.

Date/time	Sunday	Monday	Tuesday	Wednesday	Thursday	Friday	Saturday
Morning	(Self-care activity)						
Afternoon							
Evening							

4. Create a self-care journal to document your progress and the effects of each action. Use it to serve as a reminder of the positive effects self-care can have on your life.

Date	Self-care activity	How it made you feel

Great job finishing the worksheets on self-care! Remember that self-care is a process and not a one-time thing. Keep shining, and enjoy your self-care journey.

Chapter Takeaway

The emphasis of this chapter has been on the application of self-care practices for your wellbeing. To practice self-care, you must take a balanced approach that includes the seven aspects of your being. You can't take care of just one part of yourself and leave the others out.

Remember, you don't need a special, huge block of time to take care of yourself. You just need to readjust your schedule and practice the recommendations in this chapter. You can even create your own self-care practices. The goal is to ensure you're living a happy life.

Conclusion

Throughout this book, we have explored various aspects of happiness, self-compassion, emotional health, and self-care. By delving into the chapters and reflecting on the valuable insights within them, you have taken significant steps toward a happier and more fulfilling life.

In Part 1, we learned that self-compassion is a key ingredient in the recipe for happiness. Being kind to yourself and treating yourself with understanding and acceptance is the foundation of self-compassion.

Remember, it's okay to be gentle with yourself and embrace your imperfections. By practicing self-compassion, you can foster a positive relationship with yourself, leading to greater happiness.

Moving on to Part 2, we explored themes related to your emotional health. The dominant practice for having emotional stability discussed in this part was mindfulness. Mindful self-compassion emerged as a powerful tool to navigate the ups and downs of life. By practicing mindfulness and extending compassion toward yourself, you can cultivate emotional resilience and find peace within.

Additionally, we discovered the vital connection between self-esteem and happiness, understanding that building a healthy sense of self-esteem is crucial for our overall wellbeing.

Part 3 shed light on the significance of nurturing both your mental and physical health. Strengthening your mind through self-compassion, mindfulness, and a positive mindset can empower you to thrive in difficult times.

Self-care, as highlighted in Chapter 8, plays a pivotal role in your happiness journey. Taking time to care for yourself and engaging in activities that bring joy and relaxation is a powerful way to enhance your wellbeing.

Remember, happiness is a lifelong journey that requires dedication and effort. It's normal to experience setbacks and face challenges along the way. The key is to approach these obstacles with resilience, compassion, and mindfulness, grounded in the moment.

Keep in mind also that happiness is not about being in a constant state of bliss. It is an attitude. It's about finding contentment and meaning in the journey itself.

As you conclude this book, I encourage you to continue exploring, learning, and practicing the principles shared here. Embrace self-compassion, nurture your emotional wellbeing, and prioritize self-care. Cultivate a positive mindset and surround yourself with supportive relationships.

Happiness is a personal experience, and each individual's path may look different.

Final Note

God created humans to live a long, fulfilling, happy life. He provided everything we'd ever need to live a happy life. He created an enabling environment for us as well. All we had to do was take care of our habitat.

Sounds great, doesn't it?

But humans messed up that opportunity. The world is full of chaos today because the first humans messed up a golden opportunity to live happily forever.

But it's not fair to just keep blaming those first humans. We have the opportunity to make our choices today and choose how we live. We can rewrite our destiny and decide we want to live happily from now on.

First, I'm extending an invitation to you to embrace a life of unending rest and happiness. Your first and most important decision is to accept this invitation. You have to let go of the burdens of sorrow, pain, and hurt (Matthew 11:28-30).

Then, decide to trust God, the Potter, to make all things new in your life (Jeremiah 18:1-6; Isaiah 26:3; Isaiah 43:18-19).

That's how to enjoy eternal rest and peace that no human mind can comprehend.

I wish you a life filled with genuine happiness, resilience, and a deep sense of fulfillment. Embrace the lessons you've learned and carry them forward on your journey toward lasting happiness. Within you, you can find the will to create a life that brings you joy and purpose.

Now, go out there and live your happiest life!

I'd love to hear about your happiness journey! Feel free to write to me and share your feedback. If you're willing, leaving an honest review on Amazon would be greatly appreciated. Thank you so much for your support!

Thank You

Dear reader,

Your Feedback Matters!

Firstly, a massive **THANK YOU** for journeying through this bundle to the very end. Your dedication through these pages means the world!

Now, as you turn the final page of this bundle, might you **share** a fragment of your journey? Your thoughts and takeaways could become the compass for future adventurers.

Your reflections not only help future readers set their expectations, but they also paint the world with the colors of your experiences. Share a glimpse of your journey, those golden nuggets you've gleaned, or how this book has transformed your perspective.

A few seconds of your time, a few lines on Amazon can cast ripples across the reading community. Your **genuine review** on Amazon will become a guiding star for many.

Awaiting the story of your experience. Every word you pen down is a treasure.

With heartfelt gratitude,

Robert

>> Leave a review on Amazon US <<

>> Leave a review on Amazon UK <<

References

A Little Dose of Happy (2023). *52 surprisingly simple self-care ideas to boost happiness!* A Little Dose of Happy. Retrieved from https://aldohappy.com/self-care-ideas

Academy of Ideas (2015). *The ideas of Socrates.* Academy of Ideas. Retrieved from https://academyofideas.com/2015/03/the-ideas-of-socrates-trancript/

Ackerman, C. E. (2017). *Mindfulness-based stress reduction: The ultimate MBSR guide.* PositivePsychology.com. Retrieved from https://positivepsychology.com/mindfulness-based-stress-reduction-mbsr/

Ackerman, C. E. (2019). *What is happiness and why is it important? (+ definition).* PositivePsychology.com. Retrieved from https://positivepsychology.com/what-is-happiness/

Admin. (2022). *Aristotle's concept of the self.* Philo-Notes. Retrieved from https://philonotes.com/2022/05/aristotles-concept-of-the-self

Alavi, K. (2021). The role of social safeness and self-compassion in mental health problems: A model based on gilbert theory of emotion regulation systems. *Practice in Clinical Psychology, 9*(3), 237–246. https://doi.org/10.32598/jpcp.9.3.768.1

Austin, S. (2017). *3 examples of self-care in the bible.* HuffPost. Retrieved from https://www.huffpost.com/entry/3-examples-of-selfcare-in_b_13073572

Brach, T. (2023). *RAIN: A practice of radical compassion.* Tara Brach. Retrieved from https://www.tarabrach.com/rain/

Breines, J. G., & Chen, S. (2012). Self-compassion increases self-improvement motivation. *Personality and Social Psychology Bulletin, 38*(9), 1133–1143. https://doi.org/10.1177/0146167212445599

Burkett, M. (n.d.). *The seven pillars of self-care.* University of Kansas Recreation Services. Retrieved from https://recreation.ku.edu/seven-pillars-self-care

Carers Trust (n.d.). *Taking care of yourself.* Carers.org. Retrieved from https://carers.org/taking-care-of-yourself/taking-care-of-yourself

Cascio, C. N., O'Donnell, M. B., Tinney, F. J., Lieberman, M. D., Taylor, S. E., Strecher, V. J., & Falk, E. B. (2015). Self-affirmation activates brain systems associated with self-related processing and reward and is reinforced by future orientation. *Social Cognitive and Affective Neuroscience, 11*(4), 621–629. https://doi.org/10.1093/scan/nsv136

Chaieb, L., Hoppe, C., & Fell, J. (2022). Mind wandering and depression: A status report. *Neuroscience & Biobehavioral Reviews, 133*, 104505. https://doi.org/10.1016/j.neubiorev.2021.12.028

Cherry, K. (2022a). *How do psychologists define happiness?* Verywell Mind. Retrieved from https://www.verywellmind.com/what-is-happiness-4869755

Cherry, K. (2022b). *What are the signs of healthy or low self-esteem?* Verywell Mind. Retrieved from https://www.verywellmind.com/what-is-self-esteem-2795868

Cleveland Clinic (2020). *6 ways to build a healthy self-image.* Cleveland Clinic Health Essentials. Retrieved from https://health.clevelandclinic.org/ways-to-build-a-healthy-self-image/

Coates, D. (2022). *A tragic true story about low self-esteem.* Dr. Denny Coates. Retrieved from https://drdennycoates.com/a-tragic-true-story-about-low-self-esteem/

Cole, P. M., Michel, M. K., & Teti, L. O. D. (1994). The development of emotion regulation and dysregulation: A clinical perspective. *Monographs of the Society for Research in Child Development, 59*(2-3), 73–102.

Davidson, R. J., & Begley, S. (2012). *The emotional life of your brain: How its unique patterns affect the way you think, feel, and live—and how you can change them.* London: Penguin.

Education, A. D., & Bergeman, C. S. (2004). The complexity of emotions in later life. *The Journals of Gerontology: Series B, 59*(3), 117–122. https://doi.org/10.1093/geronb/59.3.p117

Fahkry, T. (2017). *Why self-compassion and self-acceptance are the foundations for optimal living.* Medium. Retrieved from https://medium.com/the-mission/why-self-compassion-and-self-acceptance-are-the-foundations-to-optimal-living-7a7df24ffd3e

Fisher, G. G., Chacon, M., & Chaffee, D. S. (2019). Chapter 2 – Theories of cognitive aging and work. *Work Across the Lifespan,* 17–45. https://doi.org/10.1016/b978-0-12-812756-8.00002-5

Foster, C. (2013). *Happiness – an emotion, a mood, a goal or a way of life?* Clare Rose Foster. Retrieved from https://www.clarerosefoster.co.uk/2013/04/happiness-an-emotion-a-mood-a-goal-or-a-way-of-life/

Frank Porter Graham Program on Mindfulness & Self-Compassion (2023). *The three components of self-compassion.* The University of North Carolina at Chapel Hill. Retrieved from https://selfcompassion.web.unc.edu/what-is-self-compassion/the-three-components-of-self-compassion/

Geller, J., Samson, L., Maiolino, N., Iyar, M. M., Kelly, A. C., & Srikameswaran, S. (2022). Self-compassion and its barriers: predicting outcomes from inpatient and residential eating disorders treatment. *Journal of Eating Disorders, 10*(1). https://doi.org/10.1186/s40337-022-00640-8

General Health Team (2022). *What is grounding and how can it improve your mental health?* (n.d.). ProMedica News Network. Retrieved from https://promedicanewsnetwork.org/general-health/what-is-grounding-and-how-can-it-improve-your-mental-health/

Gilbert, P., McEwan, K., Matos, M., & Rivis, A. (2011). Fears of compassion: Development of three self-report measures. *Psychology and Psychotherapy: Theory, Research and Practice, 84*(3), 239–255. https://doi.org/10.1348/147608310x526511

Gilbertson, T. (2010). Self-esteem vs. self-criticism. GoodTherapy. Retrieved from https://www.goodtherapy.org/blog/self-esteem-vs-self-criticism/

Gillette, H. (2021). *7 ways to practice self-compassion when you have depression.* Psych Central. Retrieved from https://psychcentral.com/depression/ways-to-practice-self-compassion-when-you-have-depression

Glowiak, M. (2020). *Why is self-care important?* Southern New Hampshire University. Retrieved from https://www.snhu.edu/about-us/newsroom/health/what-is-self-care

GoodTherapy (2018). *Compassion-focused therapy.* GoodTherapy. Retrieved from https://www.goodtherapy.org/learn-about-therapy/types/compassion-focused-therapy

Graham, B. (1955). *How you can find true happiness.* New Life Newspaper. Retrieved from https://www.newlifepublishing.co.uk/articles/how-you-can-find-true-happiness/

Gries, A. (2023). *Finding true happiness through self-awareness and self-care.* Awakenings Health. Retrieved from https://awakeningshealth.com/2023/02/06/finding-true-happiness-through-self-awareness-and-self-care/

Gross, J. J. (1998). The emerging field of emotion regulation: An integrative review. *Review of General Psychology, 2*(3), 271–299. https://doi.org/10.1037/1089-2680.2.3.271

Gupta, S. (2023). *How to improve your self-worth and why it's important.* Verywell Mind. Retrieved from https://www.verywellmind.com/what-is-self-worth-6543764

Gurwitz, K. (2019). *How self-love, self-care and self-compassion are different (and also irrelevant).* Thrive Global. Retrieved from https://community.thriveglobal.com/how-self-love-self-care-and-self-compassion-are-different-and-also-irrelevant/

Hannan, J. (2020). The power of self-acceptance and self-compassion. Morency Therapy. Retrieved from https://www.morency.co.uk/the-power-of-self-acceptance-and-self-compassion/

Hanson, R. (2013). *Hardwiring happiness: The new brain science of contentment, calm, and confidence.* New York: Harmony.

Hill, A. (2021). *Identifying "emotional complexity" in loved ones.* News Center Maine. Retrieved from https://www.newscentermaine.com/article/news/local/207/207-interview/identifying-emotional-complexity-in-loved-ones-mood-change-psychology/97-6b802c6f-bb96-4564-a722-6848e262ade4

Hoshaw, C. (2022). *What is mindfulness? A simple practice for greater wellbeing.* Healthline. Retrieved from https://www.healthline.com/health/mind-body/what-is-mindfulness

Huijer, H. (2020). *Inspiring stories on finding true happiness (by Syrian refugees).* Tracking Happiness. Retrieved from https://www.trackinghappiness.com/inspiring-stories-finding-happiness-syrian-refugees/

Jones, A. (2022). *Self-care: What is it? Why is it so important for your health?* University of Alabama at Birmingham | UAB News. Retrieved from https://www.uab.edu/news/youcanuse/item/13176-self-care-what-is-it-why-is-it-so-important-for-your-health

Kable, R. (2016). *10 mindful & powerful tips to boost your confidence.* Rachael Kable. Retrieved from https://www.rachaelkable.com/blog/mindful-and-powerful-confidence-tips

Kashyap, R. (2022). *Spice of life | Happiness is matter of choice, a state of mind.* Hindustan Times. Retrieved from https://www.hindustantimes.com/cities/chandigarh-news/spice-of-life-happiness-is-matter-of-choice-a-state-of-mind-101666914721125.html

Killingsworth, M. A., & Gilbert, D. T. (2010). A wandering mind is an unhappy mind. *Science, 330*(6006), 932. https://doi.org/10.1126/science.1192439

Lebow, H. I., & Casabianca, S. S. (2022). *Do you know how to manage your emotions and why it matters?* Psych Central. Retrieved from https://psychcentral.com/health/emotional-regulation

Lechner, T. (2019). *5 steps to detaching for a happier life.* Chopra. Retrieved from https://chopra.com/articles/5-steps-to-detaching-for-a-happier-life

Lee, D. A. (2005). The perfect nurturer: A model to develop a compassionate mind within the context of cognitive therapy. In P. Gilbert (Ed.), *Compassion: Conceptualisations, research and use in psychotherapy*, 326–351. Abingdon, UK: Routledge.

Light Program, The. (2019). *Using grounding coping skills to manage your mental health symptoms.* The Light Program. Retrieved from https://thelightprogram.pyramidhealthcarepa.com/grounding-techniques/

MacBeth, A., & Gumley, A. (2012). Exploring compassion: A meta-analysis of the association between self-compassion and psychopathology. *Clinical Psychology Review, 32*(6), 545–552. https://doi.org/10.1016/j.cpr.2012.06.003

Mayo Clinic Staff (2022). *How to stop negative self-talk.* Mayo Clinic. Retrieved from https://www.mayoclinic.org/healthy-lifestyle/stress-management/in-depth/positive-thinking/art-20043950

Mead, E. (2019). *What is mindful self-compassion? (Incl. exercises + PDF).* PositivePsychology.com. Retrieved from https://positivepsychology.com/mindful-self-compassion/

Merriam-Webster. (2023). *Self.* Merriam-Webster. Retrieved from https://www.merriam-webster.com/dictionary/self

Miller, K. (2020). *What is emotional health? (+ 11 activities & examples).* PositivePsychology.com. Retrieved from https://positivepsychology.com/emotional-health-activities/

Moore, C. (2019). *How to practice self-compassion: 8 techniques and tips.* PositivePsychology.com. Retrieved from https://positivepsychology.com/how-to-practice-self-compassion/

Nasir, I. (2019). *You are your own worst critic.* Medium. Retrieved from https://medium.com/swlh/you-are-your-own-worst-critic-fa984ff86dda

Nash, J. (2022). *ACT therapy techniques: 14+ interventions for your sessions.* PositivePsychology.com. Retrieved from https://positivepsychology.com/act-techniques/

Neff, K. (2019) *Tips for practice*. Self-Compassion.org. Retrieved from https://self-compassion.org/tips-for-practice/

Neff, K. (2020). *5 myths of self compassion*. Mindful Schools. Retrieved from https://www.mindfulschools.org/personal-practice/5-myths-of-self-compassion/

Nesse, R. M. (2000). Is depression an adaptation? *Archives of General Psychiatry, 57*(1), 14–20. https://doi.org/10.1001/archpsyc.57.1.14

Olliver, J. (2023). *The emotional reset technique: Master your emotions*. Psychosexual Alignment. Retrieved from https://www.endtheproblem.com/emotional-reset-technique-jacqui-olliver/

Purohit, V. (2022). *What is true happiness?* Times of India. Retrieved from https://timesofindia.indiatimes.com/readersblog/thetinybook/what-is-true-happiness-44628/

Recovery Editorial Staff (2018). *7 ways to combat negative self-talk*. Footprints to Recovery. Retrieved from https://footprintstorecovery.com/blog/combat-negative-self-talk/

Sakhaee, E. (2019). *Self acceptance and self compassion*. educationdln. Retrieved from https://www.linkedin.com/pulse/self-acceptance-compassion-ehssan-sakhaee-phd

Scott, E. (2022a). *Can mindfulness relieve more than stress?* Verywell Mind. Retrieved from https://www.verywellmind.com/mindfulness-the-health-and-stress-relief-benefits-3145189

Scott, E. (2022b). *How to reduce negative self-talk for a better life*. Verywell Mind. Retrieved from https://www.verywellmind.com/negative-self-talk-and-how-it-affects-us-4161304

Seppälä, E. (2021). *The power of self-compassion*. Ten Percent Happier. Retrieved from https://www.tenpercent.com/meditationweeklyblog/the-power-of-self-compassion

Seth, A. K. (2018). Consciousness: The last 50 years (and the next). *Brain and Neuroscience Advances, 2*. https://doi.org/10.1177/2398212818816019

Shethna, J. (2023). *Self-image*. EDUCBA. Retrieved from
https://www.educba.com/self-image/

Siegel, D. J. (2007). *The mindful brain: Reflection and attunement in the
cultivation of well-being*. New York: W. W. Norton & Company.

Smallwood, J., & Schooler, J. W. (2006). The restless mind. *Psychological
Bulletin, 132*(6), 946–958. https://doi.org/10.1037/0033-2909.132.6.946

Stott, R. (2007). When head and heart do not agree: A theoretical and clinical
analysis of rational-emotional dissociation (RED) in cognitive therapy.
Journal of Cognitive Psychotherapy, 21(1), 37–50.
https://doi.org/10.1891/088983907780493313

TEDx Talks (2016). *Psychology flexibility: How love turns pain into purpose /
Stephen Hayes / TEDxUniversityofNevada* [Video]. education. Retrieved
from https://www.youtube.com/watch?v=o79_gmO5ppg

Thompson, R. A. (1994). Emotion regulation: A theme in search of definition.
Monographs of the Society for Research in Child Development, 59(2-3), 25–
52, 250–283. https://doi.org/10.2307/1166137

Trzesniewski, K. H., Donnellan, M. B., Robins, R. W. (2003). Stability of self-
esteem across the life span. *Journal of Personality and Social Psychology,
84*(1), 205–220.

Turow, R. G. (2023). *Mindfulness, meditation and self-compassion – a clinical
psychologist explains how these science-backed practices can improve mental
health*. The Conversation. Retrieved from
http://theconversation.com/mindfulness-meditation-and-self-compassion-a-
clinical-psychologist-explains-how-these-science-backed-practices-can-
improve-mental-health-198731

Valerio, S. (2019). *Section 2: What philosophy says about the self*. Understanding
the Self (GED101) Digital Portfolio. Retrieved from
https://utsged101portfolio.wordpress.com/section-2-what-philosophy-says-
about-the-self/

Van Edwards, V. (2021). *10 powerful tips you can use to practice self-compassion.* Science of People. Retrieved from https://www.scienceofpeople.com/self-compassion/

Verastegui, V. (n.d.). *4 steps to help you practice self-compassion with the RAIN technique.* Rumie. Retrieved from https://learn.rumie.org/jR/bytes/4-steps-to-help-you-practice-self-compassion-with-the-rain-technique/

WebMD Editorial Contributors (2021). *What to know about emotional health.* WebMD. Retrieved from https://www.webmd.com/balance/what-to-know-about-emotional-health

Whitney, S. (2021). *Mental health exercises aren't just for lockdown.* MyProtein. Retrieved from https://www.myprotein.co.in/blog/training/boost-your-mood-with-these-mindfulness-exercises/

Williams, J. A. (2023). *5 steps to reset your emotions and find inner peace.* Heartmanity's Blog. Retrieved from https://blog.heartmanity.com/blog/5-steps-to-reset-your-emotions-and-find-inner-peace/

Williams, N. (2023). *Self-love, self-compassion & self-care.* Nicola Williams. Retrieved from https://www.nicola-williams.com/themes/self-love-and-self-care

Wolff, C. (2016). *11 surprising everyday things that can have an effect on your mood.* Bustle. Retrieved from https://www.bustle.com/articles/155648-11-surprising-everyday-things-that-can-have-an-effect-on-your-mood

Further Reading

Dan Harris's story: https://www.abc.net.au/triplej/programs/hack/dan-harris-positive-psychology-search-for-happiness/12444208

Dan Harris's story: https://www.forbes.com/sites/bryanrobinson/2020/11/04/abc-news-anchor-dan-harris-on-how-meditation-changed-his-personal-life-and-built-a-new-business/?sh=f7760e136c29

Confidence: https://parade.com/989608/marynliles/confidence-quotes/

Depression: https://parade.com/946073/parade/depression-quotes/

Emotional health: https://www.goodreads.com/quotes/tag/emotional-health

Happiness: https://www.oprah.com/spirit/10-happiness-quotes-we-love/all

Self-compassion: https://jessicadimas.com/self-compassion-quotes/

Self-kindness: https://www.goodreads.com/quotes/tag/be-kind-to-yourself

Made in the USA
Las Vegas, NV
26 March 2024